Expert Advisor Programming
for MetaTrader 5

Creating automated trading systems in the MQL5 language

Andrew R. Young

Edgehill Publishing

Published by Edgehill Publishing, Nashville, TN.

For more information on this book, including updates, news and new editions, please visit our web site at http://www.expertadvisorbook.com/

ISBN: 978-0-9826459-2-5

Table of Contents

Introduction

Since its introduction in 2005, MetaTrader 4 has become the most popular trading platform in the Forex world. It's free, supported by dozens of brokers worldwide, and offers traders the ability to program custom trading systems and indicators in the MQL language. The wide adoption of MetaTrader by Forex brokers has created a large worldwide community of users.

In 2010, MetaQuotes launched the public beta of MetaTrader 5. The new platform introduces support for additional financial instruments, including futures and stocks. A one-click trading interface allows you to open orders quickly. Charts now support custom periods. For discretionary traders, MetaTrader 5 has a built-in news calendar and a wide variety of chart objects, including Elliott, Gann and Fibonacci tools.

But the biggest change in MetaTrader 5 has been the new MQL5 programming language. The latest version of MQL has been rebuilt from the ground up as a modern object-oriented programming language. Many new features have been added, including new data types, events, chart operations and more. The redesign of MQL5 also means that it is a much different language than MQL4. Even for the experienced MQL programmer, learning MQL5 can feel like learning a new language. But once you get the hang of it, you'll see that MQL5 is much more powerful and efficient than its predecessor.

After writing *Expert Advisor Programming* for the MQL4 programming language in early 2010, I expected that the MQL5 version of the book would simply be an update to the first. But after delving into MQL5, I realized that I would have to write a whole new book. The resulting book, which you now hold in your hands, is over twice the size of the original.

Due to the continuing popularity of MetaTrader 4, the adoption of MetaTrader 5 has been slower than anticipated. As of this writing, only one major broker (Alpari) offers live MetaTrader 5 accounts, although many smaller brokers also offer live accounts. Both versions of MetaTrader will live side by side for the foreseeable future, but the advancements offered by MetaTrader 5 will likely entice many programmers and traders to make the switch.

About This Book

The purpose of this book is to give the reader the knowledge and tools necessary to create expert advisors in the MQL5 programming language. We will also review the creation of indicators, scripts and libraries.

Over the course of this book, we will be creating a framework for the rapid development of expert advisors. Using the object-oriented capabilities of MQL5, we will create classes and functions for common trading operations, such as opening, closing and managing orders. We will also create classes and functions for useful features such as money management, trailing stops, trade timers, indicators and more.

MQL5 comes with its own standard library, which provides quick access to common trading functions. The standard library is used when generating expert advisors with MetaEditor's *MQL5 Wizard*. We will not be using the MQL5 standard library in this book, although the reader is welcome to use the standard library classes in their own projects.

The MQL5 language is very powerful and extensive, much more than MQL4 was. There are many things that you can do in MQL5 that we will not be able to touch on in this book, and this book is not intended to serve as a comprehensive language reference. Once you have grasped the fundamentals of programming in MQL5, the official MQL5 website at `http://www.mq15.com`, as well as the *MQL5 Reference*, will be your guide to learning all that MQL5 is capable of.

This book assumes that the reader is familiar with MetaTrader 5 and Forex trading in general. The reader should be familiar with the usage of MQL5 programs, and have a fundamental understanding of technical analysis and trading systems. This book assumes no prior programming experience, although the reader will benefit from any programming skills acquired previously in other languages.

While every attempt has been made to ensure that the information in this book is correct, it is possible that a few errors may be present. MQL5 is still under active development, so new features may be implemented or changed after the publication of this book. If you discover any errors in the book, please email me at `contact@expertadvisorbook.com`. An errata will be available at the book's official website, and any errors will be corrected in later printings.

Source Code Download

The source code in this book is freely downloadable from the book's official website at `http://www.expertadvisorbook.com/`. The source code download contains the include files for the expert advisor framework, a printable reference sheet, and several programs that we will create over the course of this book. We will be referring to these files often, so it is recommended that you download and install these files in your MetaTrader 5 program folder.

The source code is licensed under a *Creative Commons Attribution-NonCommercial 3.0 Unported* license. This means that you can use the source code in your personal projects. You can even modify it for your own use. But you cannot use it in any commercial projects, and if you share the code, it must be attributed to the author of this book.

Conventions Used

`Fixed-width font` refers to program code, file and folder names, URLs or MQL5 language elements.

Italics are for terms that are defined or used for the first time in the text, references to the *MQL5 Reference*, keyboard commands, or interface elements in MetaEditor or MetaTrader.

Chapter 1 - MQL5 Basics

MQL5 Programs

There are three types of programs you can create in MQL5:

An *expert advisor* is an automated trading program that can open, modify and close orders. You can only attach one expert advisor at a time to a chart. The majority of this book will cover the creation of expert advisors in MQL5.

An *indicator* displays technical analysis data on a chart or in a separate window using lines, histograms, arrows, bars/candles or chart objects. You can attach multiple indicators to a chart. Chapter 21 will address the creation of indicators in MQL5.

A *script* is a specialized program that performs a specific task. When a script is attached to a chart, it will execute only once. You can only attach one script at a time to a chart. We will address the creation of scripts in Chapter 21.

File Extensions

An MQ5 file (.mq5) contains the source code of an MQL5 program, such as an expert advisor, indicator, script or library. This is the file that is created when we write an MQL5 program in MetaEditor. This file can be opened and edited in MetaEditor or any text editor.

An EX5 file (.ex5) is a compiled executable program. When an MQ5 file is compiled in MetaEditor, an EX5 file is produced with the same file name. This is the file that executes when you attach an MQL5 program to a chart. EX5 files are binary files, and cannot be opened or edited.

An MQH file (.mqh) is an include file that contains source code for use in an MQL5 program. Like MQ5 files, an MQH file can be opened and edited in MetaEditor.

Other File Types

An *include file* (.mqh) is a source code file that contains classes, functions and variables for use in an MQL program. Include files contain useful code that can be reused over and over again. When a program is compiled, the contents of any include files used in the program will be "included" in the compiled program. We will be creating many include files over the course of this book.

A *library* is an executable file that contains reusable functions, similar to an include file. Libraries are in EX5 or Windows DLL format. A library executes in memory as a separate program along with your MQL program.

Libraries are useful if you want to make your functions available to others without making the source code available. We will discuss libraries in more detail in Chapter 21.

An *expert settings* file or preset file (.set) contains trade parameters for an expert advisor. Settings files are loaded or saved in the expert advisor *Properties* dialog under the *Inputs* tab. The *Load* button loads parameters from a .set file, and the *Save* button saves the current parameters to a .set file. You can also load or save parameters in the *Strategy Tester* under the *Inputs* tab, using the right-click popup menu.

File Locations

The MetaTrader 5 program folder is located in C:\Program Files\ by default. (If you installed MetaTrader 5 to another drive or folder, your installation path may differ.) All MQL5 programs are located under the \MQL5 folder of your MetaTrader 5 program folder. Assuming the default MetaTrader 5 installation path, the path to the MQL5 folder is C:\Program Files\MetaTrader 5\MQL5. (Your broker may use a different name for the \MetaTrader 5 folder.)

Since all MQL5 programs use the same file extensions, program types are organized in subfolders in MetaTrader 5's \MQL5 folder. Here are the contents of the subfolders in the MQL5 folder:

- **\Experts** – This folder contains the MQ5 and EX5 files for expert advisors.

- **\Indicators** – This folder contains the MQ5 and EX5 files for indicators.

- **\Scripts** – This folder contains the MQ5 and EX5 files for scripts.

- **\Include** – This folder contains MQH include files.

- **\Libraries** – This folder contains the MQ5, EX5 and DLL files for libraries.

- **\Images** – If your program uses bitmap images, they must be stored in this folder in .bmp format.

- **\Files** – Any external files that you use in your programs, other than include files, libraries, images or other MQL programs, must be stored in this folder.

- **\Presets** – This is the default folder for .set files that are loaded or saved from the expert advisor *Properties* dialog or from the *Inputs* tab in the Strategy Tester.

- **\Logs** – The expert advisor logs are saved in this folder. You can view these logs in the *Experts* tab inside the *Toolbox* window in the main MetaTrader interface.

Any references to the above folders in this book assume that they are located under the \MQL5 folder of the MetaTrader 5 installation folder. So a reference to the \Experts folder would refer to the \MQL5\Experts subfolder of the MetaTrader 5 installation folder.

MetaEditor

MetaEditor is the IDE (*Integrated Development Environment*) for MQL5 that is included with MetaTrader 5. You can open MetaEditor from the MetaTrader interface by clicking the *MetaEditor* button on the *Standard* toolbar, or by pressing F4 on your keyboard. You can also open MetaEditor from the Windows Start menu.

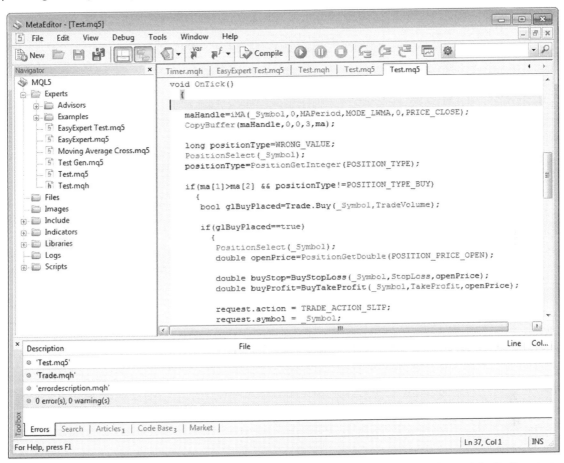

Fig. 1.1 – The MetaEditor interface. Clockwise from top left is the *Navigator* window, the code editor, and the *Toolbox* window.

MetaEditor has many useful features for creating MQL5 programs, including list names auto completion, parameter info tooltips, search tools, debugging tools and more. Figure 1.2 shows the *List Names* feature.

Type the first letters of an MQL5 language element, variable or function name, and a drop-down list will appear with all matching keywords. Scroll through the list with the up and down arrow keys, and select the keyword to auto-complete by pressing the *Enter* key. You can also select the keyword from the list with the left mouse button. You can recall the List Names drop-down box at any time by pressing *Ctrl+Space* on your keyboard, or by selecting *List Names* from the *Edit* menu.

Figure 1.3 shows the *Parameter Info* tooltip. When filling out the parameters of a function, the Parameter Info tooltip appears to remind you of the function parameters. The highlighted text in the tooltip is the current parameter.

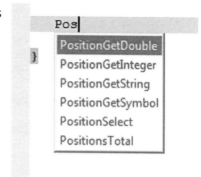

Some functions have multiple variants – the `SymbolInfoDouble()` function in Figure 1.3 has two variants, as shown by the **[1 of 2]** text that appears in the tooltip. Use the up and down arrows keys to scroll through all variants of the function. You can recall the Parameter Info tooltip at any time by pressing *Ctrl+Shift+Space* on your keyboard, or by selecting *Parameter Info* from the *Edit* menu.

Fig. 1.2 – The *List Names* dropdown.

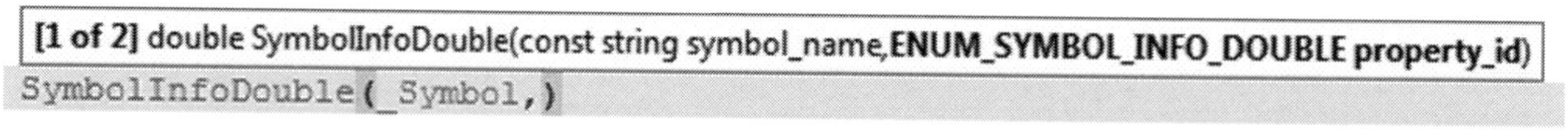

```
[1 of 2] double SymbolInfoDouble(const string symbol_name, ENUM_SYMBOL_INFO_DOUBLE property_id)
SymbolInfoDouble( _Symbol,)
```

Fig. 1.3 – The *Parameter Info* tooltip.

There are two additional windows inside the MetaEditor interface. The *Navigator* window displays the contents of the MQL5 folder in a folder tree, allowing easy access to your MQL programs. The *Toolbox* window contains several tabs, including the *Errors* tab, which displays compilation errors; the *Search* tab, which displays search results; and the *Articles, Code Base* and *Market* tabs, which list information from the MQL5 website.

MetaEditor has a built-in *MQL5 Reference*, which is useful for looking up MQL5 functions and language elements. Simply position the cursor over an MQL5 keyword and press *F1* on your keyboard. The *MQL5 Reference* will open to the appropriate page. You can also open the *MQL5 Reference* from the *Help* menu.

MQL5 Wizard

The *MQL5 Wizard* is used to create a new MQL5 program. To open the *MQL5 Wizard*, click the *New* button on the toolbar, or select *New* from the *File* menu. A window with the following options will appear:

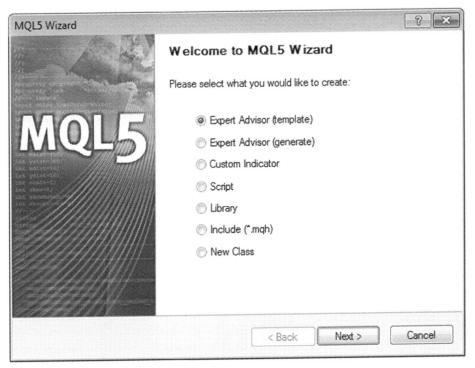

Fig. 1.4 – The *MQL5 Wizard*.

- **Expert Advisor (template)** – This will create a new expert advisor file from a built-in template. The created file is saved in the \MQL5\Experts folder or a specified subfolder.

- **Expert Advisor (generate)** – This allows the user to create an expert advisor without any coding. The generated expert advisor uses the MQL5 standard library.

- **Custom Indicator** – This will create a new custom indicator file from a built-in template. The created file is saved in the \MQL5\Indicators folder or a specified subfolder.

- **Script** – This will create a blank script file from a built-in template. The created file is saved in the \MQL5\Scripts folder or a specified subfolder.

- **Library** – This will create a blank library file from a built-in template. The created file is saved in the \MQL5\Libraries folder or a specified subfolder.

- **Include (*.mqh)** – This will create a blank include file from a built-in template with the .mqh extension. The created file is saved in the \MQL5\Include folder or a specified subfolder.

- **New Class** – This will create an include file with a class definition from a built-in template. The created file is saved in the \MQL5\Experts folder, or a specified subfolder.

We will go more in-depth into the creation of programs using the *MQL5 Wizard* throughout the book.

Compilation

To compile an MQL5 program, simply press the *Compile* button on the MetaEditor toolbar. The current MQ5 file and all included files will be checked for errors, and an EX5 file will be produced. Any compilation errors or warnings will appear in the *Errors* tab of the *Toolbox* window.

Errors will need to be fixed before an EX5 file can be generated. Chapter 22 discusses debugging and fixing program errors. Warnings should be examined, but can usually be safely ignored. A program with warnings will still compile successfully.

Syntax

MQL5 is similar to other modern programming languages such as C++, C# or Java. If you've programmed in any modern programming language with C-style syntax, the syntax and structure of MQL will be very familiar to you.

An expression or operator in MQL5 must end in a semicolon (;). An expression can span multiple lines, but there must be a semicolon at the end of the expression. Not adding a semicolon at the end of an expression is a common mistake that new programmers make.

```
// A simple expression
x = y + z;

// An expression that spans multiple lines
x = (y + z)
    / (q - r);
```

The one exception to the semicolon rule is the compound operator. A *compound operator* consists of an operator followed by a pair of brackets ({}). In the example below, the operator is the if(x == 0) expression. There is no semicolon after the closing bracket. Any expressions within the brackets must be terminated with a semicolon.

```
// A simple compound operator
if(x == 0)
{
    Print("x is equal to zero");
    return;
}
```

Identifiers

When naming variables, functions and classes, you need to use a unique and descriptive *identifier*. The identifier must not be identical to another identifier in the program, not should it be the same as an MQL5 language element.

You can use letters, numbers and the underscore character (_), although the first character in an identifier should not be a number. The maximum length for an identifier is 64 characters. This give you a lot of room to be creative, so use identifiers that are clear and descriptive.

Identifiers are case sensitive. This means that `MyIdentifier` and `myIdentifier` are not the same! Programmers use capitalization to distinguish between different types of variables, functions and classes. Here is the capitalization scheme we'll use in this book:

- Global variables, objects, classes and function names will capitalize the first letter of each word. For example: `MyFunction()` or `MyVariable`.

- Local variables and objects, which are declared inside a function, will use *camel case*. This is where the first letter is lower case, and the first letters of all other words are upper case. For example: `myVariable` or `localObject`.

- Constants are in all upper case. Use underscores to separate words, for example: `MY_CONSTANT`.

Comments

Comments are used to describe what a section of code does in a program. You'll want to use comments throughout your program to keep it organized. You can also use comments to temporarily remove lines of code from your program. Any line that is commented out is ignored by the compiler.

To add a comment, the first two characters should be a double slash (//). This will comment a single line of code:

```
// This is a comment

// The line of code below is commented out
// x = y + z;
```

To comment out multiple lines of code, use a slash-asterisk (/*) at the beginning of your comment, and an asterisk-slash (*/) at the end of your comment.

```
/* This is a multi-line comment
   These lines will be ignored by the compiler
   x = y + z;   */
```

MetaEditor has a set of useful commenting commands. Select the lines you want to comment by highlighting them with your mouse. In the *Edit* menu, under the *Comments* submenu, the *Comment Lines* menu item will comment out the selected lines, while *Uncomment Lines* will remove comments from selected lines. The *Function Header* menu item will insert a commented function header similar to those in the auto-generated MQ5 files:

```
// Function header generated by Edit menu -> Comments -> Function Header
```

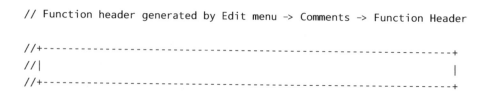

Chapter 2 - Variables & Data Types

Variables

A *variable* is the basic unit of storage in any programming language. Variables hold information that is necessary for our program to function, such as prices, indicator values or trade parameters.

Before a variable can be used, it must be *declared*. You declare a variable by specifying the data type and a unique identifier. Optionally, you can *initialize* the variable with a value. You'll generally declare a variable at the beginning of a program or function, or when it is first used. If you declare a variable more than once, or not at all, you'll get a compile error.

Here's an example of a variable declaration:

```
int myNumber = 1;
```

In this example, the data type is int (integer), the identifier is myNumber, and we initialize it with a value of 1. Once a variable has been declared, you can change its value by assigning a new value to it:

```
myNumber = 3;
```

The variable myNumber now has a value of 3. You can also assign the value of one variable to another variable:

```
int myNumber;
int yourNumber = 2;
myNumber = yourNumber;
```

The variable myNumber now has a value of 2.

If you do not initialize a variable with a value, it will be assigned a default empty value. For numerical types, the initial value will be 0, and for string types it will be a null or empty string (NULL or " ").

Data Types

When declaring a variable, the data type determines what kind of data that variable can hold. Data types in MQL can be organized into three types:

- *Integer types* are whole numbers. For example: 0, 1 and 10563.

- *Real types* are fractional numbers with a decimal point. For example: 1.35635.

- *Strings* are text comprised of Unicode characters. For example: "The brown fox jumped over the lazy dog."

Integer Types

MQL4 has only one integer type, `int`. MQL5 adds many more integer types that hold various ranges of whole numbers. Let's start by examining the signed integer types. A *signed type* can hold positive or negative numbers:

- **char** – The `char` type uses 1 byte of memory. The range of values is from -128 to 127.

- **short** – The `short` type uses 2 bytes of memory. The range of values is -32,768 to 32,767.

- **int** – The `int` type uses 4 bytes of memory. The range of values is -2,147,483,648 to 2,147,483,647.

- **long** – The `long` type uses 8 bytes of memory. The range of values is -9,223,372,036,854,775,808 to 9,223,372,036,854,775,807.

So which integer type should you use? You will frequently see the `int` or `long` type used in MQL5 functions, so those are the types you will use the most. You can use a `char` or `short` type for your variables if you wish.

There are also unsigned integer types, which do not allow negative numbers. The *unsigned types* use the same amount of memory as their signed counterparts, but the maximum value is double that of the signed type.

- **uchar** – The `uchar` type uses 1 byte of memory. The range of values is 0 to 255.

- **ushort** – The `ushort` type uses 2 bytes of memory. The range of values is 0 to 65,535.

- **uint** – The `uint` type uses 4 bytes of memory. The range of values is 0 to 4,294,967,295.

- **ulong** – The `ulong` type uses 8 bytes of memory. The range of values is 0 to 18,446,744,073,709,551,615.

In practice, you will rarely use unsigned integer types, but they are available for you to use.

Real Types

Real number types are used for storing numerical values with a fractional component, such as prices. There are two real number types in MQL5. The difference between the two types is the level of accuracy when representing fractional values.

- **float** – The float type uses 4 bytes of memory. It is accurate to 7 significant digits.

- **double** – The double type uses 8 bytes of memory. It is accurate to 15 significant digits.

You will use the double type frequently in MQL5. The float type can be used to save memory when dealing with large arrays of real numbers, but it is not used in MQL5 functions.

String Type

The string type is used to store text. Strings must be enclosed in double quotes ("). Here's an example of a string type variable declaration:

```
string myString = "This is a string";
```

If you need to use a single or double quote inside a string, use a backslash character (\) before the quote. This is called *escaping* a character.

```
string myQuote = "We are \"escaping\" double quotes";
Print(myQuote);
// Output: We are "escaping" double quotes
```

If you need to use a backslash inside a string, use two backslash characters like this:

```
string mySlash = "This is a backslash: \\";
Print(mySlash);
// Output: This is a backslash: \
```

You can also add a new line character to a string by using the \n escape character:

```
string myNewline = "This string has \n a new line character";
Print(myNewline);
// Output: This string has
//         a newline character
```

13

You can combine strings together using the *concatenation* operator (+). This combines several strings into one string:

```
string insert = "concatenated";
string myConcat = "This is an example of a " + insert + " string.";
Print(myConcat);
// Output: This is an example of a concatenated string.
```

The StringConcatenate() function can also be used to concatenate strings. It is more memory-efficient than using the concatenation operator. The first parameter of the StringConcatenate() function is the string variable to copy the concatenated string to, and the remaining parameters are the strings to concatenate:

```
string newString;
string insert = "concatenated";
StringConcatenate(newString,"This is another example of a ", insert, " string");
Print(newString);
// Output: This is another example of a concatenated string.
```

The newString variable contains the concatenated string. Note that the strings to concatenate are separated by commas inside the StringConcatenate() function.

Finally, if you have a very long string, you can split the string across multiple lines. You do not need to use the concatenation operator. Each line must be enclosed with double quotes, and there must be a semicolon at the end of the expression:

```
string myMultiline = "This is a multi-line string. "
    "These lines will be joined together.";
Print(myMultiline);
// Output: This is a multi-line string. These lines will be joined together.
```

Boolean Type

The boolean (bool) type is used to store true/false values. Technically, the boolean type is an integer type, since it takes a value of 0 (false) or 1 (true). Here's an example of a boolean type variable declaration:

```
bool myBool = true;
Print(myBool);
// Output: true
```

If a boolean variable is not explicitly initialized with a value of true, the default value will be 0, or false. Any non-zero value in a boolean variable will evaluate to true:

```
bool myBool;
Print(myBool);
// Output: false

myBool = 5;
if(myBool == true) Print("myBool is true");
// Output: myBool is true
```

In the example above, we initialize the boolean variable myBool without a value. Thus, myBool is equal to 0 or false. When we assign a value of 5 to myBool, myBool evaluates as true in a boolean operation. We'll talk more about boolean operations in Chapter 3.

Color Type

The color type is used to store information about colors. Colors can be represented by predefined color constants, RGB values, or hexadecimal values.

You'll use color constants the most. These are the same colors you'll use when choosing a color for an indicator line or a chart object. You can view the full set of color constants in the *MQL5 Reference* under *Standard Constants... > Objects Constants > Web Colors*.

Here's an example of a color variable declaration using a color constant:

```
color lineColor = clrRed;
```

The color variable lineColor is initialized using the color constant for red, clrRed. Here's an example using the RGB value for red:

```
color lineColor = C'255,0,0';
```

The RGB value for red is 255,0,0. An RGB constant begins with a capital C, and the RGB value is enclosed in single quotes. Finally, here's an example using the hexadecimal value for red:

```
color lineColor = 0xFF0000;
```

A hexadecimal value is preceded by '0x', and followed by the six-character hexadecimal value, in this case FF0000.

RGB and hexadecimal values are used for custom colors – those not defined by color constants. If you are comfortable working with RGB or hexadecimal colors, then you can define your own colors. Otherwise, you'll find the color constants to be easy and useful.

Datetime Type

The datetime type is used for storing time and date. The time and date in a datetime variable is stored in *Unix time*, which is the number of seconds elapsed since January 1, 1970. For example, January 1, 2012 at midnight in Unix time is 1,325,397,600.

If you need to initialize a datetime variable to a specific date and time, use a datetime constant. A *datetime constant* begins with a capital D, with the date and time in single quotes. The date and time is represented in the format *yyyy.mm.dd hh:mm:ss*. Here's an example:

```
datetime myDate = D'2012.01.01 00:00:00';
```

The example above initializes the variable myDate to January 1, 2012 at midnight. You can omit parts of the datetime constant if they are not used. The following examples will demonstrate:

```
datetime myDate = D'2012.01.01 00:00';        // Hour and minute
datetime myDate = D'2012.01.01 00';           // Hour only
datetime myDate = D'2012.01.01';              // Date only
```

All of these examples will initialize the variable myDate to the same time – January 1, 2012 at midnight. Since the *hh:mm:ss* part of the datetime constant is not used, we can omit it.

So what happens if you leave out the date? The compiler will substitute today's date – the date of compilation. Assuming that today is January 1, 2012, here's what happens when we use a datetime constant without a date:

```
datetime myDate = D'';            // 2012.01.01 00:00
datetime myDate = D'02:00';       // 2012.01.01 02:00
```

In the first example, the variable myDate is set to today's date at midnight. In the second example, we provide a time in the datetime constant. This sets myDate to today's date at the specified time.

MQL5 has several predefined constants for the current date and time. The __DATE__ constant returns the date of compilation. It is the same as using a blank datetime constant. The __DATETIME__ constant returns the current time and date on compilation. Note that there are two underscore characters (_) before and after each constant.

Here's an example using the __DATE__ constant. We'll assume the current date is January 1, 2012:

```
datetime myDate = __DATE__;        // 2012.01.01 00:00
datetime myDate = D'';             // 2012.01.01 00:00
```

And here's an example using the __DATETIME__ constant. We'll assume the time and date of compilation is January 1, 2012 at 03:15:05:

```
datetime myDate = __DATETIME__;    // 2012.01.01 03:15:05
```

In Chapter 18, we will examine more ways to handle and manipulate datetime values.

Constants

A *constant* is an identifier whose value does not change. A constant can be used anywhere that a variable can be used. You cannot assign a new value to a constant like you can for a variable.

There are two ways to define constants in your program. Global constants are defined in your program using the #define preprocessor directive. Any #define directives are placed at the very beginning of your program. Here's an example of a constant definition:

```
#define COMPANY_NAME "Easy Expert Forex"
```

The #define directive tells the compiler that this is a constant declaration. COMPANY_NAME is the identifier. The string "Easy Expert Forex" is the constant value. The constant value can be of any data type.

A global constant can be used anywhere in your program. Here's an example of how we can use the constant above:

```
Print("Copyright ©2012 ",COMPANY_NAME);
// Output: Copyright ©2012 Easy Expert Forex
```

The constant identifier COMPANY_NAME in the Print() function is replaced with the constant value "Easy Expert Forex".

Another way of declaring a constant is to use the const specifier. By placing a const specifier before a variable declaration, you are indicating that the value of the variable cannot be changed:

```
const int cVar = 1;
cVar = 2;              // Compile error
```

The cVar variable is set as a constant using the const specifier. If we try to assign a new value to this variable, we'll get a compilation error.

Arrays

An *array* is a variable of any type that can hold multiple values. Think of an array as a numerical list. Each number in the list corresponds to a different value. We can iterate through this list numerically, and access each of the values by its numerical index.

Here's an example of an array declaration and assignment:

```
int myArray[3];
myArray[0] = 1;
myArray[1] = 2;
myArray[2] = 3;
```

This is called a *static array*. A static array has a fixed size. When a static array is declared, the size of the array is specified in square brackets ([]). In this example, the array myArray is initialized with 3 elements. The following lines assign an integer value to each of the three elements of the array.

We can also assign the array values when first declaring the array. This line of code accomplishes the same task as the four lines of code in the previous example:

```
int myArray[3] = {1,2,3};
```

The array values are separated by commas inside the brackets ({}). They are assigned to the array in the order that they appear, so the first array element is assigned a value of 1, the second array element is assigned a value of 2, and so on. Any array elements that do not have a value assigned to them will default to an empty value – in this case, zero.

Array indexing starts at zero. So if an array has 3 elements, the elements are numbered 0, 1 and 2. See Fig. 2.1 to the right. The maximum index is always one less than the size of the array. When accessing the elements of an array, the index is specified in square brackets. In the above example, the first element, myArray[0], is assigned a value of 1, and the third element, myArray[2] is assigned a value of 3.

0
1
2

Fig. 2.1 –
Array
indexing.

Because this array has only 3 elements, if we try to access an index greater than 2, an error will occur. For example:

```
int myArray[3];
myArray[3] = 4;        // This will cause a compile error
```

Because array indexes start at 0, an index of 3 would refer to the fourth element of an array. This array has only 3 elements, so attempting to access a fourth element will result in an "array out of range" critical error.

Static arrays cannot be resized, but if you need to resize an array, you can declare a dynamic array instead. A *dynamic array* is an array that is declared without a fixed size. Dynamic arrays must be sized before they can be used, and a dynamic array can be resized at any time. The ArrayResize() function is used to set the size of a dynamic array.

Here's an example of a dynamic array declaration, sizing and assignment:

```
double myDynamic[];
ArrayResize(myDynamic,3);
myDynamic[0] = 1.50;
```

A dynamic array is declared with empty square brackets. This tells the compiler that this is a dynamic array. The ArrayResize() function takes the array name (myDynamic) as the first parameter, and the new size (3) as the second parameter. In this case, we're setting the size of myDynamic to 3. After the array has been sized, we can assign values to the array.

Dynamic arrays are used in MQL5 for storing indicator values and price data. You will frequently declare dynamic arrays for use in MQL5 functions. The functions themselves will take care of properly sizing the array and filling it with data. When using dynamic arrays in your own code, be sure to size them using ArrayResize() first.

Multi-Dimensional Arrays

Up to this point, we've been declaring one-dimensional arrays. Let's take a look at a two-dimensional array:

```
double myDimension[3][3];
myDimension[0][1] = 1.35;
```

In the example above, we declare a two-dimensional array named myDimension, with both dimensions having three elements. Think of a multi-dimensional array as an "array within an array." It will be easier if we visualize our two-dimensional array as a table. Refer to Fig. 2.2 to the right.

The first dimension will be the horizontal rows in our table, while the second dimension will be the vertical columns. So in this example, myDimension[0][0] will be the first row, first column; myDimension[1][2]

	0	1	2
0	0,0	0,1	0,2
1	1,0	1,1	1,2
2	2,0	2,1	2,2

Fig. 2.2 – Multi-dimensional array indexing.

would be the second row, third column and so forth. Two-dimensional arrays are very useful if you have a set of data that can be organized in a table format.

Only the first dimension of a multi-dimensional array can be dynamic. All other dimensions must have a static size declared. This is useful if you're not sure how many "rows" your table should have. Let's look at an example:

```
double myDimension[][3];
int rows = 5;
ArrayResize(myDimension,rows);
```

The first dimension is blank, indicating that this is a dynamic array. The second dimension is set to 3 elements. The integer variable rows is used to set the size of the first dimension of our array. We'll pass this value to the second parameter of the ArrayResize() function. So for example, if rows = 5, then the first dimension of our array will be set to 5 elements.

An array can have up to four dimensions, but it is rare that you will ever need more than two or three. In most cases, a structure would be an easier method of implementing a complex data structure. We'll cover structures later in the chapter.

Iterating Through Arrays

The primary benefit of arrays is that it allows you to easily iterate through a complete set of data. Here's an example where we print out the value of every element in an array:

```
string myArray[3] = {"cheese","bread","ale"};
for(int index = 0; index < 3; index++)
{
    Print(myArray[index]);
}

// Output:  cheese
            bread
            ale
```

We declare a string array named myArray, with a size of 3. We initialize all three elements in the array with the values of "cheese", "bread" and "ale" respectively. This is followed by a for loop. The for loop initializes a counter variable named index to 0. It will increment the value of index by 1 on each iteration of the loop. It will keep looping as long as index is less than 3. The index variable is used as the index of the array. On the first iteration of the loop, index will equal 0, so the Print() function will print the value of myArray[0] to the log – in this case, "cheese". On the next iteration, index will equal 1, so the value of myArray[1] will be printed to the log, and so on.

As mentioned earlier in the chapter, if you try to access an array element that is larger than the maximum array index, your program will fail. When looping through an array, it is important to know the size of the array. The example above uses a fixed size array, so we know the size of the array beforehand. If you're using a dynamic array, or if you don't know what size an array will be, the ArraySize() function can be used to determine the size of an array:

```
int myDynamic[];
ArrayResize(myDynamic,10);

int size = ArraySize(myDynamic);

for(int i = 0; i < size; i++)
{
    myDynamic[i] = i;
    Print(i);                          // Output: 0, 1, 2... 9
}
```

In this example, the array myDynamic has 10 elements. The ArraySize() function returns the number of elements in the array and assigns the value to the size variable. The size variable is then used to set the termination condition for the for loop. This loop will assign the value of i to each element of the myDynamic array.

We'll discuss for loops in Chapter 4. Just keep in mind that a loop can be used to iterate through all of the elements of an array, and you will frequently be using arrays for just this purpose.

Enumerations

An *enumeration* is an special integer type that defines a list of constants representing integer values. Only the values defined in an enumeration can be used in variables of that type.

For example, let's say we need to create an integer variable to represent the days of the week. There are only seven days in a week, so we don't need values that are less than 0 or greater than 7. And we'd like to use descriptive constants to specify the days of the week.

Here's an example of an enumeration that allows the user to select the day of the week:

```
enum DayOfWeek
{
    Sunday,
    Monday,
    Tuesday,
    Wednesday,
    Thursday,
    Friday,
    Saturday,
};
```

We use the type identifier enum to define this as an enumeration. The name of our enumeration is DayOfWeek. The seven days of the week are listed inside the brackets, separated by commas. The closing bracket terminates with a semicolon.

The members of an enumeration are numbered consecutively, starting at 0. So Sunday = 0, Monday = 1, Saturday = 6 and so on. These integer values happen to correspond with the values that MQL5 uses in the MqlDateTime structure for the day of the week. We'll learn more about MqlDateTime later in the book. The ENUM_DAY_OF_WEEK enumeration also uses these values.

To use our enumeration we must define a variable, using the name of our enumeration as the type identifier. This example creates a variable named Day, and assigns the value for Monday to it:

```
DayOfWeek Day;
Day = Monday;
Print(Day);     // Output: 1
```

In the first line, we use the name of our enumeration, DayOfWeek, as the type. This is an important concept to note: When we create an enumeration, the name of the enumeration becomes a type, just like the way that int, double or string are types. We then declare a variable of that type by using the enumeration name as the type identifier. This concept also applies to structures and classes, which we'll discuss shortly.

We use the constants defined in our enumeration to assign a value to our Day variable. In this case, we assign the value of the constant Monday to the Day variable. If we print the value of the Day variable to the log, the result is 1, because the integer value of the constant Monday is 1.

What if you want the enumeration to start at a number other than zero? Perhaps you'd like the members of an enumeration to have non-consecutive values? You can assign a value to each constant in an enumeration by using the assignment operator (=). Here's an example:

```
enum yearIntervals
{
    month = 1,
    twoMonths,          // 2
    quarter,            // 3
    halfYear = 6,
    year = 12,
};
```

This example was adapted from the *MQL5 Reference*. The name of our enumeration is yearIntervals. The first member name is month, which is assigned a value of 1. The next two members, twoMonths and quarter, are incremented by one and assigned the values of 2 and 3 respectively. The remaining members are assigned their respective values.

One area where enumerations are useful is to provide the user a set of values to choose from. For example, if you're creating a timer feature in your EA, and you want the user to choose the day of the week, you can use the DayOfWeek enumeration defined earlier as one of your input parameters. The user will see a drop-down list of constants in the expert advisor *Properties* dialog to choose from.

There are many predefined standard enumerations in MQL5. All of the standard enumerations in MQL5 begin with ENUM_ and are all uppercase with underscore characters. You can view the standard enumerations in the *MQL5 Reference* under *Standard Constants... > Enumerations and Structures*.

Structures

A *structure* is a set of related variables of different types. The concept is similar to an enumeration, but the members of a structure can be of any type. There are several predefined structures in MQL5, and we will be using them often. You probably won't need to create your own structures very often, but it's important to know how they work.

Let's look at an example of a structure. This structure could be used to store trade settings:

```
struct tradeSettings
{
    ulong slippage;
    double price;
    double stopLoss;
    double takeProfit;
    string comment;
};
```

EXPERT ADVISOR PROGRAMMING FOR METATRADER 5

The type identifier struct defines this as a structure. The name of the structure is tradeSettings. There are six member variables defined inside the brackets. Although you can assign a default value to a member variable using the assignment operator (=), typically we assign values after an object has been initialized.

Here's an example of how we would use our structure in code:

```
tradeSettings trade;
trade.slippage = 50;
trade.stopLoss = StopLoss * _Point;
```

Using our structure name tradeSettings as the type, we define an object named trade. This object allows us to access the member variables of the structure. We'll talk more about objects in Chapter 6. To access the structure members, we use the dot operator (.) between the object name and the member name. In this case, we assign the value 50 to the structure member slippage, and assign a calculated stop loss value to the structure member stopLoss.

The predefined structures in MQL5 are often used to return values from the trade server. For example, the MqlTick structure stores the most recent time, price and volume for an instrument. Here is the definition of the MqlTick structure:

```
struct MqlTick
{
    datetime      time;        // Time of the last prices update
    double        bid;         // Current Bid price
    double        ask;         // Current Ask price
    double        last;        // Price of the last deal (Last)
    ulong         volume;      // Volume for the current Last price
};
```

To use the MqlTick structure, we initialize an object of type MqlTick. Then we use the SymbolInfoTick() function to fill the object with the time, price and volume data for the current symbol from the trade server:

```
MqlTick price;
SymbolInfoTick(_Symbol,price);
Print(price.bid);                      // Returns the current Bid price
```

We define an object named price, using the structure name MqlTick as the type. We pass the object to the SymbolInfoTick() function. The function returns the object, filled with the current price information from the server. To access this price information, we use the dot operator (.) between the object name and the member variable name. The expression price.bid will return the current Bid price, while price.ask would return the current Ask price.

We'll cover the `MqlTick` structure as well as other commonly-used structures in-depth later in the book.

Typecasting

The process of converting a value from one type to another is called *typecasting*. When you copy the contents of a variable into another variable of a different type, the contents are *casted* into the proper type. This can produce unexpected results if you're not careful.

When copying numerical values from one variable to another, there is the possibility of data loss if copying from one type to another, smaller type. Remember our discussion of integer types on page 12. If you copy an `int` value into a `long` variable, there is no possibility of data loss, since the `long` type can hold a larger range of values.

You can freely copy smaller numerical types into larger ones. A `float` value copied into a `double` variable would suffer no data loss. However, a `double` value copied into a `float` variable would result in the `double` value being truncated. The same can result if you copy an `int` value into a `short` variable. This is especially true if you are casting a floating-number type (such as a `double`) into an integer type. Anything after the decimal point will be lost. This is fine if you don't need the fractional part of the number though.

If you are casting a value of a larger type into a variable of a smaller type, the compiler will warn you with the message "possible loss of data due to type conversion." If you are certain that the value of the larger type won't overflow the range of the smaller type, then you can safely ignore the message. Otherwise, you can *explicitly* typecast the new value to make the warning go away.

For example, if you have a `double` value that you need to pass to a function that requires an integer value, you'll get the "possible loss of data due to type conversion" error. You can cast the new value as an integer by prefacing the variable with (`int`). For example:

```
double difference = (high - low) / _Point;
BuyStopLoss(_Symbol,(int) difference);
```

The double variable `difference` is calculated by dividing two floating-point values. The `BuyStopLoss()` function requires an integer value for the second parameter. Passing the `difference` variable will cause a compiler warning. By prefacing the `difference` variable name with (`int`), we cast the value of `difference` to an integer, effectively rounding the value down and avoiding the compiler error.

Input Variables

The *input variables* of an MQL5 program are the only variables that can be changed by the user. These variables consist of trade settings, indicator settings, stop loss and take profit values, and so on. They are displayed under the *Inputs* tab of the program's *Properties* window.

An input variable is preceded by the `input` keyword. Input variables are placed at the beginning of your program, before any functions or other program code. Input variables can be of any type, including enumerations. Arrays and structures cannot be used as input variables. The identifiers for input variables should be clear and descriptive.

Here's an example of some input variables that you may see in an expert advisor:

```
input int MAPeriod = 10;
input ENUM_MA_METHOD MAMethod = MODE_SMA;
input double StopLoss = 20;
input string Comment = "ea";
```

These input variables set the period and calculation method for a moving average indicator, set a stop loss for the order, and add a comment to the order.

You can set a user-friendly display name in the *Inputs* tab by appending an input variable with a comment. The comment string will appear in the *Variable* column of the *Inputs* tab. Here are the input variables defined above with a descriptive comment:

```
input int MAPeriod = 10;                    // Moving average period
input ENUM_MA_METHOD MAMethod = MODE_SMA;   // Moving average method
input double StopLoss = 20;                 // Stop loss (points)
input string Comment = "ea";                // Trade comment
```

A *static* input variable can be defined by using the `sinput` keyword. The value of a static input variable can be changed, but it cannot be optimized in the Strategy Tester. Static input variables are useful for logical grouping of input parameters. Simply declare an `sinput` variable of the string type and include a comment:

```
sinput string MASettings;     // Moving average settings
```

Fig. 2.3 below shows how the input variables above will appear in the *Inputs* tab of the *Properties* window:

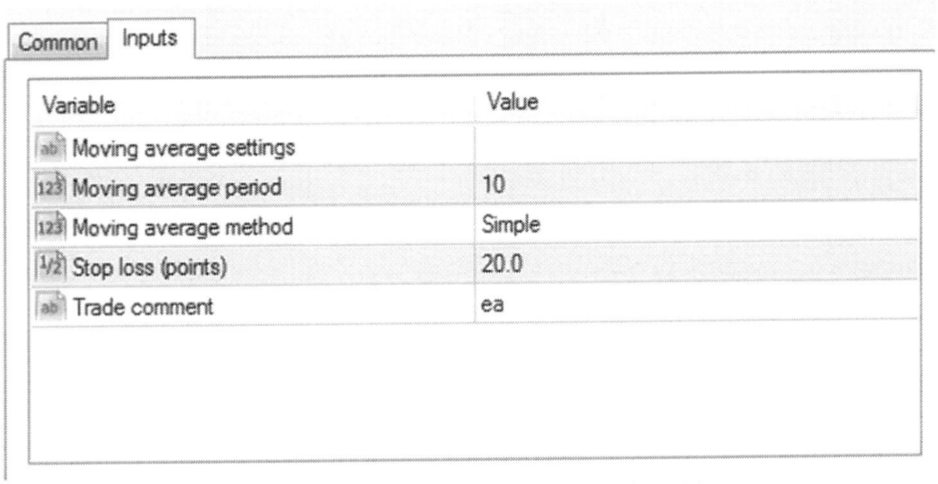

Common	Inputs	
Variable		**Value**
ab Moving average settings		
123 Moving average period		10
123 Moving average method		Simple
1/2 Stop loss (points)		20.0
ab Trade comment		ea

Fig. 2.3 – The *Inputs* tab, showing comments in lieu of variable names.

To use an enumeration that you've created as an input variable type, you'll need to define the enumeration before the input variable itself. We'll use the DayOfWeek enumeration that we defined earlier in the book:

```
enum DayOfWeek
{
    Sunday,
    Monday,
    Tuesday,
    Wednesday,
    Thursday,
    Friday,
    Saturday,
};

input DayOfWeek Day = Monday;
```

This creates an input variable named Day, using the DayOfWeek enumeration as the type, with a default value of Monday or 1. When the user attempts to change the value of the Day input variable, a drop-down box will appear, containing all of the values of the enumeration.

Local Variables

A *local variable* is one that is declared inside a function. Local variables are allocated in memory when the function is first run. Once the function has exited, the variable is cleared from memory.

In this example, we'll create a simple function. We'll discuss functions in more detail in Chapter 5. We will declare a local variable inside our function. When the code in this function is run, the variable is declared and used. When the function exits, the variable is cleared from memory:

```
void myFunction()
{
    int varInt = 5;
    Print(varInt);     // Output: 5
}
```

The name of this function is myFunction(). This function would be called and executed from somewhere else in our program. The variable varInt is local to this function. This is referred to as the *variable scope*. Local variables cannot be referenced from outside of the function, or anywhere else in the program. They are created when the function is run, and disposed of when the function exits.

Let's take a closer look at *variable scope*. A local variable's scope is limited to the block that is is declared in. A *block* is defined as a function or a compound operator within a function. A block is surrounded by opening and closing brackets ({}). Any variables declared inside a block are local only to that block. Let's take a look at a modified example of our function:

```
void myFunction()
{
    bool varBool = true;

    if(varBool == true)
    {
        int varInt = 5;
        Print(varInt);        // Output: 5
    }
}
```

We've added a new local variable, a boolean variable named varBool. We've also added an if operator block. The if operator, its accompanying brackets and the code inside them are a compound operator. Any variables declared inside the brackets are local to the if operator block.

The if expression can be read as: "If varBool contains the value of true, then execute the code inside the brackets." In this case, the expression is true, so the code inside the brackets is run. The varInt variable is declared, and the value is printed to the log.

The varInt variable is local to the if operator block. That means that varInt cannot be referenced outside the block. Once the block is exited, varInt is out of scope. If we attempt to reference it from outside the if operator block, we'll get a compilation error:

```
if(varBool == true)
{
    int varInt = 5;
    Print(varInt);              // Output: 5
}

varInt = 7;                     // Both of these expressions
Print(varInt);                  // will produce an error
```

The expression varInt = 7 will produce an error on compilation. The variable varInt that we declared inside the if operator block is out of scope. If we want to correct this code, we can simply declare the varInt variable that is outside the if operator block:

```
if(varBool == true)
{
    int varInt = 5;
    Print(varInt);              // Output: 5
}

int varInt = 7;                 // This is a different variable!
Print(varInt);                  // Output: 7
```

Now we have a variable named varInt in this scope. Note that this is a different variable than the varInt variable declared inside the if operator block, even though they both have the same name!

Here's another example: The variable varInt is declared at the top of the function, and another variable of the same name and type is declared inside the if operator block nested inside the function.

```
void myFunction()
{
    bool varBool = true;
    int varInt = 7;

    if(varBool == true)
    {
        int varInt = 5;
        Print(varInt);          // Output: 5
    }

    Print(varInt);              // Output: 7
}
```

An integer variable named varInt is declared at the top of the function, and assigned a value of 7. A second integer variable named varInt is declared inside the if operator block and initialized with a value of 5. When we print the value of varInt inside the if operator block, it prints a value of 5.

When the if operator block is exited, and we print the value of varInt again, this time it prints a value of 7 – the same value that was declared at the top of the function! In other words, the varInt variable that was declared inside the if operator block overrides the one declared in the scope of the function. By the way, if you try to compile this, you'll get a warning message stating "declaration of 'varInt' hides local declaration..." The example above is not considered good practice, so renaming the second varInt variable would fix the warning.

Just to clarify things, let's see what would happen if we declared the varInt variable once outside of the if operator block, and then referenced it inside the if operator block:

```
void myFunction()
{
    bool varBool = true;
    int varInt = 5;

    if(varBool == true)
    {
        Print(varInt);        // Output: 5
    }
}
```

This will work as expected, because the varInt variable is declared outside of the if operator block, in the function scope. A variable declared in a higher scope is still in scope inside any nested blocks, as long as those nested blocks don't have a variable of the same name and type.

This may seem arbitrary and confusing, but most modern programming languages treat variable scope this way. By requiring that variables be local only inside the block in which they are declared, programming errors are prevented when variables share the same name. Also note that this is different than the way local variables are handled in MQL4. In MQL4, a local variable declared inside a function is valid anywhere inside that function, even if it was declared inside a compound operator or block.

Global Variables

A *global variable* is one that is declared outside of any function. Global variables are defined at the top of your program, generally after the input variables. The scope of a global variable is the entire program.

As demonstrated in the previous section, a local variable declared inside a block will override any variable of the same name and type in a higher scope. If you do this to a global variable, you'll get a compilation warning:

"Declaration of variable hides global declaration." There is no practical reason to override a global variable this way, so watch for this.

The value of a global variable can be changed anywhere in the program, and those changes will be available to all functions in the program. Here's an example:

```
// Global variable
int GlobalVarInt = 5;

void functionA()
{
    GlobalVarInt = 7;
}

void functionB()
{
    Print(GlobalVarInt);            // Output: 7
}
```

The global variable `GlobalVarInt` is declared at the top of the program, and assigned a value of 5. We'll assume that `functionA()` is executed first. This changes the value of `GlobalVarInt` to 7. When `functionB()` is run, it will print the changed value of `GlobalVarInt`, which is now 7.

If you have a variable that needs to be accessed by several functions throughout your program, declare it as a global variable at the top of your program. If you have a local variable whose value needs to be retained between function calls, use a static variable instead.

Static Variables

A *static variable* is a local variable that remains in memory even when the program has exited the variable's scope. We declare a static variable by prefacing it with the `static` modifier. Here's an example of a static variable within a function. On each call of the function, the static variable is incremented by 1. The value of the static variable is retained between function calls:

```
void staticFunction()
{
    static int staticVar = 0;
    staticVar++;                  // Increments staticVar by 1
    Print(staticVar);             // Output: 1, 2, 3, etc.
}
```

A static integer variable named `staticVar` is declared with the `static` modifier. On the first call of the function, `staticVar` is initialized to 0. The variable is incremented by 1, and the result is printed to the log. The first entry in the log will read 1. On the next call of the function, `staticVar` will have a value of 1. (Note that it will not be reinitialized to zero!) The variable is then incremented by 1, and a value of 2 is printed to the log, and so on.

Predefined Variables

MQL5 has several predefined variables to access commonly used values. The predefined variables are prefaced by the underscore character (_). All of these variables have equivalent functions as well, but since they are frequently used as function parameters, the predefined variables are easier to read.

Here is a list of commonly-used predefined variables in MQL5. All of these variables refer to the properties of the chart that the program is currently attached to:

- **_Symbol** – The symbol of the financial security on the current chart.

- **_Period** – The period, in minutes, of the current chart.

- **_Point** – The point value of the current symbol. For five-digit Forex currency pairs, the point value is 0.00001, and for three-digit currency pairs (JPY), the point value is 0.001.

- **_Digits** – The number of digits after the decimal point for the current symbol. For five-digit Forex currency pairs, the number of digits is 5. JPY pairs have 3 digits.

Chapter 3 - Operations

Operations

We can perform mathematical operations and assign the result to a variable. You can even use other variables in an operation. Let's demonstrate how to perform basic mathematical operations in MQL5.

Addition & Multiplication

```
// Addition
int varAddA = 3 + 5;                    // Result: 8
double varAddB = 2.5 + varAddA;         // Result: 10.5

// Multiplication
int varMultA = 5 * 3;                   // Result: 15
double varMultB = 2.5 * varMultA;       // Result: 37.5
```

In the first example of each operation, we add or multiply two integers together and assign the result to an `int` variable (`varAddA` and `varMultA`). In the second example, we add or multiply a real number (or floating-point number) by a variable containing an integer value. The result is stored in a `double` variable (`varAddB` or `varMultB`).

If you know that two values will be of integer types, then it's fine to store them in an integer variable. If there's any possibility that one value will be a floating-point number, then use a real number type such as `double` or `float`.

Subtraction & Negation

```
// Subtraction
int varSubA = 5 - 3;                    // Result: 2
double varSubB = 0.5 - varSubA;         // Result: -1.5

// Negation
int varNegA = -5;
double varNegB = 3.3 - varNegA;         // Result: 8.3
```

In the subtraction example, we first subtract two integers and assign the value to an `int` variable, `varSubA`. Then we subtract our integer variable from a floating point number, 0.5. The result is a negative floating point number that is assigned to a `double` variable, `varSubB`.

You can specify a numerical constant as a negative number simply by placing a minus sign (-) directly in front of it. The int variable varNegA has a value of -5 assigned to it. Next, we subtract -5 from 3.3 and assign the result to varNegB. Since we are subtracting a negative number from a positive number, the result is an addition operation that results in a value of 8.3.

Division & Modulus

```
// Division
double varDivA = 5 / 2;        // Result: 2.5
int varDivB = 5 / 2;           // Result: 2

// Modulus
int varMod = 5 % 2;            // Result: 1
```

The first division example, varDivA, divides two integers and stores the result in a double variable. Note that 5 / 2 doesn't divide equally, so there is a fractional remainder. Because of the possibility of fractional remainders, you should always use a real number type when dividing!

The second example demonstrates: We divide 5 / 2 and store the result in an int variable, varDivB. Because integer types don't store fractional values, the value is rounded down to the nearest whole number.

The modulus example divides 5 by 2, and stores the integer remainder in varMod. You can only use the modulus operator (%) on two integers. Therefore, it is safe to store the remainder in an int variable.

Assignment Operations

Sometimes you will need to perform a mathematical operation using a variable, and then assign the result back to the original variable. Here's an example using addition:

```
int varAdd = 5;
varAdd = varAdd + 3;
Print(varAdd);          // Output: 8
```

We declare the variable varAdd and initialize it to a value of 5. Then we add 3 to varAdd, and assign the result back to varAdd. The result is 8. Here's a shorter way to do this:

```
int varAdd = 5;
varAdd += 3;            // varAdd = 8
```

Here we combine a mathematical operator (+) with the assignment operator (=). This can be read as "Add 3 to varAdd, and assign the result back to varAdd." We can do this with other mathematical operators as well:

```
varSub  -= 3;           // Subtraction assignment
varMult *= 3;           // Multiplication assignment
varDiv  /= 3;           // Division assignment
varMod  %= 3;           // Modulus assignment
```

Relation Operations

You will often have to compare two values in a greater than, less than, equal or non-equal relationship. The operation evaluates to a boolean result, either `true` or `false`. Let's take a look at greater than and less than operations:

```
a > b       // Greater than
a < b       // Less than
```

In the first example, if a is greater than b, the result is true, otherwise false. In the second example, if a is less than b, the result is true. You can also check for equality as well:

```
a >= b      // Greater than or equal to
a <= b      // Less than or equal to
```

In the first example, if a is greater than or equal to b, the result is true. In the second example, if a is less than or equal to b, the result is true. Let's look at equal and non-equal operations:

```
a == b      // Equal to
a != b      // Not equal to
```

In the first example, if a is equal to b, the result is true. In the second example, if a is not equal to b, the result is true. Note that the equality operator (==) is not the same as the assignment operator (=)! This is a common mistake made by new programmers.

When using real numbers, it is important to normalize or round the numbers to a specific number of decimal places. This is done using the `NormalizeDouble()` function. The first argument is the `double` value to normalize. The second argument is the number of digits after the decimal point to round to. Here's an example:

```
double normalA = 1.35874934;
double normalB = 1.35873692;

normalA = NormalizeDouble(normalA,4);       // Result: 1.3587
normalB = NormalizeDouble(normalB,4);       // Result: 1.3587
```

```
if(normalA == normalB)
{
    Print("Equal");
}
```

In this example, we have two double variables containing fractional values to 8 decimal places. We use the NormalizeDouble() function to round these numbers to 4 decimal places and assign the results to their original variables. We can then compare them in an equality statement. In this case, normalA and normalB are equal, so the string "Equal" is printed to the log.

If we tried to perform an equality operation on two prices without normalizing the numbers, it's unlikely we would ever get an equal result. Internally, prices and indicator values are calculated out to a large number of significant digits. By normalizing the numbers, we can check for equality using a smaller number of digits.

Boolean Operations

A boolean operation compares two or more operations (mathematical, boolean or relation) using logical operators, and evaluates whether the expression is true or false. There are three logical operations: AND, OR and NOT.

Let's take a look at an example of an AND operation. An AND operation is true if all of the operations in the expression are true. The logical operator for AND is && (two ampersands):

```
int a = 1;
int b = 1;
int c = 2;

if(a == b && a + b == c)
{
    Print(true);                // Result: true
}
```

First we declare and initialize three integer variables: a, b and c. We use an if operator to evaluate our boolean operation. If the operation is true, the code inside the brackets is run.

The value of a is 1, and the value of b is 1. The expression a == b is true, so we go on to the next expression. The addition operation a + b equals 2. The value of c is also 2, so this expression is true. The boolean operation AND evaluates to true, so a value of true is printed to the log.

Let's see what happens if we have a false expression in our AND boolean operation:

```
int a = 1;
int b = 1;
int c = 3;

if(a == b && a + b == c)
{
    Print(true);
}
else
{
    Print(false);              // Result: true
}
```

In this example, we initialize the value of c to 3. Since a + b is not equal to c, the expression evaluates to false, and thus the boolean AND operation evaluates to false. In this case, the execution skips to the else operator, and a value of false is printed to the log.

Next, we'll examine the OR boolean operation. An OR operation is true if any of the expressions evaluates to true. The OR operator is || (two pipes):

```
int a = 1;
int b = 1;
int c = 3;

if(a == b || a + b == c)
{
    Print(true);               // Result: true
}
```

This code is almost identical to the previous example, except we are using an OR operator. The expression a == b is true, but a + b == c is not. Since at least one of the expressions is true, the boolean OR operation evaluates to true, and a value of true is printed to the log.

Finally, we'll examine the NOT boolean operation. The NOT operator (!) is applied to a single boolean expression. If the expression is true, the NOT operation evaluates to false, and vice versa. Essentially, the NOT operator reverses the true/false value of a boolean expression. Here's an example:

```
bool not = false;

if(!not)
{
    Print(true);               // Result: true
}
```

The variable not is initialized to false. The boolean expression !not evaluates to true. Thus, a value of true is printed to the log. The NOT operator works on more complex expressions as well:

```
int a = 1;
int b = 2;

if(!(a == b))
{
    Print(true);                // Result: true
}
```

The expression a == b is false. By enclosing the expression in parentheses and applying the NOT operator, the expression evaluates to true and a value of true is printed to the log.

Chapter 4 - Conditional & Loop Operators

Conditional Operators

One of the most basic functions of any program is making decisions. Conditional operators are used to make decisions by evaluating a true/false condition. There are three conditional operators in MQL5: the `if-else` operator, the ternary operator, and the `switch-case` operator.

The if Operator

You've already been introduced to the *if* operator. The `if` operator is the most common conditional operator in MQL5, and one that you'll use often. It is a compound operator, meaning that there is usually more than one expression contained inside the operator.

The `if` operator evaluates a condition as true or false. The condition can be a relational or boolean operation. If the condition is true, the expression(s) inside the compound operator are executed. If the condition is false, control passes to the next line of code. Let's look at a simple `if` expression:

```
bool condition = true;

if(condition == true)          // If the condition in parentheses is true...
{
    Print(true);               // Execute the code inside the brackets
}
```

We declare a boolean variable named `condition`, and set its value to `true`. Next, we evaluate the boolean condition in the `if` operator. In this case, `condition == true`, so we execute the code inside the brackets, which prints a value of `true` to the log.

When an `if` compound operator has only one expression, you can omit the brackets and place it on the same line as the `if` operator. You can even place the expression on the next line. Note that this only works with a single expression, and that expression must be terminated with a semicolon:

```
// Single line
if(condition == true) Print(true);

// Multi line
if(condition == true)
    Print(true);
```

You can have multiple if expressions next to each other. Each if expression will be evaluated individually. In the example below, two if operators evaluate a relational operation. Both Print() functions will be executed, since 2 is greater than 1 and less than 3:

```
int number = 2;

if(number > 1) Print("number is greater than 1");
if(number < 3) Print("number is less than 3");

// Result:  number is greater than 1
//          number is less than 3
```

The else Operator

The *else* operator is the companion to the if operator. The else operator is placed after an if operator. When the if operator evaluates to false, the expression(s) inside the else operator are executed instead:

```
bool condition = false;

if(condition == true) Print(true);      // If condition is true
else Print(false);                      // If condition is false
                                        // Result: false
```

In this example, the if operator evaluates to false, so the expression inside the else operator is run and a value of false is printed to the log. The else operator is useful if you have a default action that you want to be carried out when all other conditions are false.

The else operator can be combined with the if operator, allowing multiple conditions to be evaluated. When one or more else if operators are placed in an if-else block, the first true condition will end execution of the if-else block. An else if operator must be placed after the first if operator, and before any else operator:

```
int oneOrTwo = 2;

if(oneOrTwo == 1)
    Print("oneOrTwo is 1");

else if(oneOrTwo == 2)                          // If previous if operator is false
    Print("oneOrTwo is 2");

else                                            // If both if operators are false
    Print("oneOrTwo is not 1 or 2");            // Result: oneOrTwo is not 1 or 2
```

40

In this example, we declare an integer variable, oneOrTwo, and assign a value of 2. The condition for the if operator, oneOrTwo == 1, is false, so we move on to the else if operator. The else if operator condition, oneOrTwo == 2 is true, so the string "oneOrTwo is 2" is printed to the log.

The if and else if operators are evaluated in order until one of them evaluates to true. Once an if or else if operator evaluates to true, the expression(s) inside the operator are executed, and the program resumes execution after the if-else block. If none of the if or else if operators evaluate to true, then the expression(s) inside the else operator will execute instead.

For example, if oneOrTwo is assigned a value of 1, the expression in the first if operator, oneOrTwo == 1, will be true. The message "oneOrTwo is 1" will be printed to the log. The following else if and else operators will not be evaluated. The program will resume execution after the else operator.

If all of the if and else if operators are false, the expression in the else operator is executed. In this case, the message "oneOrTwo is not 1 or 2" will be printed to the log:

```
int oneOrTwo = 3;

if(oneOrTwo == 1)
    Print("oneOrTwo is 1");

else if(oneOrTwo == 2)
    Print("oneOrTwo is 2");

else                                    // Result: oneOrTwo is not 1 or 2
    Print("oneOrTwo is not 1 or 2");
```

Note that the else operator is not required in any if-else block. If it is present, it must come after any if or else if operators. You can have multiple else if operators, or none at all. It all depends on your requirements.

Ternary Operator

The *ternary* operator is a single-line shortcut for the if-else operator. A ternary operator consists of three parts. The first part is the true/false condition to be evaluated. The second part is the expression to be executed if the condition is true. The third part is the expression to be executed if the condition is false. The result of the expression is assigned to a variable. Here's an example:

```
bool condition = true;
bool result = condition ? true : false;

Print(result);                          // Output: true
```

We declare a boolean variable named condition, and set the value to true. This variable is used as the condition for the ternary operator. A question mark (?) separates the condition from the expressions. The first expression assigns a value of true to the boolean variable result. The second expression assigns a value of false to the variable result. The expressions are separated by a colon (:).

In this case, condition == true, so the first expression, true, is assigned to the variable result. Here's how we would express this using the if-else operator:

```
bool condition = true;
bool result;

if(condition == true) result = true;
else result = false;

Print(result);                                  // Output: true
```

We saved two lines of code using the ternary operator. Whichever you prefer to use is up to you.

Switch Operator

The *switch* operator compares an expression to a list of constant values using the case operator. When a constant value is matched, the accompanying expressions are executed. Here's an example:

```
int x = 1;

switch(x)
{
    case 1:
        Print("x is 1");                // Output: x is 1
        break;

    case 2:
        Print("x is 2");
        break;

    default:
        Print("x is not 1 or 2");
}
```

We declare an integer variable, x, and assign a value of 1. The switch operator contains the expression to evaluate. In this case, the expression is the variable x. The case operators are labels, each assigned a different constant value. Since x is equal to 1, the string "x is 1" will be printed to the log. The break operator ends execution of the switch operator.

If the expression inside the `switch` operator does not match any of the `case` operators, the optional `default` operator will execute instead. For example, if x does not match any of the `case` operators, the expressions after the `default` operator are executed instead. So if x were assigned a value of 3, the string "x is not 1 or 2" is printed to the log.

Unlike an `if-else` block, execution of the `switch` operator block does not stop when a `case` constant is matched. Unless a `break` operator is encountered, execution will continue until all remaining expressions in the `switch` operator have been executed. Here's an example:

```
int x = 1;

switch(x)
{
    case 1:

    case 2:

    case 3:
        Print("x is 1, 2 or 3");          // Output: x is 1, 2 or 3
        break;

    default:
        Print("x is not 1, 2, or 3");
        break;
}
```

Note that there are no expressions following the `case` 1 or `case` 2 labels. If either of these labels are matched, the program will begin executing any expressions following the case labels until a `break` operator is encountered, a `default` operator is encountered, or the `switch` operator ends.

In this example, the variable x has a value of 1. The expression x matches the first `case` label. Execution continues past the `case` 3 label, to the `Print()` function. The string "x is 1, 2 or 3" is printed to the log, and the `break` operator exits the `switch` block. If x did not match any of the `case` labels, then the expressions in the `default` operator would execute instead.

The `switch` operator is useful is a few specific situations. In most cases, an `if-else` block will work just as well, although a `switch-case` block may be more efficient and compact. Here's a useful example of a `switch-case` block. This code will evaluate the chart period in minutes, and return a string if the chart period matches several common chart periods:

```
int period = _Period;
string printPeriod;
```

```
switch(period)
{
    case 60:
        printPeriod = "H1";
        break;

    case 240:
        printPeriod = "H4";
        break;

    case 1440:
        printPeriod = "D1";
        break;

    default:
        printPeriod = "M" + period;
}
```

The integer variable period is assigned the period of the current chart, in minutes, using the predefined _Period variable. The switch operator compares period to several common chart periods, including H1, H4 and D1. If period matches any of the common chart periods, the appropriate string is assigned to the string variable printPeriod. In the event that none of these chart periods are matched, a chart period string is constructed using the prefix "M" and the period in minutes.

For example, if period == 240, the variable printPeriod is assigned the string "H4". If period == 15, the expression following the default operator will execute, and printPeriod is assigned the string "M15". The variable printPeriod can be used to print a user-friendly chart period to the log or to the screen.

Loop Operators

Sometimes it is necessary for a program to repeat an action over and over again. For this, we use loop operators. There are three loop operators in MQL: *while*, *do-while* and *for*.

The while Operator

The while loop is the simplest loop in MQL. The while operator checks for a boolean or relational condition. If the condition is true, the code inside the brackets will execute. As long as the condition remains true, the code inside the brackets will continue to execute in a loop. Here is an example:

```
bool loop = true;
int count = 1;
```

```
while(loop == true)
{
    Print(count);                    // Output: 1, 2, 3, 4, 5
    if(count == 5) loop = false;
    count++;
}
```

We start by declaring a boolean variable named `loop` to use as the loop condition. We also declare an integer variable named `count` and initialize it to 1. The `while` operator checks to see if the variable `loop == true`. If so, the code inside the brackets is run.

We print the value of the `count` variable to the log. Next we check to see if `count == 5`. If so, we set `loop = false`. Finally we increment `count` by 1, and check the loop condition again. The result of this loop is that the numbers 1 - 5 are printed to the log.

When `count == 5`, the `loop` variable is set to `false`, and the condition for the `while` operator is no longer true. Thus, the loop stops executing and control passes to the expression following the closing bracket. Let's look at a second example, using a relational condition:

```
int count = 1;

while(count <= 5)
{
    Print(count);                    // Output: 1, 2, 3, 4, 5
    count++;
}
```

This code produces the same result as the loop above. In this example, the `count` variable is used as the loop condition. If `count` is less than or equal to 5, the loop will execute. On each execution of the loop, `count` will be incremented by 1 and the result printed to the log. Once `count` is greater than 5, the loop will exit.

The `while` loop condition is checked at the beginning of the loop. If the condition is false, the loop is never run. If you need to check the condition at the end of the loop, or you need the loop to run at least once, then use the do-while loop.

The do-while Operators

The do-while operators check the loop condition at the end of the loop, instead of the beginning. This means that the loop will always run at least once. Here's an example:

```
int count = 1;
```

45

```
    do
    {
        Print(count);                    // Output: 1, 2, 3, 4, 5
        count++;
    }
    while(count < 5)
```

Again, this is identical to the previous while loop example, except in this case, the value of count will be printed to the log at least once. For example, if count == 1, the numbers 1-5 will be printed to the log. If count == 6, the number 6 will be printed to the log.

In both the while and do-while loops, the condition to halt loop execution must occur sometime during the loop, or independently of the loop (such as an external event). If the condition to stop the loop does not occur, you'll end up with an infinite loop and your program will freeze. Here's an example:

```
    bool loop = true;
    int count;

    do
    {
        Print(count);
        count++;
    }
    while(loop == true)
```

This example will loop infinitely because the variable loop is always equal to true.

If you don't know how many times a loop will need to execute, or if you need to use a boolean condition as the loop condition, then use a while or do-while loop. If you know how many times a loop needs to execute, or if you need more advanced iteration, then use a for loop instead.

The for Operator

If you are using an integer variable to iterate through a loop (such as the count variable in the previous examples), the for loop is a better choice. The for operator contains three expressions separated by semicolons:

- The first expression is a variable(s) to initialize at the start of the loop. This variable is generally used to iterate through the loop.

- The second expression is the loop condition. This is generally a relational expression. When this expression is true, the loop executes. When it is false, the loop exits.

- The third expression is executed at the end of each loop. This is generally a mathematical expression to increment the iterator variable.

Here's an example of a for loop:

```
for(int count = 1; count <= 5; count++)
{
    Print(count);
}
```

The first expression in the for operator, int count = 1, declares an integer variable named count and initializes it to 1. The second expression, count <= 5, is the loop condition. If count is less than or equal to 5, the loop will execute. The third expression, count++, is executed at the end of each loop. This expression increments the count variable by 1. Note that there are semicolons after the first and second expressions, but not after the third expression.

Like the previous examples, this code prints the numbers 1-5 to the log. If you compare the code above to the while loop example on the previous page, the for loop requires fewer lines of code. Just about anything you can do with a while loop can also be done with a for loop.

You can omit any of the three expressions in the for loop, but the semicolons separating them must remain. If you omit the second expression, the loop is considered to be constantly true, and thus becomes an infinite loop.

You can declare multiple variables in the first expression of a for loop, as well as calculate multiple expressions in the third expression of a for loop. The additional expressions must be separated by commas. For example:

```
for(int a = 1, b = 2; a <= 5; a++, b += 2)
{
    Print("a=",a," b=",b);                    // Output: "a=1 b=2", "a=2 b=4", etc...
}
```

We declare two integer variables, a and b, and initialize them with the values of 1 and 2 respectively. The loop will execute when a is less than or equal to 5. On each iteration of the loop, a is incremented by 1, while b is incremented by 2. The values of a and b are printed to the log on each iteration.

The break Operator

Sometimes you need to exit a loop before it has finished iterating, or when a certain condition is met. The break operator immediately exits the nearest while, do-while or for loop. It also exits the switch operator, as explained on page 42.

Generally, the break operator is used to exit a loop when a certain condition is met. For example:

```
for(int count = 1; count <= 5; count++)
{
    if(count == 3) break;
    Print(count);              // Output: 1, 2
}
```

In this example, when count == 3, the break operator is called and the for loop is exited.

The continue Operator

The continue operator works similar to the break operator. Instead of exiting the loop entirely, the continue operator exits the current iteration of the loop and skips to the next iteration.

```
int count = 1;

while(count <= 5)
{
    if(count == 3) continue;
    Print(count);              // Output: 1, 2, 4, 5
    count++
}
```

This example will print the value of count to the log for every value except for 3.

Chapter 5 - Functions

Functions

A *function* is a block of code that performs a specific task, such as placing an order or adjusting the stop loss of a position. We will be creating our own functions to carry out many trading-related activities in this book. In addition, MQL5 has dozens of built-in functions that do everything from retrieving order information to performing complex mathematical operations.

Functions are designed to be flexible and reusable. Whenever you need to perform a specific action, such as placing an order, you call a function to perform that action. The function contains all of the code and logic necessary to perform the task. All you need to do is pass the required parameters to the function, if necessary, and handle any values returned by the function.

When you place an order, for example, you will call an order placement function. You will pass parameters to the function that instruct it to place an order on the specified symbol, at the specified price with the specified number of lots. Once the function has finished executing, it will return a value such as an order confirmation.

A function declaration consists of a return type, an identifier, and an optional list of parameters. Here's an example of a function declaration:

```
double BuyStopLoss(string pSymbol, int pStopPoints, double pOpenPrice)
{
    // Function body
}
```

The name of our function is BuyStopLoss(). This function will calculate the stop loss for a buy order. The return type is double, which means that this function will calculate a value of type double, and return that value to our program.

This function has three parameters: pSymbol, pStopPoints and pOpenPrice. In this book, we will preface all function parameter identifiers with a lower case "p". The parameters are separated by commas. Each parameter must have a type and an identifier. A parameter can also have a default value. We'll discuss default values in more detail shortly.

All three parameters are required – which means they must be passed to the function when the function is called. The first parameter, pSymbol, is a string value representing the symbol of the instrument. The second parameters, pStopPoints, is an integer value representing the stop loss value in points. The third parameter, pOpenPrice, is a double value representing the order opening price.

Here is the function in its entirety. This function will be placed somewhere on the global scope of our program – which means that it can't be inside another function. It can be placed in an include file, or even inside another program that is included in our program:

```
double BuyStopLoss(string pSymbol, int pStopPoints, double pOpenPrice)
{
    double stopLoss = pOpenPrice - (pStopPoints * _Point);
    stopLoss = NormalizeDouble(stopLoss,_Digits);
    return(stopLoss);
}
```

This function will calculate the stop loss by multiplying pStopPoints by the symbol's point value, represented by the predefined variable _Point (usually 0.00001 or 0.001), and subtracting that value from pOpenPrice. The result is assigned to the variable stopLoss. The value of stopLoss is normalized to the number of digits in the price using the NormalizeDouble() function, and the return operator returns the normalized value of stopLoss to the program.

Here's an example of how we would call this function in our program:

```
// Input variables
input int StopLoss = 500;

// OnTick() event handler
double orderPrice = SymbolInfoDouble(_Symbol,SYMBOL_ASK);
double useStopLoss = BuyStopLoss(_Symbol,StopLoss,orderPrice);
```

The input variable StopLoss is an integer variable that contains the stop loss value in points. This will be located at the beginning of our program, and will be set by the user. The double variable orderPrice is a local variable that will contain the opening price of our order – in this case, the current Ask price.

We call the BuyStopLoss() function, and pass the current chart symbol (_Symbol), the StopLoss variable and the orderPrice variable as the function parameters. The BuyStopLoss() function calculates the stop loss and stores the return value in the useStopLoss variable. This variable would then be used to modify the currently opened position and add a stop loss.

Default Values

A function parameter can be assigned a default value when the function is first declared. If a parameter has a default value, it must be placed at the end of the parameter list. Let's add a default value to one of the parameters in our BuyStopLoss() function:

```
double BuyStopLoss(string pSymbol, int pStopPoints, double pOpenPrice = 0)
{
    double stopLoss = pOpenPrice - (pStopPoints * _Point);
    stopLoss = NormalizeDouble(stopLoss,_Digits);
    return(stopLoss);
}
```

The pOpenPrice parameter is assigned a default value of zero. Any parameter that has a default value must be at the end of the parameter list. If you are using the default value when calling the function, the parameter can be omitted:

```
BuyStopLoss(_Symbol,StopLoss);
```

In the above example, the default value of 0 will be used for the pOpenPrice parameter.

You can have multiple parameters with default values, but they must all be at the end of the parameter list. If a function has multiple parameters with default values, and you are passing a value to a parameter with a default value, then any parameters before it must have values passed as well. Here's an example:

```
int MyFunction(string pSymbol, int pDefault1 = 0, int pDefault2 = 0)
{
    // Function body
}
```

MyFunction() has two parameters with default values: pDefault1 and pDefault2. If you need to pass a non-default value to pDefault2, but not to pDefault1, then a value must be passed to pDefault1 as well:

```
int nonDefault = 5;
MyFunction(_Symbol,0,nonDefault);
```

The parameter pDefault1 is passed the default value of 0, while pDefault2 is passed a value of 5. You cannot skip parameters when calling a function, unless all remaining parameters are using their default values. Of course, if you don't need to pass a value to pDefault1 and pDefault2, or just pDefault2, then you can omit it from the function call:

```
int point = 5;
MyFunction(_Symbol,point);
```

In this example, pDefault1 is passed a value of 5, but pDefault2 uses its default value of 0. If you are using the default value for pDefault1 as well, the only parameter that needs to be specified is pSymbol.

In summary, any function parameter(s) with a default value must be at the end of the parameter list. You cannot skip parameters when calling the function, so if a parameter with a default value is passed a different value when calling the function, then any parameters before it must have a value passed to it as well.

The return Operator

Any function that returns a value must have at least one return operator. The return operator contains the variable or expression to return to the calling program. The type of the expression must match the return type of the function. Generally, the return operator is the last line in your function, although you may have several return operators in your function, depending on your requirements.

The return type of a function can be of any type, including structures and enumerations. You cannot return an array from a function, although you can return an element from an array. If you need a function to return an array, you can pass an array to a function by reference. We'll discuss passing by reference shortly.

Here is our BuyStopLoss() function again. This function returns a value of type double. The value of the double variable stopLoss, which is local to the function, is returned to the calling program using the return operator:

```
double BuyStopLoss(string pSymbol, int pStopPoints, double pOpenPrice = 0)
{
    double stopLoss = pOpenPrice - (pStopPoints * _Point);
    stopLoss = NormalizeDouble(stopLoss,_Digits);
    return(stopLoss);
}
```

The void Type

Not every function needs to return a value. There is a special type called void, which specifies a function that does not return a value. A void function can accept parameters, but does not need to have a return operator. Here is an example of a function of void type with no parameters:

```
void TradeEmail()
{
    string subject = "Trade placed";
    string text = "A trade was placed on " + _Symbol;
    SendMail(subject,text);
}
```

This function will send an email using the mail settings specified in the *Tools* menu > *Settings* > *Email* tab. Note that there is no return operator because the function is of void type.

Passing Parameters by Reference

Normally, when you pass parameters to a function, the parameters are passed by *value*. This means that the value of the parameter is passed to the function, and the original variable remains unchanged.

You can also pass parameters by *reference*. Any changes made to a variable inside a function will be reflected in the original variable. This is useful when you need a function to modify an array or a structure. You will frequently pass arrays and structures by reference into MQL5 functions.

Here's an example of passing a structure by reference using the SymbolInfoTick() function. Here is the definition of the SymbolInfoTick() function from the *MQL5 Reference*:

```
bool SymbolInfoTick(
    string    symbol,      // symbol name
    MqlTick&  tick         // reference to a structure
);
```

The ampersand (&) before the tick parameter means that this parameter is passed by reference. Here is how we would use the SymbolInfoTick() function in code:

```
MqlTick myTick;
SymbolInfoTick(_Symbol,myTick);
Print(myTick.bid);
```

The first line declares an object named myTick, using the built-in MqlTick structure as the type. The MqlTick structure stores current price information from the server. The SymbolInfoTick() function fills an MqlTick object with the current price information of the specified symbol. The second parameter in the SymbolInfoTick() function call, myTick, is passed by reference. The myTick structure is modified by the function, and filled with the current price information from the trade server. The Print() function prints the current Bid price to the log by referencing the bid variable of the myTick object.

Here's another example of passing by reference using an array. In this example, we'll pass a dynamic array to a function by reference. We specify that a parameter is being passed by reference by prefixing the identifier with an ampersand (&):

```
void FillArray(int &array[])
{
    ArrayResize(array,3);
    array[0] = 1;
    array[1] = 2;
    array[2] = 3;
}
```

53

The sole parameter of the FillArray() function, &array[], is passed by reference. The dynamic array passed to the &array[] parameter will be modified by the function. Here is how we would call this function from our program:

```
int fill[];
FillArray(fill);
Print(fill[0]);        // Output: 1
```

The array fill[] now contains the values that were modified inside the FillArray() function.

Overloading Functions

Sometimes you may need to create multiple functions that perform essentially the same task. Each of these functions will have different input parameters, but the end result is the same. In MQL4, it would be necessary to give these functions different identifiers. MQL5 introduces *function overloading*, which allows you to have multiple functions with the same name.

Each identically-named function must have different parameters, either in number or in type. Let's demonstrate by using two trailing stop functions that we'll create later in this book. Both functions have the same name, and do basically the same thing. The difference is that the first function has an integer parameter named pTrailPoints, and the second has a double parameter named pTrailPrice:

```
bool TrailingStop(string pSymbol, int pTrailPoints, int pMinProfit = 0, int pStep = 10);
bool TrailingStop(string pSymbol, double pTrailPrice, int pMinProfit = 0, int pStep = 10);
```

The int parameter in the first function, pTrailPoints, accepts a trailing stop value in points. This is used to calculate a trailing stop price, relative to the current Bid or Ask price. The double parameter in the second function, pTrailPrice, accepts a price to be used as the trailing stop price.

By having two identically-named functions with different parameters, we have some flexibility as to how to administer the trailing stop, depending on the trading system. Since both functions share the same name, the programmer does not have to remember two (or more) different function names. In the end, this simply makes life easier for the programmer.

The compiler will know which function to use based on its unique parameter signature. The first function has a string parameter, followed by three integer parameters. The second has a string parameter, followed by a double parameter and two integer parameters. Here's how we would call the first variant of the function:

```
// Input variables
input int TrailingPoints = 500;

// OnTick() event handler
TrailingStop(_Symbol,TrailingPoints);
```

An int input variable named TrailingPoints allows the user to set a trailing stop in points. This value is used as the second parameter in the TrailingStop() function call. Because the TrailingPoints variable is of type int, the compiler knows to use the first variant of the function. Since we are using the default values for the pMinProfit and pStep parameters, we have omitted them from the function call.

And here's how we would call the second variant of the function:

```
// Input variables
input int TrailingPoints = 500;

// OnTick() event handler
double trailingPrice = SymbolInfoDouble(_Symbol,SYMBOL_ASK) - (TrailingPoints * _Point);
TrailingStop(_Symbol,trailingPrice);
```

The local double variable trailingPrice will contain a price to use as the trailing stop. Since the second parameter of the TrailingStop() function call is of type double, the compiler knows to use the second variant of the function.

Chapter 6 - Object-oriented Programming

One of the most exciting new features in MQL5 is the addition of object-oriented programming. *Object-oriented programming* (OOP for short) encourages code reuse and hides unnecessary implementation details from the user. This allows a much more flexible and compact style of programming.

The concepts of object-oriented programming are abstract in nature and often confounded by technical jargon. They can be difficult for the new programmer to grasp. But once you learn the fundamentals of OOP, you'll find them to be incredibly useful.

Object-oriented programming is based around the concepts of classes and objects. A *class* is a collection of variables and functions that perform a set of related tasks. The variables and functions contained inside a class are referred to as the *members* of a class.

A class is like a blueprint for an object. Take a car, for example. A car has a steering wheel, a gear shifter, a turn signal, headlights and so on. A class for a car object would contain all of the variables describing the car's state (speed, gear, whether the headlights are on and off), and all of the functions to perform a specific task (accelerating or decelerating, shifting gears, turning the headlights on and off, etc.)

An *object* is created using the class as a template. The class describes the car, while the object is the car itself. Each object has a unique name, similar to how each car has a unique vehicle identification number. You can create as many objects as necessary, just like a manufacturer can build many different cars of the same model. The variables of an object are distinct from the variables of other objects, just like how different cars are going different speeds on the highway.

For example, in an expert advisor you may have several indicators. For a moving average cross, you will have at least two moving average indicators. Each moving average will have a different period setting, and may have different calculation mode and price settings.

A moving average indicator can be represented by a class. The moving average indicator class contains all of the variables and functions necessary to create the indicator and retrieve the current indicator value during program execution. Using this class, we create one or more objects, each of which will have their own identifier, settings and indicator values.

We don't have to worry about creating a dynamic series array to hold the indicator values, nor do we need to think about initializing the indicator, storing the indicator handle and copying the indicator values from the buffers to the array. All of these details are handled in the class implementation. All we need to do is create an object, and use the class functions to carry out these tasks.

Classes

Classes are declared on the global scope, just like functions. A class can be placed inside your program or inside an include file. A class declaration uses the `class` keyword, followed by a unique identifier. The members of the class are placed inside the brackets, sorted by *access keywords*. The closing bracket of a class declaration is terminated with a semicolon.

Here's an example of a class declaration for an indicator object:

```
class CIndicator
{
    protected:
        int handle;
        double main[];

    public:
        double Main(int pShift=0);
        void Release();
        CIndicator();
};
```

The name of the class is `CIndicator`. It has three public members and two protected members. Notice that every function and variable declaration inside the class declaration is terminated with a semicolon. The closing bracket of the class declaration itself is terminated with a semicolon as well. The public members of the `CIndicator` class include the `Main()` function, the `Release()` function, and a default constructor with the same name as our class. The protected members include the `handle` variable and the `main[]` array.

We'll discuss the `CIndicator` class in more detail in Chapter 17, so don't worry if you don't understand how it works just yet. In this chapter, we will be using the `CIndicator` class as an example to explain the concepts of object-oriented programming.

Access Modifiers

The labels `public`, `private` and `protected` are access keywords. They determine whether a variable or function is available for use outside of a class. Here are the descriptions of the access keywords:

- **Public** members of a class are available for use outside of the class. This is the method by which the program interacts with an object. Public members are generally functions that perform important tasks. Public functions can access and modify the private and protected members of a class.

- **Private** members of a class are only available for use by functions inside the class. A private member cannot be accessed outside the class. Classes that are derived from this class will not inherit these members. (We'll discuss inheritance shortly.) Private members are generally internal functions and variables that are accessed by public members of a class.

- **Protected** members of a class are essentially private members that will be inherited by a derived class. Use the protected keyword unless you're certain that you won't be deriving any classes from the current class.

This concept of hiding class members from the rest of the program is an OOP concept referred to as *encapsulation*. By hiding class members, we ensure that they won't be used or modified unnecessarily.

The CIndicator class is meant to be used as a parent class for other indicator classes, such as a moving average indicator class. We've created this class to implement features that every indicator will use. For example, every indicator requires a variable to store the indicator handle, so we've created an integer variable named handle. We'll also need at least one dynamic array to hold indicator values. The first (and sometimes only) buffer in an indicator is referred to as the *main buffer,* so we've declared a double array named main[]. Both of these variables are protected, which means they can't be accessed outside of our class, and can only be accessed by public members of the class.

For the public members of our class, we've created a function named Main() to update the indicator values and access the values in the main[] array, and a Release() function to release the indicator from memory. Let's take a closer look at the public functions of our class. We'll start with the Main() function. This function copies indicator data to the main[] array using the handle variable to identify the indicator, and returns the value for the specified bar. Here is the function declaration for the Main() function:

```
double CIndicator::Main(int pShift=0)
{
    CopyBuffer(handle,0,0,MAX_COUNT,main);
    double value = NormalizeDouble(main[pShift],_Digits);
    return(value);
}
```

This function declaration is placed on the global scope, after the CIndicator class declaration. Note the CIndicator:: right before the function identifier. The double-colon operator (::) is the *scope resolution* operator. It identifies a function as belonging to a specific scope – in this case, the scope is the CIndicator class.

Notice also that our protected handle and main[] variables are used as parameters for the CopyBuffer() function. The only way we can access protected and private members of our class is through a public class function. If you attempt to access these members from elsewhere in your program, you'll get a compilation error.

The preferred way to declare class functions is the method used above. But you can also declare a function in-line, inside the class declaration itself. This is useful for very short functions that consists of a single line or two. Here's an example using our `Release()` function:

```
class CIndicator
{
    public:
        void Release() { IndicatorRelease(handle); }

    // ...
};
```

The `Release()` function is declared on a single line inside our class declaration. It consists of a call to the `IndicatorRelease()` function. The contents of the function are contained within the brackets. It is not required to have a semicolon after the closing bracket, although the compiler will not complain if you do.

Constructors

When an object is created from a class, a function called the *constructor* is executed automatically. The constructor is used to initialize the variables inside our object. If no constructor is explicitly defined, then the compiler creates a default constructor to initialize the variables. This default constructor is not visible to the programmer.

In our `CIndicator` function, we have declared our own default constructor, also called `CIndicator()`. The name of a constructor must match that of the class identifier. It is not necessary to specify a return type for a default constructor, as the type is always `void`. The access level of a constructor must be `public`.

Here is the `CIndicator()` constructor declaration inside the `CIndicator` class declaration:

```
class CIndicator
{
    public:
        CIndicator();

    // ...
};
```

And here is our explicitly defined class constructor. The only purpose of our constructor is to set our `main[]` array as a series array. We'll talk more about series arrays later in the book:

```
CIndicator::CIndicator(void)
{
    ArraySetAsSeries(main,true);
}
```

Remember, you do not need to explicitly declare a default constructor if you do not need one. If there are actions you want carried out automatically upon the creation of an object, then create a default constructor to do this.

There are more advanced things you can do with constructors, such as parametric constructors and initialization lists. There is also the destructor, which is called upon destruction of an object. Since we won't be using those features in this book, it will be up to the reader to learn more. You can learn about constructors and destructors in the *MQL5 Reference* under *Language Basics > Data Types > Structures and Classes*.

Derived Classes

One of the most useful features of OOP is the concept of *inheritance*. In OOP, you can create a class using another class as a template. The new class inherits all of the functions and variables of the parent class (except for those that use the private access keyword). You can then extend upon that class by adding new functions and variables.

This is exactly what we'll do with our CIndicator class. Remember that the CIndicator class is meant to be a parent class for other indicator classes. The specifics of implementing a particular indicator are handled in the derived class, while the basic variables and functions are already defined in the parent class.

Here's an example of a derived class for a moving average indicator. This class contains one function, Init(), which initializes the moving average indicator:

```
class CiMA : public CIndicator
{
    public:
        int Init(string pSymbol,ENUM_TIMEFRAMES pTimeframe, int pMAPeriod,
            int pMAShift,ENUM_MA_METHOD pMAMethod, ENUM_APPLIED_PRICE pMAPrice);
};
```

The name of our derived class is CiMA. Notice the colon (:), followed by public CIndicator in the class declaration. This specifies that the CiMA class is derived from the CIndicator class. All of the public and protected members of the CIndicator class are now part of the CiMA class.

The public keyword specifies that all public and protected members of the base class will remain public or protected in any classes derived from this one. You can also specify the protected or private keywords, which changes the access level of all public and protected members of the parent class to protected or private in any derived classes. However, you won't need to do this very often, if at all.

Here is the function declaration for our `Init()` function. This function passes the moving average indicator settings to the `iMA()` function, which returns an indicator handle. Note the usage of the `handle` variable from the `CIndicator` class:

```
int CiMA::Init(string pSymbol, ENUM_TIMEFRAMES pTimeframe, int pMAPeriod,
    int pMAShift, ENUM_MA_METHOD pMAMethod, ENUM_APPLIED_PRICE pMAPrice)
{
    handle = iMA(pSymbol,pTimeframe,pMAPeriod,pMAShift,pMAMethod,pMAPrice);
    return(handle);
}
```

Virtual Functions

Sometimes, you will need to change the way a function operates in a derived class. Or you may want to define a function in a parent class, but take care of the implementation details in the derived class. You can accomplish this by using *virtual functions*.

Let's use the example of a car again: A car class would have a function to change gears. However, the process of changing gears in a car with a manual transmission is different than changing gears with an automatic transmission. Therefore, we would declare a virtual gear changing function in our parent class, and then write the actual function in our derived classes.

Here's what a car class would look like in code:

```
class Car
{
    public:
        virtual int ShiftGears(int gear) { return(gear); }
};
```

The name of our class is `Car`. We've declared a single function – a virtual function named `ShiftGears()`. We've added an empty function body to the `ShiftGears()` declaration, containing only a single `return` operator. The `ShiftGears()` function is declared with the `virtual` keyword. This means that the function will be defined in the derived classes.

Let's create a derived class for a manual transmission car:

```
class ManualCar : public Car
{
    public:
        int ShiftGears(int gear);
};
```

This class is named ManualCar, and is for a manual transmission vehicle. Here is where we define the ShiftGears() function. The function is declared with the same type and parameters as the function in the Car class. Notice that we do not use the virtual keyword here. The body of the function is defined elsewhere, and contains the logic for shifting gears using a manual transmission. Other classes derived from the Car class would define ShiftGears() in a similar manner.

If a derived class has a function with the same name as a function in the parent class, the function in the derived class will override the function in the parent class. This process of redefining functions in derived classes is an OOP concept known as *polymorphism*.

The Init() function in our CiMA class can be declared as a virtual function in our CIndicator class. This ensures that any class derived from CIndicator must implement the Init() class:

```
class CIndicator
{
    protected:
        int handle;

    public:
        virtual int Init() { return(handle); }
};
```

The Init() function is declared as a public member of the class. The virtual keyword specifies that the implementation of the function will be carried out in any derived classes. The body of the function is declared on the same line. In this example, the function simply returns the value of the handle variable. When we create a derived class based on CIndicator, the Init() function must be implemented in the new class.

Objects

Now that we've created a class for a moving average indicator, let's create an object. You create an object the same way you create a variable, enumeration or structure: The class name is used as the type, and the object is given a unique identifier:

```
CiMA objMa;
```

This creates an object named objMa, based on the class CiMA. When an object is created, the constructor for that object is executed automatically. Since the CiMA class is derived from the CIndicator class, the constructor from the CIndicator class is made available to the CiMA class, and will execute automatically upon creation of an object based on the CiMA class. Thus, the CIndicator() constructor is called, and the main[] array is set as a series array upon creation of the object:

```
CIndicator::CIndicator(void)
{
    ArraySetAsSeries(main,true);
}
```

Once the object is declared, we can access any public members using the dot (.) operator. The first thing we'll need to do is initialize our indicator with the Init() function:

```
objMa.Init(_Symbol,0,MAPeriod,0,MAMethod,MAPrice);
```

Remember that the Init() function was declared as a virtual function in the CIndicator class, and defined in the CiMA class. The Init() function creates an indicator handle for the moving average indicator using the specified settings. The indicator handle is stored in the protected variable handle, which is defined in the CIndicator class.

Next, we'll use the Main() function to fill the main[] array with indicator values, and retrieve the indicator value for a specific bar. Since the main[] array is a protected class member, we can only access it through a public function such as the Main() function. This line of code prints the moving average value for the current bar to the log:

```
Print(objMa.Main());
```

You can create as many objects as necessary for your program. If you need a second moving average indicator, then declare it using a different unique identifier, and access the public members of the object as shown above. By creating classes to perform common tasks, you save time and reduce errors, as well as reducing the amount of code in your program. The remainder of the book on expert advisors will focus on the creation of classes to perform common trading tasks.

Chapter 7 - The Structure of an MQL5 Program

Before we start developing MQL5 programs, let's take a minute to address the structure of an MQL5 program. All MQL5 programs share the same basic structure. At the top of the file will be the preprocessor directives. Next are the input and global variables. Finally, the functions, classes and event handlers of the program are defined.

Preprocessor Directives

The *preprocessor directives* are used to set program properties, define constants, include files and import functions. Preprocessor directives are typically declared at the very top of the program file. Let's start with the `#property` preprocessor directive, which you'll see in nearly every MQL5 program.

#property Directive

The `#property` directive defines properties for the program, such as descriptive information, indicator, script and library properties. We'll discuss properties for indicators, scripts and libraries in the appropriate chapters.

When you create a program using the *MQL5 Wizard*, the author, `link` and `version` properties will be inserted automatically. You can also add the `description` property manually. These will be displayed on the *Common* tab in the expert advisor *Properties* dialog. This is useful if you decide to distribute your program.

The `#property` directives will be placed at the very top of your program. They must be defined in your main program file, as any property directives in include files will be ignored. Here's an example of the descriptive `#property` directives:

```
#property copyright "Andrew R. Young"
#property link "http://www.expertadvisorbook.com"
#property version "1.02"
#property description "Dual moving average cross with trailing stop"
```

And here's how these `#property` directives above will display in the *Common* tab of the expert advisor *Properties* window:

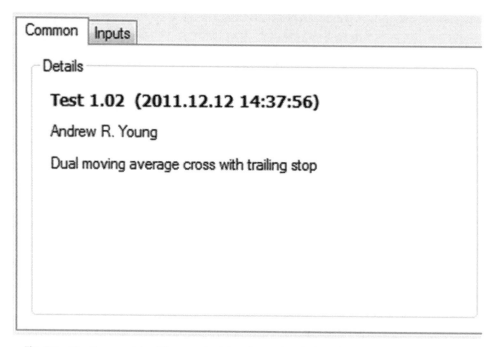

Fig. 7.1 – The *Common* tab of the expert advisor *Properties* window, displaying the `#property` directives defined in the source code file.

The `copyright` property above ("Andrew R. Young") doubles as a hyperlink. Placing the mouse over it and clicking will take the user to the website defined in the `link` property.

#define Directive

The `#define` directive is used to define constants for use throughout the program. We addressed constants earlier on page 17. To summarize, the `#define` directive specifies an identifier with a constant value. The convention is to use all capital letters for the identifier name. Here are some examples of constants using the `#define` directive:

```
#define PI 3.14159265
#define MAX_BARS 100
#define COMPANY_NAME "Easy Expert Forex"
```

To use a constant, you substitute the identifier name for the constant value. If you wanted to use the value of Pi in your program, the identifier PI would be interpreted as 3.14159265 by the compiler:

```
double diameter = 5;
double circumference = PI * diameter;
Print(circumference);                    // Output: 15.70796325
```

The example above calculates the circumference of a circle by multiplying the value of Pi by the diameter of a circle.

There a a second variant of the #define directive called the parametric form. The parametric form of the #define directive accepts parameters, just like a function would. You can have up to eight parameters in a parametric #define directive. The result is an expression that is calculated and substituted in the program:

```
#define PI 3.14159265
#define CIRC(dia) PI * dia
```

The define directive CIRC(dia) takes a single argument, dia, which is the diameter of a circle. The value of dia will be multiplied by the constant PI, and the result returned to the program.

```
double diameter = 5;
double circumference = CIRC(diameter);
Print(circumference);                    // Output: 15.70796325
```

The example above calculates the circumference of a circle by using the CIRC(dia) parametric constant. The value of the diameter variable is passed to the CIRC(dia) constant as the parameter. The dia parameter is multiplied by the PI constant, and the result is placed in the circumference variable.

If you have a simple mathematical expression that is used frequently, then the parametric form of the #define directive can be a good substitute for writing a dedicated function. However, a function would allow for more advanced manipulation, such as normalizing a result to a specified number of digits.

#include Directive

The #include directive specifies an include file to be included in the program. An include file contains variables, function and classes to be used in the main program. There are two variations of the #include directive:

```
#include <Trade.mqh>
#include "Trade.mqh"
```

The first variant of the #include directive encloses the include file name in angle brackets (<>). This indicates that the compiler will look for the include file in the default include directory, which is the \MQL5\Include subfolder of your MetaTrader 5 install folder. This is the preferred method of including files, and the one we will use in this book.

The second variant of the #include directive encloses the include file name in double quotes ("). This tells the compiler to look for the include file in the same directory as the program file. If for some reason you've stored the include file in the same directory as your program, then use double quotes in your #include directive.

There is an additional preprocessor directive, the #import directive, which is used to import functions from libraries and DLLs. We'll address the usage of the #import directive in Chapter 21.

Input and Global Variables

After the preprocessor directives, the next section of your MQL5 program will be the input and global variable declarations. It doesn't necessarily matter which comes first, but the convention is to put the input variable declarations first. As you will recall, input variables are the user-adjustable settings for your program.

Any global variables that you're using must be declared outside of any functions or event handlers. The convention is to put them at the top of the file, after the input variables. This ensures that they won't be called by any functions before they have been declared.

Classes and Functions

Custom classes or functions can be defined anywhere in your program, especially in include files that are included using the #include directive. Generally, any classes or functions that are present in the main program file can go before or after the event handlers, but should be placed below any input or global variables in the file.

Event Handlers

An *event handler* is a function that is executed whenever a certain event occurs. Event handlers are the method by which an MQL5 program runs. For example, when an incoming price quote is received by an expert advisor, the *NewTick* event occurs. This causes the OnTick() event handler to execute. The OnTick() event handler contains code that runs every time a price change occurs.

Each program type has its own event handlers. Expert advisors and indicators use the *Init* event to execute the OnInit() event handler, which runs once at the start of the program. Scripts use the *Start* event, which is handled by the OnStart() event handler. Indicators use the *Calculate* event and the OnCalculate() event handler to execute indicator calculations. We'll go into more detail on event handlers for each program type in the relevant chapters.

An Example Program

Here's a brief example showing all of the elements described above and how they would fit into an MQL5 program. Not every element will be in every program – for example, an #include directive is not needed if you're not including functions and variables from an external file. The #property directives are usually optional. Most programs will have input variables, but global variables are optional. And you may or may not need to create your own classes or functions.

The event handlers will vary depending on the program type. This example shows an expert advisor program with the OnInit() and OnTick() event handlers:

```
// Preprocessor directives
#property copyright "Andrew R. Young"
#property link "http://www.expertadvisorbook.com"
#property description "An example of MQL5 program structure"

#define PI 3.14159265

// Input variables
input double Radius = 1.5;

// Global variables
double RadiusSq;

// Event handlers
int OnInit()
{
    RadiusSq = MathPow(Radius,2);
    return(0);
}

void OnTick()
{
    double area = CalcArea();
    Print("The area of a circle with a radius of "+Radius+" is "+area);
}

// Functions
double CalcArea()
{
    double result = PI * RadiusSq;
    return result;
}
```

Above is a simple program that calculates the area of a circle, given the radius. The #property directives come first, with some descriptive information about the program. A #define directive defines a constant for Pi. An input variable named Radius allows the user to enter the radius of a circle. Finally, a global variable named RadiusSq is available to all functions of the program.

This program has two event handlers. The OnInit() event handler runs once at the start of the program. The square of the Radius variable is calculated and stored in the global variable RadiusSq. After OnInit() has run, the OnTick() event handler will run on each incoming price change.

The OnTick() event handler calls the function CalcArea(), which is defined at the bottom of our program. The function calculates the area of a circle, and returns the result to the OnTick() function. The Print() function will print the following string to the log, assuming that the default value for Radius is used:

```
The area of a circle with a radius of 1.5 is 7.0685834625
```

That's it. We haven't added any trading functions to this program, as we simply want to demonstrate the basic structure of an MQL5 program. In the next chapter, we'll begin creating expert advisors.

Chapter 8 - Expert Advisor Basics

Orders, Deals and Positions

Before delving into the specifics of creating expert advisors, let's address the way that MetaTrader 5 executes trades. There are significant changes in trade execution compared to MetaTrader 4. It is important to understand these differences, as it may affect whether your trading strategy is appropriate for MetaTrader 5.

There are three steps to executing a trade in MetaTrader 5: *order*, *deal*, and *position*. An order is a request to open a trade at a specified price and volume for a specific financial security, such as the EURUSD. When an order is filled, a deal occurs, and a trade is placed at the specified price with the specified volume. A position is the net long or short result of one or more deals. As an MQL5 programmer, you will be using orders to modify your current position in a security. The deal is the intermediate step, and while you can access deal information in MQL5, we won't need to do so.

There can be only one position open at any time on a security. You can add orders to a position, or open orders in the opposite direction to reduce or even change the direction of a position. You can also adjust the stop loss or take profit of a position at any time. But unlike MetaTrader 4, it is not possible to have multiple, separate orders open on a security at one time. It is also not possible to hedge a position.

Let's demonstrate with an example: A buy order is opened on EURUSD for 1.00 lots. This results in a net long position of 1 lot on EURUSD. If we then open a sell order for 0.50 lots, the result is a net long position of 0.5 lots. The sell order effectively closed part of the existing long position. If we opened a second sell order of 0.5 lots, the remaining long position would be closed out, leaving us with no position.

Here's another example: We have a long position of 1 lot on EURUSD. We then open a sell order for 2.00 lots. The result is a net short position of 1 lot. Our position changed from long to short in a single deal. Thus, it is possible to close out an existing position and open a new position in the opposite direction with a single trade.

When multiple orders in the same direction are added to a position, the position price is changed. The new position price is calculated as a weighted average. For example, if we have a net long position of 1 lot on EURUSD at 1.35712, and add a second buy order of 0.5 lots at 1.35825, the new position price would be 1.357496. If an order is opened in the opposite direction to close out part of an existing position, the position price does not change.

Depending on the order type and the market execution type, a stop loss and take profit can be set when the order is placed. Otherwise, the position can be modified at any time to add or change the stop loss and take profit. If another order is placed with a different stop loss and/or take profit, the new stop loss and/or take profit price will be applied to the entire position.

For example, a buy position of 0.75 lots is opened on EURUSD at 1.35674, with a stop loss at 1.3517 and no take profit. A second buy order of 0.25 lots is placed with a stop loss of 1.3532 and a take profit of 1.3632. The stop loss of the entire position is changed to 1.3532, and the take profit is changed to 1.3632.

To summarize, it is not possible to have several open orders with different lot sizes and stop loss and/or take profit prices as is possible in MetaTrader 4. However, you can use pending orders to scale out of a position at predetermined price levels. We'll examine this in more detail in Chapter 13.

Market Orders

A *market order* is a request to open a trade at the current market price. The order type is either *buy* or *sell*. Buy orders are opened at the current Ask price, while sell orders are opened at the current Bid price. Conversely, when a position is closed, a buy position is closed at the current Bid price, while a sell position is closed at the current Ask price.

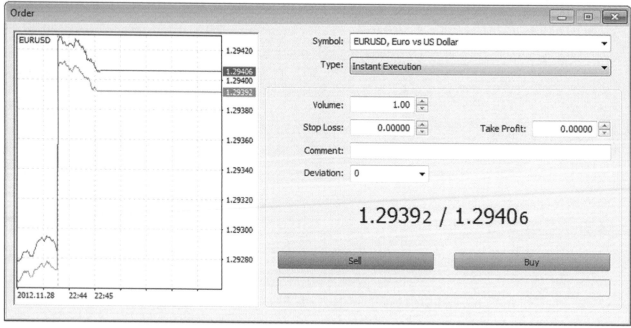

Fig 8.1 – The *New Order* dialog. This broker uses Instant Execution.

The process by which an order is executed depends on the trade server's *execution type*. There are four execution types in MetaTrader 5. The execution type is determined by the broker, and is indicated in the *Type* field of the *New Order* dialog box. Most Forex brokers use either market or instant execution. ECN brokers use exchange execution. The request execution type is intended for non-Forex instruments, and is not commonly used.

Instant execution is the classic execution mode familiar to MetaTrader 4 users. The trader specifies the trade type, the symbol to trade, the trade volume, a stop loss and take profit price, and the deviation in points. If the current market price deviates from the last quoted price by the number of points specified in the *Deviation* field, a requote is triggered, and the trader is asked to accept or reject the new price. Otherwise, the trade is placed at the current market price.

One advantage of instant execution is that the trader can specify a stop loss and take profit when placing the order, which saves a step when trading manually. In the event of rapidly moving prices and significant price deviation (also referred to as *slippage*), the trader has the option to reject the order and wait for calmer market conditions.

The disadvantage of instant execution is slippage. When the slippage exceeds the specified deviation, the order will not be placed, which creates difficulties when auto trading. Even if the order is placed, the stop loss and take profit price will be a few points off relative to the order execution price.

Most brokers now use market or exchange execution. With the *market execution* type, the trader specifies the trade volume and the fill policy. The trade is executed at the current market price, with no requotes. No stop loss or take profit is placed with the market execution type. The trader will have to modify the position to add a stop loss and take profit after the order is filled.

Exchange execution is used by ECN brokers, and allows traders to execute trades with no intermediate dealing desk. For all intents and purposes, the exchange execution type works similarly to the market execution type. For the *request execution* type, the trader must specify the trade volume, stop loss and take profit first. Then, the terminal requests a current market price from the trade server. As of this writing, no MetaTrader brokers are known to be using request execution.

The *fill policy* determines the action to take when there is insufficient liquidity in the market. *Fill or Kill* means that if the trade server cannot place the order for the full trade volume at the specified price, then the order is canceled. *Fill or Cancel* (also called *Immediate or Cancel*) means that the trade server will attempt to partially fill an order. Any remaining volume that is not filled will be canceled. *Return* means that the trade server will always attempt to fill any unfilled volume.

Expert Advisor Event Handlers

At the end of the last chapter, we discussed the structure of an MQL5 program and introduced the reader to event handlers. Let's discuss the event handlers that are used in expert advisor programs:

OnInit()

The OnInit() event handler runs when the *Init* event occurs. The Init event occurs when the program is initialized. Normally, the OnInit() event handler runs once at the start of a program. If there are any changes in the expert advisor properties, or if the current chart symbol or period is changed, the expert advisor will reinitialize and the OnInit() function will run again.

If there are any actions you wish to execute once at the start of the program, place them in the OnInit() event handler. The OnInit() event handler is not required in your program, but it is recommended. We will use OnInit() to initialize certain variables and carry out one-time actions.

OnDeinit()

The OnDeinit() event handler runs when the *Deinit* event occurs. The Deinit event occurs when the program is deinitialized. If the expert advisor properties are changed, the current chart symbol or period is changed, or if the program is exited, the OnDeinit() event will run.

If there are any actions you wish to execute when the program ends, place them in the OnDeinit() event handler. The OnDeinit() event handler is not required in your program. One use of the OnDeinit() event handler is to remove objects from the chart when removing an indicator or program that has placed them.

OnTick()

The OnTick() event handler runs when the *NewTick* event occurs. The NewTick event occurs when a price change is received from the server. Depending on current market activity, price changes can occur several times a minute or even several times a second. Each time a price change occurs, the OnTick() event handler will run.

The OnTick() event handler is the most important event handler in your program, and is required in your expert advisor. Almost all of your trading system logic will occur in the OnTick() event handler, and many of the code examples in this book will go inside the OnTick() event handler.

OnTrade()

The OnTrade() event handler runs when the *Trade* event occurs. The Trade event occurs whenever there is a change in the order pool. This includes placing and modifying orders, closing and modifying positions, and triggering of pending orders. If there are any actions you want to execute when changes in order status occur, then place them in the OnTrade() event handler. The OnTrade() event handler is optional.

OnTimer()

The OnTimer() event handler runs when the *Timer* event occurs. The Timer event occurs when a timer defined by the EventSetTimer() function is activated. This allows you to execute actions at specified intervals. The OnTimer() event handler is optional. We'll discuss the usage of the OnTimer() event handler in Chapter 18.

Creating An Expert Advisor in MetaEditor

The easiest way to create an expert advisor file in MetaEditor is to use the *MQL5 Wizard*. If you have a template that you want to use to create your expert advisors (like the one included in the source code download), you can open the file and save it under a different name in the \MQL5\Experts directory. Unfortunately, MetaEditor for MQL5 does not allow the use of predefined template files.

Click the *New* button on the MetaEditor toolbar to open the *MQL5 Wizard*. Ensure that *Expert Advisor (template)* is selected, and click *Next*. The *Properties* dialog allows you to enter a file name and some descriptive information about your program. You can optionally add input variables in the *Parameters* window. The path to the \MQL5\Experts folder is already included in the file name. Type the name of your expert advisor, preserving the "Experts\" path preceding it. Fig. 8.2 shows the *Properties* dialog.

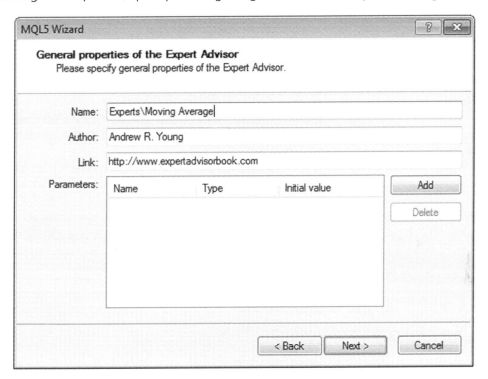

Fig 8.2 – The Expert Advisor properties dialog of the *MQL5 Wizard*.

Click *Next*, and you'll be prompted to insert additional event handlers. The OnTrade() event handler is checked by default. If you need to add an event handler to your program, check it and click *Finish* at the bottom. Fig. 8.3 shows the event handler dialog. After clicking *Finish*, a new expert advisor MQ5 file is created in the \MQL5\Experts folder, and the file is opened in MetaEditor.

Fig. 8.3 – The event handlers dialog of the *MQL5 Wizard*.

Here is what an empty expert advisor template looks like with the basic event handlers added:

```
//+------------------------------------------------------------------+
//|                                         Simple Expert Advisor.mq5 |
//|                                                     Andrew Young  |
//|                                      http://www.easyexpertforex.com |
//+------------------------------------------------------------------+
#property copyright "Andrew Young"
#property link      "http://www.easyexpertforex.com"
#property version   "1.00"
//+------------------------------------------------------------------+
//| Expert initialization function                                   |
//+------------------------------------------------------------------+
int OnInit()
  {
//---

//---
   return(0);
  }
```

```
//+------------------------------------------------------------------+
//| Expert deinitialization function                                 |
//+------------------------------------------------------------------+
void OnDeinit(const int reason)
  {
//---

  }
//+------------------------------------------------------------------+
//| Expert tick function                                             |
//+------------------------------------------------------------------+
void OnTick()
  {
//---

  }
//+------------------------------------------------------------------+
```

The expert advisor file generated by the MQL5 Wizard includes three descriptive #property directives and the OnInit(), OnDeinit() and OnTick() functions by default. If you specified any additional event handlers or input parameters in the MQL5 Wizard, they will appear here as well.

Chapter 9 - Order Placement

OrderSend()

The OrderSend() function is used to place, modify and close orders. The usage of the function has changed from MQL4. Here is the function definition for OrderSend():

```
bool OrderSend(MqlTradeRequest& request, MqlTradeResult& result)
```

The OrderSend() function has two parameters: an MqlTradeRequest object that contains the order parameters, and an MqlTradeResult object that returns the results of the order request. The ampersands (&) in the function definition indicate that both objects are passed by reference.

The MqlTradeRequest Structure

Let's examine the MqlTradeRequest structure. We previously addressed structures on page 23. We will declare an object of the MqlTradeRequest type, and assign the trade parameters to the member variables of the object. Here is the MqlTradeRequest structure definition from the *MQL5 Reference*:

```
struct MqlTradeRequest
{
    ENUM_TRADE_REQUEST_ACTIONS action;     // Trade operation type
    ulong magic;                           // Magic number
    ulong order;                           // Order ticket (for modifying pending orders)
    string symbol;                         // Symbol
    double volume;                         // Volume in lots
    double price;                          // Order opening price
    double stoplimit;                      // Stop limit price (for stop limit orders)
    double sl;                             // Stop loss price
    double tp;                             // Take profit price
    ulong deviation;                       // Deviation in points
    ENUM_ORDER_TYPE type;                  // Order type
    ENUM_ORDER_TYPE_FILLING type_filling;  // Execution type
    ENUM_ORDER_TYPE_TIME type_time;        // Expiration type
    datetime expiration;                   // Expiration time
    string comment;                        // Order comment
}
```

To declare an MqlTradeRequest object, simply declare an object using MqlTradeRequest as the type:

```
MqlTradeRequest request;
```

This creates an object named `request`. An `MqlTradeRequest` object is generally declared early in the `OnTick()` event handler of your program, or as a class member. We can now assign the trade parameters to the variables of the object using the dot (.) operator:

```
request.symbol = _Symbol;
request.volume = 0.5;
request.type = ORDER_TYPE_BUY;
```

Let's take a closer look at the members of the `MqlTradeRequest` structure:

- **action** – The trade operation type. Required. This variable accepts a value of the ENUM_TRADE_REQUEST_ACTIONS enumeration:

  - TRADE_ACTION_DEAL – The `OrderSend()` function will place a market order.

  - TRADE_ACTION_PENDING – The `OrderSend()` function will place a pending order.

  - TRADE_ACTION_SLTP – The `OrderSend()` function will modify the stop loss and/or take profit of the current position.

  - TRADE_ACTION_MODIFY – The `OrderSend()` function will modify a previously placed pending order.

  - TRADE_ACTION_REMOVE – The `OrderSend()` function will cancel a previously placed pending order.

- **magic** – The "magic number". This number uniquely identifies orders as being placed by a certain expert advisor. Optional.

- **order** – The order ticket of a previously placed pending order. Required if the `action` variable is set to TRADE_ACTION_MODIFY or TRADE_ACTION_REMOVE.

- **symbol** – The symbol of the financial security to trade, for example, "EURUSD" or `_Symbol`. Required.

- **volume** – The trade volume in lots. Required.

- **price** – The order opening price. For a pending order, the price can be any valid price above or below the current market price. For a market order, the price must be the current Ask price (for buy orders) or the current Bid price (for sell orders). Brokers that use market or exchange execution do not require this parameter when placing market orders. Otherwise, required if action is set to TRADE_ACTION_DEAL, TRADE_ACTION_PENDING or TRADE_ACTION_MODIFY.

- **stoplimit** – This is the limit order price for stop limit orders. The `action` variable must be set to `TRADE_ACTION_PENDING`, and the `type` variable below must be set to `ORDER_TYPE_BUY_STOP_LIMIT` or `ORDER_TYPE_SELL_STOP_LIMIT`. Required for stop limit orders.

- **sl** – The stop loss price. Required for market orders if the broker uses the request or instant execution types. Also required for pending orders. If the broker uses market or exchange execution, the stop loss is not placed.

- **tp** – The take profit price. Required for market orders if the broker uses the request or instant execution types. Also required for pending orders. If the broker uses market or exchange execution, the take profit is not placed.

- **deviation** – The maximum deviation in points. Required for request or instant execution of market orders.

- **type** – The order type. This variable accepts a value of the `ENUM_ORDER_TYPE` enumeration. Required.

    - `ORDER_TYPE_BUY` – A buy market order.

    - `ORDER_TYPE_SELL` – A sell market order.

    - `ORDER_TYPE_BUY_STOP` – A buy stop pending order.

    - `ORDER_TYPE_SELL_STOP` – A sell stop pending order.

    - `ORDER_TYPE_BUY_LIMIT` – A buy limit pending order.

    - `ORDER_TYPE_BUY_STOP_LIMIT` – A buy stop limit pending order.

    - `ORDER_TYPE_SELL_STOP_LIMIT` – A sell stop limit pending order.

- **type_filling** – The fill policy of the order. This variable accepts a value of the `ENUM_ORDER_TYPE_FILLING` enumeration. If not specified, the trade server default will be used.

    - `ORDER_FILLING_FOK` – *Fill or Kill*. If the order cannot be filled at the requested trade volume and price, the order will not be placed.

    - `ORDER_FILLING_IOC` – *Immediate or Cancel* (also known as Fill or Cancel). If the order cannot be filled at the requested trade volume and price, a partial order will be filled.

    - `ORDER_FILLING_RETURN` – *Return*. If an order cannot be filled at the requested trade volume and price, the trade server will place an additional order for the unfilled volume.

- **type_time** – The expiration type for a pending order. This variable accepts a value of the ENUM_ORDER_TYPE_TIME enumeration. Optional. If not specified, the trade server default (usually *Good Til Canceled*) will be used.

  - ORDER_TIME_GTC – Good Til Canceled. The pending order will not expire.

  - ORDER_TIME_DAY – The pending order will expire at the end of the trading day.

  - ORDER_TIME_SPECIFIED – The pending order will expire at the date and time specified in the expiration variable below.

- **expiration** – The pending order expiration time. Required if the type_time variable is set to ORDER_TIME_SPECIFIED. The value must be of datetime type, and must be set sometime in the future.

- **comment** – A text string to use as an order comment.

Market Order

Let's demonstrate how the MqlTradeRequest structure can be used to place a market order. The first thing we need to do is to declare MqlTradeRequest and MqlTradeResult objects. We'll cover the MqlTradeResult structure in the next section:

```
MqlTradeRequest request;
MqlTradeResult result;
```

This example will place a buy market order of 1.00 lot on the current chart symbol with no stop loss or take profit:

```
request.action = TRADE_ACTION_DEAL;
request.type = ORDER_TYPE_BUY;
request.symbol = _Symbol;
request.volume = 1;
request.type_filling = ORDER_FILLING_FOK;
request.price = SymbolInfoDouble(_Symbol,SYMBOL_ASK);
request.sl = 0;
request.tp = 0;
request.deviation = 50;

OrderSend(request,result);
```

The action variable is set to TRADE_ACTION_DEAL, which indicates that this is a market order. The type variable is set to ORDER_TYPE_BUY, which indicates this is a buy order. We assign the predefined _Symbol variable to the `symbol` variable to indicate that we will place an order on the current chart symbol. The `volume` variable is set to 1 lot. The `type_filling` variable sets the fill type to Fill or Kill. All execution types require the above five variables to be specified. (If `type_filling` is not specified, it will default to the server's default fill policy.)

We use the `SymbolInfoDouble()` function to return the current Ask price for the current chart symbol, and assign that value to the `price` variable. Remember that a buy market order is placed at the current Ask price. The `sl` and `tp` variables are both set to zero. The `deviation` variable sets the deviation to 50 points.

Brokers using the market or exchange execution types will ignore the `price`, `sl`, `tp` and `deviation` variables. However, since we want our code to work on all brokers, regardless of execution type, we will assign values to these variables for brokers that use the instant or request execution types.

Notice that we don't have a stop loss or take profit defined. Since market and exchange execution brokers will ignore the stop loss and take profit, we will add a stop loss and take profit to the position after the order has been placed. This also ensures accurate placement of the stop loss and take profit relative to the position opening price.

Finally, we call the `OrderSend()` function, passing our `request` and `result` objects as parameters. The trade server will attempt to place the order, and return the result in the `result` object variables.

Add Stop Loss & Take Profit

After we've placed a market order, we'll add a stop loss and take profit, if one has been specified. For simplicity's sake, we'll simply assign a valid stop loss and take profit price to the `sl` and `tp` variables in this example:

```
request.action = TRADE_ACTION_SLTP;
request.symbol = _Symbol;
request.sl = 1.3500;
request.tp = 1.3650;

OrderSend(request,result);
```

The `action` variable is set to `TRADE_ACTION_SLTP`, which indicates that we will be modifying the stop loss and take profit on the current position. The `symbol` variable specifies that we will modify the open position on the current chart symbol. We've set a stop loss and take profit price that would be valid on a buy position, assuming that the position opening price is between 1.3500 and 1.3650.

All of the above variables must be specified when modifying a position, regardless of whether the stop loss or take profit value remains unchanged. If you do not want to set either the stop loss or take profit value, set the appropriate variable to zero.

Pending Order

Next, let's demonstrate the placement of a pending order. We'll add a stop loss, take profit and expiration time to this order. All of the variables below must be specified when placing a pending order:

```
request.action = TRADE_ACTION_PENDING;
request.type = ORDER_TYPE_BUY_STOP;
request.symbol = _Symbol;
request.volume = 1;
request.price = 1.3550;
request.sl = 1.3500;
request.tp = 1.3650;
request.type_time = ORDER_TIME_SPECIFIED;
request.expiration = D'2012.01.10 15:00';
request.type_filling = ORDER_FILLING_FOK;
request.stoplimit = 0;

OrderSend(request,result);
```

The action variable is set to TRADE_ACTION_PENDING, indicating that we are placing a pending order. The type variable is set to ORDER_TYPE_BUY_STOP, indicating a buy stop order. The symbol, volume, price, sl and tp variables are all assigned appropriate values.

The type_time variable is set to ORDER_TIME_SPECIFIED, which indicates that the order will have an expiration time. A datetime constant for January 10, 2012 at 15:00 is assigned to the expiration variable. The type_filling variable sets the fill type to Fill or Kill. The stoplimit variable is only needed when placing a stop limit order, but we'll assign a value of 0.

Modify Pending Order

Let's demonstrate how to modify a pending order. You'll need the order ticket of a pending order to be able to modify it. To retrieve the order ticket, use the OrderGetTicket() function to iterate through the order pool and select the appropriate pending order. We'll discuss pending order management in Chapter 13. For now, we'll assume that the ticket variable holds the correct order ticket number:

```
request.action = TRADE_ACTION_MODIFY;
request.order = ticket;
request.price = 1.3600;
request.sl = 1.3550;
request.tp = 1.3700;
request.type_time = ORDER_TIME_SPECIFIED;
request.expiration = D'2012.01.10 18:00';
```

```
OrderSend(request,result);
```

The action variable is set to TRADE_ACTION_MODIFY, indicating that we are modifying a current order. The order variable is assigned the ticket number of the order that we wish to modify, which is stored in the ticket variable. The price, sl, tp and expiration variables are assigned appropriate values, and the order will be modified to reflect these changes.

Remove Pending Order

Finally, we'll demonstrate how to remove a pending order. The only variables necessary are the action and order variables:

```
request.action = TRADE_ACTION_REMOVE;
request.order = ticket;

OrderSend(request,result);
```

The action variable is set to TRADE_ACTION_REMOVE, indicating that we wish to delete a pending order. As before, the ticket number is stored in the ticket variable, and assigned to the order variable of the request object. Calling the OrderSend() function with the above parameters will delete the pending order that matches the ticket number in the order variable.

The MqlTradeResult Structure

Once we've placed an order using the OrderSend() function, we'll check the MqlTradeResult object to see if the order was successful. The variables of the MqlTradeResult object contain the return code from the trade server, the ticket number of the trade, the volume and price of the trade, and the current bid and ask prices.

Here is the definition of the MqlTradeResult structure from the *MQL5 Reference*:

```
struct MqlTradeResult
{
    uint retcode;        // Return code
    ulong deal;          // Deal ticket (for market orders)
    ulong order;         // Order ticket (for pending orders)
    double volume;       // Deal volume
    double price;        // Deal price
    double bid;          // Current Bid price
    double ask;          // Current Ask price
    string comment;      // Broker comment to operation
}
```

As demonstrated earlier in the chapter, we declare an `MqlTradeResult` object named `result`, and pass the object as the second parameter of the `OrderSend()` function. The trade server fills the object with the results of the trade request. After the `OrderSend()` function is called, we check the variables of the `MqlTradeResult` object to verify that the trade was placed correctly. Depending on the type of trade operation, not all of the `MqlTradeResult` variables will be filled.

The most important variable of the `MqlTradeResult` structure is `retcode`, which is the *return code* from the trade server. The return code indicates whether or not the request was successful. If the trade was not placed, the return code indicates the error condition.

The next page has a complete list of return codes from the *MQL5 Reference*:

Code	Constant	Description
10004	TRADE_RETCODE_REQUOTE	Requote
10006	TRADE_RETCODE_REJECT	Request rejected
10007	TRADE_RETCODE_CANCEL	Request canceled by trader
10008	TRADE_RETCODE_PLACED	Order placed
10009	TRADE_RETCODE_DONE	Request completed
10010	TRADE_RETCODE_DONE_PARTIAL	Only part of the request was completed
10011	TRADE_RETCODE_ERROR	Request processing error
10012	TRADE_RETCODE_TIMEOUT	Request canceled by timeout
10013	TRADE_RETCODE_INVALID	Invalid request
10014	TRADE_RETCODE_INVALID_VOLUME	Invalid volume in the request
10015	TRADE_RETCODE_INVALID_PRICE	Invalid price in the request
10016	TRADE_RETCODE_INVALID_STOPS	Invalid stops in the request
10017	TRADE_RETCODE_TRADE_DISABLED	Trade is disabled
10018	TRADE_RETCODE_MARKET_CLOSED	Market is closed
10019	TRADE_RETCODE_NO_MONEY	There is not enough money to complete the request
10020	TRADE_RETCODE_PRICE_CHANGED	Prices changed
10021	TRADE_RETCODE_PRICE_OFF	There are no quotes to process the request
10022	TRADE_RETCODE_INVALID_EXPIRATION	Invalid order expiration date in the request
10023	TRADE_RETCODE_ORDER_CHANGED	Order state changed
10024	TRADE_RETCODE_TOO_MANY_REQUESTS	Too frequent requests
10025	TRADE_RETCODE_NO_CHANGES	No changes in request
10026	TRADE_RETCODE_SERVER_DISABLES_AT	Autotrading disabled by server
10027	TRADE_RETCODE_CLIENT_DISABLES_AT	Autotrading disabled by client terminal
10028	TRADE_RETCODE_LOCKED	Request locked for processing
10029	TRADE_RETCODE_FROZEN	Order or position frozen
10030	TRADE_RETCODE_INVALID_FILL	Invalid order filling type
10031	TRADE_RETCODE_CONNECTION	No connection with the trade server
10032	TRADE_RETCODE_ONLY_REAL	Operation is allowed only for live accounts
10033	TRADE_RETCODE_LIMIT_ORDERS	The number of pending orders has reached the limit
10034	TRADE_RETCODE_LIMIT_VOLUME	The volume of orders and positions has reached the limit

Each return code is represented by a constant. The most common return codes are TRADE_RETCODE_PLACED (10008) and TRADE_RETCODE_DONE (10009), both of which indicate that the trade was placed successfully. Almost all other return codes indicate a problem placing the trade. The return code description will indicate the nature of the problem.

Depending on the return code, you may want to take various actions, such as emailing a trade confirmation or printing an error message to the screen. Here's a simple example of how to handle the return code from the server:

```
OrderSend(request,result);

if(result.retcode == TRADE_RETCODE_DONE || result.retcode == TRADE_RETCODE_PLACED)
{
    Print("Trade placed");
}
else
{
    Print("Trade not placed. Error code ",result.retcode);
}
```

After the OrderSend() function sends the trade request to the server and fills the variables of the result object, we check the request.retcode variable for the return code. If the return code equals TRADE_RETCODE_DONE or TRADE_RETCODE_PLACED, we print a message to the log indicating that the trade was placed successfully. Otherwise, we print a message indicating that the trade was not placed, along with the return code indicating an error state.

The other variables of the result object can be used to confirm order placement or to troubleshoot a failed order placement. The example below prints a message to the log containing the volume, price, bid and ask values returned from the trade server:

```
OrderSend(request,result);

if(result.retcode == TRADE_RETCODE_DONE || result.retcode == TRADE_RETCODE_PLACED)
{
    Print("Trade placed");
}
else
{
    Print("Trade not placed. Error code ",result.retcode);
}

Print("Return Code:",result.retcode,", Volume: ",result.volume,
    ", Price: ",result.price,", Bid: ",result.bid,", Ask: ",result.ask);
```

In the next chapter, we will add code to our order placement functions to assist us in troubleshooting errors, as well as retrying order placement on recoverable errors.

A Simple Expert Advisor

Let's demonstrate how the OrderSend() function works in a simple expert advisor. This trading strategy will open a buy market order when the current close price is greater than the moving average, or open a sell market order when the close price is less than the moving average. The user has the option to specify a stop loss and take profit in points, as well as a trade volume.

```
// Input variables
input double TradeVolume=0.1;
input int StopLoss=1000;
input int TakeProfit=1000;
input int MAPeriod=10;

// Global variables
bool glBuyPlaced, glSellPlaced;

// OnTick() event handler
void OnTick()
{
    // Trade structures
    MqlTradeRequest request;
    MqlTradeResult result;
    ZeroMemory(request);

    // Moving average
    double ma[];
    ArraySetAsSeries(ma,true);

    int maHandle=iMA(_Symbol,0,MAPeriod,MODE_SMA,0,PRICE_CLOSE);
    CopyBuffer(maHandle,0,0,1,ma);

    // Close price
    double close[];
    ArraySetAsSeries(close,true);
    CopyClose(_Symbol,0,0,1,close);

    // Current position information
    bool openPosition = PositionSelect(_Symbol);
    long positionType = PositionGetInteger(POSITION_TYPE);

    double currentVolume = 0;
    if(openPosition == true) currentVolume = PositionGetDouble(POSITION_VOLUME);
```

```
    // Open buy market order
    if(close[0] > ma[0] && glBuyPlaced == false
        && (positionType != POSITION_TYPE_BUY || openPosition == false))
    {
        request.action = TRADE_ACTION_DEAL;
        request.type = ORDER_TYPE_BUY;
        request.symbol = _Symbol;
        request.volume = TradeVolume + currentVolume;
        request.type_filling = ORDER_FILLING_FOK;
        request.price = SymbolInfoDouble(_Symbol,SYMBOL_ASK);
        request.sl = 0;
        request.tp = 0;
        request.deviation = 50;

        OrderSend(request,result);

        // Modify SL/TP
        if(result.retcode == TRADE_RETCODE_PLACED || result.retcode == TRADE_RETCODE_DONE)
        {
            request.action = TRADE_ACTION_SLTP;

            do Sleep(100); while(PositionSelect(_Symbol) == false);
            double positionOpenPrice = PositionGetDouble(POSITION_PRICE_OPEN);

            if(StopLoss > 0) request.sl = positionOpenPrice - (StopLoss * _Point);
            if(TakeProfit > 0) request.tp = positionOpenPrice + (TakeProfit * _Point);

            if(request.sl > 0 && request.tp > 0) OrderSend(request,result);

            glBuyPlaced = true;
            glSellPlaced = false;
        }
    }

    // Open sell market order
    else if(close[0] < ma[0] && glSellPlaced == false && positionType != POSITION_TYPE_SELL)
    {
        request.action = TRADE_ACTION_DEAL;
        request.type = ORDER_TYPE_SELL;
        request.symbol = _Symbol;
        request.volume = TradeVolume + currentVolume;
        request.type_filling = ORDER_FILLING_FOK;
        request.price = SymbolInfoDouble(_Symbol,SYMBOL_BID);
        request.sl = 0;
        request.tp = 0;
        request.deviation = 50;
```

```
        OrderSend(request,result);

        // Modify SL/TP
        if((result.retcode == TRADE_RETCODE_PLACED || result.retcode == TRADE_RETCODE_DONE)
            && (StopLoss > 0 || TakeProfit > 0))
        {
            request.action = TRADE_ACTION_SLTP;

            do Sleep(100); while(PositionSelect(_Symbol) == false);
            double positionOpenPrice = PositionGetDouble(POSITION_PRICE_OPEN);

            if(StopLoss > 0) request.sl = positionOpenPrice + (StopLoss * _Point);
            if(TakeProfit > 0) request.tp = positionOpenPrice - (TakeProfit * _Point);

            if(request.sl > 0 && request.tp > 0) OrderSend(request,result);

            glBuyPlaced = false;
            glSellPlaced = true;
        }
    }
}
```

Let's go through this one section at a time:

```
// Input variables
input double TradeVolume=0.1;
input int StopLoss=1000;
input int TakeProfit=1000;
input int MAPeriod=10;
```

These are the input variables that are visible to the end user. These allow the user to adjust the trade volume, the stop loss and take profit in points, and the period of the moving average.

```
// Global variables
bool glBuyPlaced, glSellPlaced;
```

These are global variables that are visible to our entire program. Global variables will have a gl prefix throughout this book. The glBuyPlaced and glSellPlaced variables will determine whether a buy or sell position was previously opened. This prevents another position from opening in the same direction after the current position has closed at a stop loss or take profit price.

```
// OnTick() event handler
void OnTick()
{
    // Trade structures
    MqlTradeRequest request;
    MqlTradeResult result;
    ZeroMemory(request);
```

The beginning of the OnTick() event handler contains the declarations for the request and result objects. The ZeroMemory() function ensures that the member variables of the request object are zeroed out. Not including the ZeroMemory() function may cause order execution errors.

```
    // Moving average
    double ma[];
    ArraySetAsSeries(ma,true);

    int maHandle=iMA(_Symbol,0,MAPeriod,MODE_SMA,0,PRICE_CLOSE);
    CopyBuffer(maHandle,0,0,1,ma);


    // Close price
    double close[];
    ArraySetAsSeries(close,true);
    CopyClose(_Symbol,0,0,1,close);
```

The code above initializes the arrays that hold the moving average values and the close prices. We'll discuss price and indicator data in Chapters 16 and 17. The ma[] array holds the moving average indicator values, while the close[] array holds the close price of each bar.

```
    // Current position information
    bool openPosition = PositionSelect(_Symbol);
    long positionType = PositionGetInteger(POSITION_TYPE);

    double currentVolume = 0;
    if(openPosition == true) currentVolume = PositionGetDouble(POSITION_VOLUME);
```

Before opening an order, we'll need to check and see if there is a position already open. The PositionSelect() function returns a value of true if a position is open on the current symbol. The result is assigned to the openPosition variable. The PositionGetInteger() function with the POSITION_TYPE parameter returns the type of the current position (buy or sell), and assigns it to the positionType variable. If a position is currently open, the PositionGetDouble() function with the POSITION_VOLUME parameter assigns the current position volume to the currentVolume variable. We'll discuss position information in Chapter 12.

```
// Open buy market order
if(close[0] > ma[0] && glBuyPlaced == false
    && (positionType != POSITION_TYPE_BUY || openPosition == false))
{
    request.action = TRADE_ACTION_DEAL;
    request.type = ORDER_TYPE_BUY;
    request.symbol = _Symbol;
    request.volume = TradeVolume + currentVolume;
    request.type_filling = ORDER_FILLING_FOK;
    request.price = SymbolInfoDouble(_Symbol,SYMBOL_ASK);
    request.sl = 0;
    request.tp = 0;
    request.deviation = 50;

    OrderSend(request,result);
```

This is the code that checks for the buy market order condition. The close[0] array refers to the close price for the current bar, while ma[0] is the current moving average value. If the close of the current bar is greater than the moving average, that indicates a buy signal. But first we need to check for the existence of an open position, and determine whether the previous order was a buy order.

If the glBuyPlaced global variable is true, this indicates that the last order placed was a buy order. Our trading system will place one order when a trading signal occurs. When that order is closed at a stop loss or take profit price, we will wait for a new trade signal before opening another order. A trading signal in the opposite direction will set the glBuyPlaced variable to false.

We also need to check the type of the open position. If the positionType variable is not equal to the value of the POSITION_TYPE_BUY constant, then we can assume that a buy position is not currently open. We also need to check the openPosition variable to see if a position is currently open. We do this because the positionType variable will contain a value of 0 if a position is not open. The integer value for POSITION_TYPE_BUY just happens to be 0. So the openPosition variable is needed to confirm the existence of a buy position.

To summarize the buy order conditions – if the close price is greater than the moving average, the last order opened was not a buy order and a position is not currently open (or the currently open position is a sell position), then we open a buy market order.

The request variables followed by the OrderSend() function should already be familiar to you. Note the request.volume assignment. We add the value of the TradeVolume input variable to the value of the currentVolume local variable. If a sell position is currently open, we want to open a larger buy order so that the sell position is closed out, and we are left with a net long position equal to the amount entered in TradeVolume.

```
// Modify SL/TP
if(result.retcode == TRADE_RETCODE_PLACED || result.retcode == TRADE_RETCODE_DONE)
{
    request.action = TRADE_ACTION_SLTP;

    do Sleep(100); while(PositionSelect(_Symbol) == false);
    double positionOpenPrice = PositionGetDouble(POSITION_PRICE_OPEN);

    if(StopLoss > 0) request.sl = positionOpenPrice - (StopLoss * _Point);
    if(TakeProfit > 0) request.tp = positionOpenPrice + (TakeProfit * _Point);

    if(request.sl > 0 && request.tp > 0) OrderSend(request,result);

    glBuyPlaced = true;
    glSellPlaced = false;
}
}
```

After the buy market order has been placed, we check to see if the trade was successful. If so, we go ahead and modify the position to add the stop loss and take profit. The first thing to do is to check the value of the result.retcode variable to see if the order was placed successfully. Depending on the execution type, a return code value of TRADE_RETCODE_PLACED or TRADE_RETCODE_DONE indicates a successful order. If the retcode variable matches either of these values, then we calculate the stop loss and take profit prices and modify the order.

We assign the TRADE_ACTION_SLTP value to the request.action variable to indicate that we are modifying the stop loss and take profit. Next, we use a do-while loop to pause the program's execution using the Sleep() function before checking the output of the PositionSelect() function. Because of the way that MetaTrader 5's trade structure works, it may take several milliseconds until the order that was just placed appears as a currently opened position. If we attempt to call PositionSelect() immediately, it will sometimes return a value of false, making it impossible to retrieve the order opening price. After pausing the execution, we check the output of the PositionSelect() function to see if it returns true. If not, the loop continues until PositionSelect() returns true.

Once the current position has been selected, we retrieve the position opening price using PositionGetDouble() with the POSITION_PRICE_OPEN parameter, assigning the result to the positionOpenPrice variable. If the StopLoss and/or TakeProfit input variables are greater than zero, we calculate the stop loss and/or take profit price by adding or subtracting the relevant value from the positionOpenPrice variable, and assigning the result to request.sl or request.tp. If either request.sl or request.tp contains a value greater than zero, we call the OrderSend() function to modify our position with the new stop loss and/or take profit prices.

Lastly, we need to set the glBuyPlaced and glSellPlaced variables. Since our buy order was placed successfully, we will set glBuyPlaced to true. This will prevent a second buy order from opening if our buy position is closed by stop loss or take profit. We also set glSellPlaced to false, which allows a sell position to open if the close price crosses the moving average in the opposite direction.

If this all looks a little overwhelming to you, don't worry. The example expert advisor above shows the process of placing orders in MQL5, but the actual implementation of this code will be hidden in classes and functions that we will create in the next few chapters. The file name of this expert advisor is Simple Expert Advisor.mq5, and you can view the code in the \MQL5\Experts\Mql5Book folder.

Chapter 10 - Creating An Order Placement Class

You've learned how to place and modify orders of all types using the `OrderSend()` function. Now it is time to create reusable classes for placing, modifying and closing orders. Our order placement class will take care of filling the `MqlTradeRequest` variables, placing the order, and checking the `MqlTradeResult` variables to verify the order result. All you have to do is declare an object based on the class and pass the relevant parameters to the order placement function of the object.

First, we'll need to create an include file to hold our order placement classes. Include files are stored in the `\MQL5\Include` directory by default. We will store our include files in a subfolder named Mql5Book. If you download the source code from `http://www.expertadvisorbook.com`, the include files used in this book will be in the `\MQL5\Include\Mql5Book` folder.

The `#include` directives in our program files will reference the Mql5Book path. The first include file we'll create is named `Trade.mqh`. So the `#include` directive to include this file in our expert advisor programs will be:

```
#include <Mql5Book\Trade.mqh>
```

Assuming that there is an empty include file named `Trade.mqh` in the `\MQL5\Include\Mql5Book` folder, let's create our trade class. The convention for class names that we'll use in this book is a capital "C", followed by a capitalized class name. The name of our trade class will be `CTrade`.

Note that some of our class names will be identical to class names in the MQL5 standard library. We will not be using the MQL5 standard library in this book, so keep in mind that any identical class names found in the *MQL5 Reference* refer to the standard library, and not to the classes found in this book.

CTrade Class

Let's start by creating a class declaration for our trade class. We'll add the `MqlTradeRequest` and `MqlTradeResult` objects to our declaration, as they will be used in most of our class functions:

```
class CTrade
{
    private:
        MqlTradeRequest request;

    public:
        MqlTradeResult result;
};
```

We've made the `request` object private, since there is no reason for the programmer to be able to access the `request` object members outside of the class. The `result` object is public, because the programmer may want to access the result object members outside of the class to determine the result of the last trade.

The OpenPosition() Function

Our first class function will place market orders. We'll name the function `OpenPosition()`, since it opens a trade position as opposed to a pending order. We're going to make the `OpenPosition()` function private instead of public. Later on in the chapter, we'll create public helper functions to place specific types of orders.

Here is the `OpenPosition()` function declaration inside our class declaration:

```
class CTrade
{
    private:
        MqlTradeRequest request;
        bool OpenPosition(string pSymbol, ENUM_ORDER_TYPE pType, double pVolume,
            double pStop = 0, double pProfit = 0, string pComment = NULL);

    public:
        MqlTradeResult result;
};
```

The return type of the `OpenPosition()` function is `bool`. The function will return `true` if the order was placed successfully, and `false` if it was not. This function has six parameters. You will recognize these as the request parameters from the previous chapter. All of our function parameter variables are prefaced with a lower-case "p" (short for "parameter"). This indicates that the variable is a function parameter that is local to the function.

Here are the descriptions of the `OpenPosition()` function parameters:

- `pSymbol` – The symbol of the financial security to open the market order on.

- `pType` – The order type. Accepts a value of the ENUM_ORDER_TYPE enumeration.

- `pVolume` – The volume in lots of the market order.

- `pStop` – The stop loss price. Optional.

- `pProfit` – The take profit price. Optional.

- `pComment` – An order comment. Optional.

The only required parameters are the symbol, the order type and the trade volume. Although the stop loss and take profit parameters are provided, we will add the stop loss and take profit to the position after the order has been placed. We will cover this in the next chapter.

Next, we'll define the function itself. This is done below the class declaration:

```
bool CTrade::OpenPosition(string pSymbol, ENUM_ORDER_TYPE pType, double pVolume,
    double pStop = 0, double pProfit = 0, string pComment = NULL)
{

}
```

Notice the `CTrade::` before `OpenPosition()`. The double colon (`::`) is the scope resolution operator, which identifies the `OpenPosition()` function as being part of the `CTrade` class. The class name and scope resolution operator must be present before the class function identifier.

Let's begin adding code to our empty function. We'll start by filling in the `request` object variables:

```
request.action = TRADE_ACTION_DEAL;
request.symbol = pSymbol;
request.type = pType;
request.sl = pStop;
request.tp = pProfit;
request.comment = pComment;
```

This should be familiar to you from the previous chapter. `TRADE_ACTION_DEAL` defines the trade operation as a market order. The function parameters are assigned to their respective `request` variables.

Next we'll need to determine the trade volume. The purpose of this function is to open a net position of the indicated type (buy or sell) and volume. If there is a position currently open in the opposite direction, we'll need to close it out when opening our order. For example, if we are opening a buy position of 1 lot, and there is a sell position of 1 lot currently opened, we'll need to open a buy position of 2 lots to result in a net buy position of 1 lot.

To do this, we need to determine whether there is a position currently open on the selected symbol, and in what direction. We'll use the `PositionSelect()` function to select the position, if one exists. If a position exists, we'll retrieve the order type and volume of the current position:

```
double positionLots = 0;
long positionType = WRONG_VALUE;
```

```
if(PositionSelect(pSymbol) == true)
{
    positionLots = PositionGetDouble(POSITION_VOLUME);
    positionType = PositionGetInteger(POSITION_TYPE);
}
```

First, we declare a double variable named positionLots to hold the lot size of the current position. Next, we declare a long variable named positionType to hold the position type. This is initialized to the constant WRONG_VALUE. The integer value of the WRONG_VALUE constant is -1. This sets the variable to a neutral state. The reason we don't initialize positionType to 0 is because 0 is a valid position type value.

The PositionSelect() function queries whether there is a position open on the symbol contained in the pSymbol variable. If there is a position open, the PositionSelect() function returns a value of true and selects the current position for processing. If PositionSelect() returns true, we execute the expressions inside the brackets.

The PositionGetDouble() function with the POSITION_VOLUME parameter returns the volume of the current position, and assigns it to the positionLots variable. The PositionGetInteger() function with the POSITION_TYPE parameter returns the position type and assigns it to the positionType variable.

The position type is a value of the ENUM_POSITION_TYPE enumeration, either POSITION_TYPE_BUY or POSITION_TYPE_SELL. Since POSITION_TYPE_BUY has an integer value of 0, this is why we initialized the positionType variable above to WRONG_VALUE, or -1.

Now that we have information on the current position, we need to calculate the appropriate trade volume. If the current position is a buy position, and the market order type as identified by the pType variable is a sell order (or vice versa), then we need to add the current position volume to the value of the pVolume variable to get the total trade volume:

```
if((pType == ORDER_TYPE_BUY && positionType == POSITION_TYPE_SELL)
    || (pType == ORDER_TYPE_SELL && positionType == POSITION_TYPE_BUY))
{
    request.volume = pVolume + positionLots;
}
else request.volume = pVolume;
```

There are two boolean AND operations (&&) inside the if operator, separated by an OR operation (||). If the market order type (the pType variable) is a buy order (ORDER_TYPE_BUY) and the position type (the positionType variable) is a sell position (POSITION_TYPE_SELL), then we add the value of the pVolume parameter to the value of the positionLots variable to get the total trade volume. This is assigned to the

100

request.volume variable. If the market order type is a sell order, and the position type is a buy position, then the same applies.

In either case, the existing position will be closed out, and the result will be a net position of the type indicated by the pType variable. If there is no position open, or if the currently opened position is of the same type as the market order, then we simply assign the value of pVolume to the request.volume variable.

The last thing we need to do before placing the order is to assign the current market price to the request.price variable. This depends on whether the order type is buy or sell. If it is a buy order, the order opening price will be the current Ask price. If it is a sell order, the order opening price will be the current Bid price:

```
if(pType == ORDER_TYPE_BUY) request.price = SymbolInfoDouble(pSymbol,SYMBOL_ASK);
else if(pType == ORDER_TYPE_SELL) request.price = SymbolInfoDouble(pSymbol,SYMBOL_BID);
```

If the pType variable indicates a buy order, the SymbolInfoDouble() function retrieves the current Ask price for the symbol indicated by the pSymbol variable. If pType indicates a sell order, then SymbolInfoDouble() retrieves the current Bid price.

Now all we need to do is to call the OrderSend() function to place the market order.

```
OrderSend(request,result);
```

Error Handling

When a trade error occurs, we need to notify the user so they can take appropriate action. We will also log relevant trade information to assist in troubleshooting. Some error conditions (such as requotes, timeouts and connection errors) are self-correcting if we simply retry the order placement again.

The first thing we need to do is check the return code from the server. As you'll recall, the MqlTradeResult object that we pass to the OrderSend() function contains the return code from the server in the retcode variable. The complete list of return codes is on page 87.

Return codes 10008 (TRADE_RETCODE_PLACED) and 10009 (TRADE_RETCODE_DONE) indicate that the trade has been placed successfully. If any other code is returned from the server, this indicates a likely error condition. We will create a function to check the return code and evaluate whether the return code indicates an error condition or a successful order placement.

First, we will create an enumeration that will be used as a return value to determine whether an order was placed successfully. This enumeration will be defined in our Trade.mqh file:

```
enum ENUM_CHECK_RETCODE
{
    CHECK_RETCODE_OK,
    CHECK_RETCODE_ERROR,
};
```

The constant CHECK_RETCODE_OK indicates that the trade operation was successful, while the constant CHECK_RETCODE_ERROR indicates that the trade operation has failed.

Next, we'll create a function to check the return code. The CheckReturnCode() function will use the switch-case operators to evaluate a list of return code constants. Depending on the return code passed to the function, the switch operator will return one of the constants from the ENUM_CHECK_RETCODE enumeration above.

Here is the CheckReturnCode() function. This will be placed in the Trade.mqh file:

```
int CheckReturnCode(uint pRetCode)
{
    int status;
    switch(pRetCode)
    {
        case TRADE_RETCODE_DONE:
        case TRADE_RETCODE_DONE_PARTIAL:
        case TRADE_RETCODE_PLACED:
        case TRADE_RETCODE_NO_CHANGES:

            status = CHECK_RETCODE_OK;
            break;

        default: status = CHECK_RETCODE_ERROR;
    }

    return(status);
}
```

The CheckReturnCode() function accepts one parameter, a uint variable named pRetCode. This contains the return code from the MqlTradeResult object.

We declare an integer variable named status, which will hold a value from our ENUM_CHECK_RETCODE enumeration. The switch operator compares the value of pRetCode against a list of return code constants indicated by the case operators. If the value of pRetCode matches any of the case operators, program execution will continue until a break operator is reached, or the switch operator ends.

First, we check for a successful order placement. We've added several return codes that indicate a successful order placement or a non-error condition. If the pRetCode value matches any of the return codes in this list, the status variable is assigned the CHECK_RETCODE_OK constant. Otherwise, the default label is executed and the status variable is assigned the CHECK_RETCODE_ERROR constant. The value of status is returned to the program, and the function exits.

Let's return to our market order placement function and add the CheckReturnCode() function:

```
int checkCode = 0;
OrderSend(request,result);

checkCode = CheckReturnCode(result.retcode);
```

We declare an integer variable named checkCode. This will hold the return value of the CheckReturnCode() function. We call the OrderSend() function to place the order. Then we pass the result.retcode variable to the CheckReturnCode() function, and store the return value in checkCode.

Next, we will check the value of the checkCode variable to determine whether the return code indicates a successful trade or an error condition. In the event of an error, an alert will be displayed to the user:

```
if(checkCode == CHECK_RETCODE_ERROR)
{
    string errDesc = TradeServerReturnCodeDescription(result.retcode);
    Alert("Open market order: Error ",result.retcode," - ",errDesc);
    break;
}
```

If checkCode contains the value of CHECK_RETCODE_ERROR, we obtain an error description from the TradeServerReturnCodeDescription() function. This function is contained in the errordescription.mqh file, which is installed with MetaTrader 5. To add this file to our project, we place this #include directive at the top of our Trade.mqh file:

```
#include <errordescription.mqh>
```

The TradeServerReturnCodeDescription() function returns a string with a description of the error code. This is stored in the errDesc variable. The Alert() function shows the alert popup window with the return code and description:

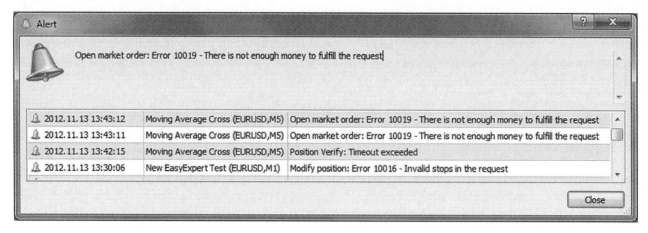

Fig 10.1 – The *Alert* dialog, displaying an error message from our `OpenPosition()` function.

Next, we will print the order information to the log for troubleshooting purposes. If an error has occurred, this information may be helpful. We will print the order type, the deal number, the return code and description, as well as the order price and the current Bid and Ask prices.

We've created a function to check the order type constant and return a descriptive string describing the order type:

```
string CheckOrderType(ENUM_ORDER_TYPE pType)
{
    string orderType;
    if(pType == ORDER_TYPE_BUY) orderType = "buy";
    else if(pType == ORDER_TYPE_SELL) orderType = "sell";
    else if(pType == ORDER_TYPE_BUY_STOP) orderType = "buy stop";
    else if(pType == ORDER_TYPE_BUY_LIMIT) orderType = "buy limit";
    else if(pType == ORDER_TYPE_SELL_STOP) orderType = "sell stop";
    else if(pType == ORDER_TYPE_SELL_LIMIT) orderType = "sell limit";
    else if(pType == ORDER_TYPE_BUY_STOP_LIMIT) orderType = "buy stop limit";
    else if(pType == ORDER_TYPE_SELL_STOP_LIMIT) orderType = "sell stop limit";
    else orderType = "invalid order type";
    return(orderType);
}
```

This function is defined in the `Trade.mqh` file. It is a public function that can be used anywhere in our program. The pType parameter contains a value of the ENUM_ORDER_TYPE enumeration. We use `if-else` operators to evaluate the value of pType and assign the appropriate string value to the `orderType` string variable. The string is then returned to the program. Note that we could have used the `switch-case` operators here, but we wanted to keep this function simple, and it doesn't require the advanced functionality of the `switch` operator that was necessary in our `CheckReturnCode()` function.

We'll use the `CheckOrderType()` and `TradeServerReturnCodeDescription()` functions to retrieve strings describing our order type and return code. Then we'll call the `Print()` function to print the trade information to the log:

```
string orderType = CheckOrderType(pType);

string errDesc = TradeServerReturnCodeDescription(result.retcode);

Print("Open ",orderType," order #",result.deal,": ",result.retcode," - ",errDesc,
    ", Volume: ",result.volume,", Price: ",result.price,", Bid: ",result.bid,
    ", Ask: ",result.ask);
```

If we examine the experts log, here is what the `Print()` function output will look like for a successful buy market order:

```
Open Buy order #105624: 10009 - Request is completed, Volume: 0.1, Price: 1.31095,
Bid: 1.31076, Ask: 1.31095
```

Finally, we will evaluate the return code to determine whether to return a `true` or `false` value to the program. If the order was placed successfully, we will print a comment to the chart:

```
if(checkCode == CHECK_RETCODE_OK)
{
    Comment(orderType," position opened at ",result.price," on ",pSymbol);
    return(true);
}
else return(false);
```

If the `checkCode` variable contains the value of `CHECK_RETCODE_OK`, we will print a comment to the chart and return a value of `true`, indicating that the trade operation was successful. Otherwise, we will return a value of `false`. Fig. 10.2 shows a chart comment placed on successful order completion.

Retry On Error

We can make our expert advisor more reliable and robust by retrying the trade operation depending on the return code. Some error conditions such as requotes, off quotes and server connection issues can be self-correcting if we simply retry the trade operation.

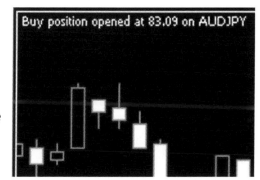

Fig 10.2 – Chart comment placed by the `Comment()` function.

105

To determine whether to retry the trade operation, we will modify our CheckReturnCode() function to return a third value. We will define a third constant in our ENUM_CHECK_RETCODE enumeration named CHECK_RETCODE_RETRY, which indicates that the error condition defined by the return code is potentially recoverable:

```
enum ENUM_CHECK_RETCODE
{
    CHECK_RETCODE_OK,
    CHECK_RETCODE_ERROR,
    CHECK_RETCODE_RETRY
};
```

Let's add this constant to our CheckReturnCode() function:

```
int CheckReturnCode(uint pRetCode)
{
    int status;
    switch(pRetCode)
    {
        case TRADE_RETCODE_REQUOTE:
        case TRADE_RETCODE_CONNECTION:
        case TRADE_RETCODE_PRICE_CHANGED:
        case TRADE_RETCODE_TIMEOUT:
        case TRADE_RETCODE_PRICE_OFF:
        case TRADE_RETCODE_REJECT:
        case TRADE_RETCODE_ERROR:

            status = CHECK_RETCODE_RETRY;
            break;

        case TRADE_RETCODE_DONE:
        case TRADE_RETCODE_DONE_PARTIAL:
        case TRADE_RETCODE_PLACED:
        case TRADE_RETCODE_NO_CHANGES:

            status = CHECK_RETCODE_OK;
            break;

        default: status = CHECK_RETCODE_ERROR;
    }

    return(status);
}
```

We have seven return code constants assigned to the case operators highlighted in bold. These errors are ones that we have determined are possibly self-correcting. If the pRetCode parameter matches any of these constants, the CHECK_RETCODE_RETRY constant is assigned to the status variable.

We will have to modify our market order placement function to add the order retry logic. We will use a do-while loop to handle the order retry functionality. The updated code is highlighted in bold:

```
int retryCount = 0;
int checkCode = 0;

do
{
    if(pType == ORDER_TYPE_BUY) request.price = SymbolInfoDouble(pSymbol,SYMBOL_ASK);
    else if(pType == ORDER_TYPE_SELL) request.price = SymbolInfoDouble(pSymbol,SYMBOL_BID);

    OrderSend(request,result);

    checkCode = CheckReturnCode(result.retcode);

    if(checkCode == CHECK_RETCODE_OK) break;
    else if(checkCode == CHECK_RETCODE_ERROR)
    {
        string errDesc = TradeServerReturnCodeDescription(result.retcode);
        Alert("Open market order: Error ",result.retcode," - ",errDesc);
        break;
    }
    else
    {
        Print("Server error detected, retrying...");
        Sleep(RETRY_DELAY);
        retryCount++;
    }
}
while(retryCount < MAX_RETRIES);
```

First, we declare an integer variable named retryCount. This will be the counter that keeps track of how many times we have retried the order placement. The entire order placement and error handling code from the previous section is placed inside a do-while loop.

The first thing we do inside the do loop is retrieve the current Bid or Ask price. Since these prices can change between trade operations, we will always retrieve the most current price before calling the OrderSend() function.

After placing the order and calling the CheckReturnCode() function, we examine the checkCode variable to determine which action to take. If the trade was successful, and checkCode contains the CHECK_RETCODE_OK constant, then we break out of the do loop. Otherwise, if checkCode contains the CHECK_RETCODE_ERROR constant, we display an alert and break out of the loop.

If the checkCode variable contains the CHECK_RETCODE_RETRY constant, the code in the else operator is executed. We print a message to the log indicating that an error was detected, and the program will retry the trade operation. The Sleep() function will pause program execution temporarily, using the value in milliseconds indicated by the RETRY_DELAY constant. Then the retryCount variable is incremented by 1.

The while operator at the end of the loop checks the retryCount variable and compares the value to a constant named MAX_RETRIES. The MAX_RETRIES constant is the maximum number of times to retry the order placement. If retryCount is less than MAX_RETRIES, the do-while loop will execute again. Otherwise, the loop will exit.

The RETRY_DELAY and MAX_RETRIES constants are defined at the beginning of the Trade.mqh include file. We set these to a reasonable default value. You can change these if you like, or substitute them with input variables that can be changed by the user.

```
#define MAX_RETRIES 5
#define RETRY_DELAY 3000
```

The MAX_RETRIES constant is set to retry the trade operation up to 5 times. The RETRY_DELAY is 3000 milliseconds, or 3 seconds. You can change these if you wish, and recompile any expert advisors that use this file.

If the trade operation was not successful even after several retries, we need to alert the user. This code goes right after our do-while loop, before we print the order information to the log:

```
if(retryCount >= MAX_RETRIES)
{
    string errDesc = TradeServerReturnCodeDescription(result.retcode);
    Alert("Max retries exceeded: Error ",result.retcode," - ",errDesc);
}
```

If retryCount is greater than or equal to MAX_RETRIES, we send an alert to the user's screen indicating that the order placement failed, with the last known error code and description.

This completes the OpenPosition() function for the CTrade class. You can view the full code of the function in the \MQL5\Include\Mql5Book\Trade.mqh file.

Setting the Deviation and Fill Type

If your broker uses the instant execution type, you can specify a deviation in points. The deviation is the maximum allowed slippage when placing an order. If the current market price is more than the specified number of points away from the requested price, then the order will not be placed.

We've created a function that allows the user to set the deviation in the expert advisor properties. The `CTrade::Deviation()` function sets the value of the `request.deviation` variable for use in the order placement functions:

```
void CTrade::Deviation(ulong pDeviation)
{
    request.deviation = pDeviation;
}
```

Since the `request` object is created is created when an object based on the `CTrade` class is created, we only need to assign a value to the `request.deviation` variable once. Here's how we would use the `Deviation()` function in our program:

```
#include <Mql5Book\Trade.mqh>
CTrade Trade;

// Input variables
input int Slippage = 20;

// OnInit() event handler
int OnInit()
{
    Trade.Deviation(Slippage);
    return(0);
}
```

We include the `Trade.mqh` file and declare an object named `Trade`, based on the `CTrade` class, at the top of the program file. The `Slippage` input variable allows the user the set the deviation in points. The `Trade.Deviation()` function is placed in the `OnInit()` event handler, which sets the value of the `request.deviation` variable at the start of the program. This deviation is then used when placing market orders.

The fill type can also be set if you want to use a different fill type than the server default. Here is a function that will set the `request.type_filling` variable for later use:

```
void CTrade::FillType(ENUM_ORDER_TYPE_FILLING pFill)
{
    request.type_filling = pFill;
}
```

The fill type must be specified using a constant of the ENUM_ORDER_TYPE_FILLING enumeration. Here's how we can set the fill type using the FillType() function:

```
#include <Mql5Book\Trade.mqh>
CTrade Trade;

// Input variables
input ENUM_ORDER_TYPE_FILLING FillType = ORDER_FILLING_RETURN;

// OnInit() event handler
int OnInit()
{
    Trade.FillType(FillType);
    return(0);
}
```

The above code sets the fill type to Return. Note that the type of the FillType input variable is ENUM_ORDER_TYPE_FILLING. As before, the Trade.FillType() function is placed in the OnInit() event handler, setting the request.type_filling variable for later use.

Using the OpenPosition() Function

Let's simplify the order placement process by creating some helper functions to place buy and sell positions:

```
class CTrade
{
    public:
        bool Buy(string pSymbol, double pVolume, double pStop = 0,
            double pProfit = 0, string pComment = NULL);
        bool Sell(string pSymbol, double pVolume, double pStop = 0,
            double pProfit = 0, string pComment = NULL);
};
```

We've declared two public functions in our CTrade class: Buy() and Sell(). We'll use these classes to call our private OpenPosition() function. This way, we don't need to remember the enumeration constants for the order types. Here are the function definitions:

```
bool CTrade::Buy(string pSymbol, double pVolume, double pStop = 0, double pProfit = 0,
    string pComment = NULL)
{
    bool success = OpenPosition(pSymbol,ORDER_TYPE_BUY,pVolume,pStop,pProfit,pComment);
    return(success);
}

bool CTrade::Sell(string pSymbol, double pVolume, double pStop = 0, double pProfit = 0,
    string pComment = NULL)
{
    bool success = OpenPosition(pSymbol,ORDER_TYPE_SELL,pVolume,pStop,pProfit,pComment);
    return(success);
}
```

Both functions call the OpenPosition() function with the appropriate order type constant. The Buy() function uses the ORDER_TYPE_BUY constant for the second parameter of the OpenPosition() function, while Sell() uses ORDER_TYPE_SELL. The remainder of the input parameters are assigned to the appropriate OpenPosition() function parameters. We'll use the Buy() and Sell() functions to open market orders in our expert advisors.

Let's revisit the simple expert advisor we created in the previous chapter. We'll substitute the request variables and the OrderSend() function with the Buy() and Sell() functions that we just created:

```
#include <Mql5Book\Trade.mqh>
CTrade Trade;

// Input variables
input double TradeVolume=0.1;
input int StopLoss=1000;
input int TakeProfit=1000;
input int MAPeriod=10;

// Global variables
bool glBuyPlaced, glSellPlaced;

// OnTick() event handler
void OnTick()
{
    // Trade structures
    MqlTradeRequest request;
    MqlTradeResult result;
    ZeroMemory(request);
```

```
// Moving average
double ma[];
ArraySetAsSeries(ma,true);

int maHandle=iMA(_Symbol,0,MAPeriod,MODE_LWMA,0,PRICE_CLOSE);
CopyBuffer(maHandle,0,0,1,ma);

// Close price
double close[];
ArraySetAsSeries(close,true);
CopyClose(_Symbol,0,0,1,close);

// Current position information
bool openPosition = PositionSelect(_Symbol);
long positionType = PositionGetInteger(POSITION_TYPE);

double currentVolume = 0;
if(openPosition == true) currentVolume = PositionGetDouble(POSITION_VOLUME);

// Open buy market order
if(close[0] > ma[0] && glBuyPlaced == false
    && (positionType != POSITION_TYPE_BUY || openPosition == false))
{
    glBuyPlaced = Trade.Buy(_Symbol,TradeVolume);

    // Modify SL/TP
    if(glBuyPlaced == true)
    {
        request.action = TRADE_ACTION_SLTP;

        do Sleep(100); while(PositionSelect(_Symbol) == false);
        double positionOpenPrice = PositionGetDouble(POSITION_PRICE_OPEN);

        if(StopLoss > 0) request.sl = positionOpenPrice - (StopLoss * _Point);
        if(TakeProfit > 0) request.tp = positionOpenPrice + (TakeProfit * _Point);

        if(request.sl > 0 && request.tp > 0) OrderSend(request,result);

        glSellPlaced = false;
    }
}
```

```
    // Open sell market order
    else if(close[0] < ma[0] && glSellPlaced == false && positionType != POSITION_TYPE_SELL)
    {
        glSellPlaced = Trade.Sell(_Symbol,TradeVolume);

        // Modify SL/TP
        if(glSellPlaced == true)
        {
            request.action = TRADE_ACTION_SLTP;

            do Sleep(100); while(PositionSelect(_Symbol) == false);
            double positionOpenPrice = PositionGetDouble(POSITION_PRICE_OPEN);

            if(StopLoss > 0) request.sl = positionOpenPrice + (StopLoss * _Point);
            if(TakeProfit > 0) request.tp = positionOpenPrice - (TakeProfit * _Point);

            if(request.sl > 0 && request.tp > 0) OrderSend(request,result);

            glBuyPlaced = false;
        }
    }
```

The changes are highlighted in bold. At the top of the program, we add an #include directive to include the Trade.mqh file that contains our trade classes. Next, we create an object based on the CTrade class. We will name this object Trade.

Moving on to the order placement code, we've replaced the request variables and the OrderSend() function with our Trade.Buy() and Trade.Sell() class functions. The glBuyPlaced and glSellPlaced global boolean variables will contain the result of the trade operation. If the trade was placed successfully, the value of these variables will be true.

After the order has been placed, we check the value of the glBuyPlaced or glSellPlaced variable. If the value is true, we calculate the stop loss and take profit price, and add it to the position. Finally, we set the opposite glBuyPlaced or glSellPlaced variable to false.

Note that the position modification code still uses the request and result objects defined earlier in the program. We do not need to use these objects when placing our orders, since we now use the Trade.Buy() and Trade.Sell() functions, which contain their own request and result objects. In the next chapter, we will create functions that will simplify the process of modifying the position, and eliminate having to declare these objects altogether.

These changes can be found in the file \MQL5\Experts\Mql5Book\Simple Expert Advisor with Functions.mq5. We will be making changes to this program several more times in this book.

Chapter 11 - Stop Loss & Take Profit

Calculating A Fixed Stop Loss and/or Take Profit Price

Many trading strategies place the stop loss and take profit a fixed distance from the order opening price. The trader specifies the number of points for the stop loss and take profit in the expert advisor properties. The stop loss and take profit prices are then calculated relative to the order or position opening price.

For a market order, the opening price is the current Bid or Ask price at the moment the order is filled. After the order is placed, we will retrieve the position's opening price using the `PositionSelect()` and `PositionGetDouble()` functions, and calculate the stop loss and take profit relative to that price. For a pending order, the opening price is the price we specify when opening the order. We will calculate the stop loss and take profit relative to the order opening price prior to placing the order.

Stop Loss

For a buy order, the stop loss is calculated by subtracting the stop loss value in points from the opening price. For a sell order, the stop loss is calculated by adding the stop loss value in points to the opening price.

First, we multiply the stop loss value by the symbol's point value. For example, a Forex symbol with five digits after the decimal point will have a point value of 0.00001. If we have specified a stop loss of 500 points, we multiply 500 by 0.00001 to get a value of 0.005. Then we add or subtract this value from the opening price to find the stop loss price.

Here's an example of adding a stop loss to a buy position:

```
// Input variables
input int StopLoss = 500;

// OnTick() event handler
MqlTradeRequest request;
MqlTradeResult result;
ZeroMemory(request);

request.action = TRADE_ACTION_SLTP;
request.symbol = _Symbol;

// Calculate the stop loss for a buy position
PositionSelect(_Symbol);
double positionPrice = PositionGetDouble(POSITION_PRICE_OPEN);
```

```
    double stopLossPoint = StopLoss * _Point;
    request.sl = positionPrice - stopLossPoint;

    OrderSend(request,result);
```

The StopLoss input variable is defined at the beginning of the program. The code that follows is placed in the OnTick() event handler. We'll assume that a buy position is currently open. The request.action variable identifies this trade operation as a position modification (TRADE_ACTION_SLTP), and the request.symbol variable identifies the position to modify (the current chart symbol).

To calculate the stop loss price, first we retrieve the opening price of the current position. The PositionSelect() function selects the open position on the current chart symbol for further processing. Then, the PositionGetDouble() function with the POSITION_PRICE_OPEN parameter returns the position open price and stores it in the variable positionPrice.

Next, we multiply the StopLoss input variable by the symbol's point value (_Point). The result is stored in the variable stopLossPoint. Finally, we subtract stopLossPoint from positionPrice to calculate the stop loss price, and assign the result to the result.sl variable. The OrderSend() function will then modify the stop loss of the position.

The stop loss calculation for a sell position is nearly identical. We are simply reversing the operation from subtraction to addition:

```
    // Calculate the stop loss for a sell position
    PositionSelect(_Symbol);
    double positionPrice = PositionGetDouble(POSITION_PRICE_OPEN);

    double stopLossPoint = StopLoss * _Point;
    request.sl = positionPrice + stopLossPoint;
```

For a pending order, the stop loss is calculated prior to placing the order. In this example, we'll set the buy stop order price 100 points above the current Ask price:

```
    // Input variables
    input int StopLoss = 500;
    input int PendingPrice = 100;

    // OnTick() event handler
    MqlTradeRequest request;
    MqlTradeResult result;
    ZeroMemory(request);
```

```
request.action = TRADE_ACTION_PENDING;
request.type = ORDER_TYPE_BUY_STOP;
request.symbol = _Symbol;
request.volume = 1;
request.type_time = ORDER_TIME_GTC;

// Calculate the stop loss for a pending buy order
request.price = SymbolInfoDouble(_Symbol,SYMBOL_ASK) + (PendingPrice * _Point);
double stopLossPoint = StopLoss * _Point;
request.sl = request.price - stopLossPoint;

OrderSend(request,result);
```

We have defined a `PendingPrice` input variable to calculate the pending order price relative to the current Ask price. The `request.action` variable is set to `TRADE_ACTION_PENDING`, indicating that this is a pending order operation. The `request.type` variable indicates that this is a buy stop order. We specify the symbol, a trade volume, and the expiration type (`ORDER_TIME_GTC`), indicating that the pending order does not expire.

The pending order price (`request.price`) is calculated by multiplying the `PendingPrice` input variable by the current symbol's point value (`_Point`), and adding that to the current Ask price, which is retrieved using the `SymbolInfoDouble()` function. This sets the pending order price 100 points above the current Ask price.

The `stopLossPoint` value is calculated as before, and the stop loss price is calculated by subtracting `stopLossPoint` from the pending order price (`request.price`). The result is assigned to the `request.sl` variable, and the pending order request is then sent to the trade server.

Let's look at the stop loss calculation for a pending sell order:

```
// Calculate the stop loss for a pending sell order
request.price = SymbolInfoDouble(_Symbol,SYMBOL_BID) - (PendingPrice * _Point);
double stopLossPoint = StopLoss * _Point;
request.sl = request.price + stopLossPoint;
```

The pending order price is calculated by subtracting (`PendingPrice * _Point`) from the current Bid price, and the stop loss price is calculated by adding `stopLossPoint` to the pending order price.

The method for calculating a fixed stop loss is the same regardless of the pending order type. For buy orders, the stop loss is placed below the pending order price, and for sell orders, the stop loss is placed above the pending order price.

Take Profit

The take profit price is calculated the same way as a stop loss price – only in reverse. The take profit price for a buy order is placed above the opening price, while the take profit price for a sell order is placed below the opening price.

Here is the calculation of the take profit price for a buy position:

```
// Input variables
input int TakeProfit = 1000;

// OnTick() event handler
MqlTradeRequest request;
MqlTradeResult result;
ZeroMemory(request);

request.action = TRADE_ACTION_SLTP;
request.symbol = _Symbol;

// Calculate the take profit for a buy position
PositionSelect(_Symbol);
double positionPrice = PositionGetDouble(POSITION_PRICE_OPEN);

double takeProfitPoint = TakeProfit * _Point;
request.tp = positionPrice + takeProfitPoint;

OrderSend(result,request);
```

We declare an input variable named TakeProfit, with a default take profit value of 1000 points. The following code is similar to the stop loss modification from earlier. We select the current position and retrieve the current position opening price first. Next we calculate the take profit price by multiplying TakeProfit by _Point and storing the result in the takeProfitPoint variable. Then we add takeProfitPoint to positionPrice to calculate the take profit price. The result is assigned to the request.tp variable.

And here is the code to calculate the take profit price for a sell position:

```
// Calculate the take profit for a sell position
double takeProfitPoint = TakeProfit * _Point;
PositionSelect(_Symbol);
double positionPrice = PositionGetDouble(POSITION_PRICE_OPEN);
request.tp = positionPrice - takeProfitPoint;
```

The value of takeProfitPoint is subtracted from positionPrice to get the take profit price.

For pending orders, the same logic applies. Add the take profit value to the pending order price for a pending buy order, and subtract it for a pending sell order.

Creating Stop Calculation Functions

We're going to create a set of functions that will allow us to calculate a stop loss or take profit price for a buy or sell order. This way it won't be necessary to remember the calculation for a stop loss or take profit. All you need to specify is the symbol, the stop loss or take profit value in points, and optionally an order or position opening price.

Let's start with the stop loss functions. The function to calculate the stop loss for a buy order is called BuyStopLoss(). This function is located in the Trade.mqh include file:

```
double BuyStopLoss(string pSymbol,int pStopPoints, double pOpenPrice = 0)
{
    if(pStopPoints <= 0) return(0);

    double openPrice;
    if(pOpenPrice > 0) openPrice = pOpenPrice;
    else openPrice = SymbolInfoDouble(pSymbol,SYMBOL_ASK);

    double point = SymbolInfoDouble(pSymbol,SYMBOL_POINT);
    double stopLoss = openPrice - (pStopPoints * point);

    long digits = SymbolInfoInteger(pSymbol,SYMBOL_DIGITS);
    stopLoss = NormalizeDouble(stopLoss,(int)digits);

    return(stopLoss);
}
```

The BuyStopLoss() function accepts three parameters: the symbol name (pSymbol), the stop loss value in points (pStopPoints), and an optional opening price (pOpenPrice).

The first line in the function will exit the function immediately and return a value of 0 if pStopPoints is less than or equal to 0. Next, we declare a double variable named openPrice, which will hold the order opening price. If the order opening price is specified with pOpenPrice, then pOpenPrice will be assigned to openPrice. Otherwise, the current Ask price for the symbol specified by pSymbol will be used.

We use the SymbolInfoDouble() function with the SYMBOL_POINT parameter to retrieve the point value for the symbol specified by the pSymbol parameter. This is assigned to the point variable. Next, we calculate the stop loss price by multiplying pStopPoints by point, and subtracting that value from openPrice. The result is saved to the stopLoss variable.

119

The last step is to normalize the stop loss value to the number of digits in the symbol price. Forex symbols have either three or five digits after the decimal point, so we will round the stop loss to the appropriate number of digits. The SymbolInfoInteger() function with the SYMBOL_DIGITS parameter will retrieve the digits value for pSymbol, and assign it to the long variable digits.

The NormalizeDouble() function rounds the stopLoss value to the number of digits specified by the digits variable. The (int) before the digits variable in the NormalizeDouble() function explicitly casts the value of digits into the int type. This is not absolutely necessary, but we insert it to avoid the "possible data loss due to type conversion" warning. Finally, we return the normalized value of stopLoss to the program.

Let's look at the function to calculate the take profit price for a buy order. The code is nearly identical. In this case, we are simply adding the take profit value to the opening price:

```
double BuyTakeProfit(string pSymbol,int pProfitPoints, double pOpenPrice = 0)
{
    if(pProfitPoints <= 0) return(0);

    double openPrice;
    if(pOpenPrice > 0) openPrice = pOpenPrice;
    else openPrice = SymbolInfoDouble(pSymbol,SYMBOL_ASK);

    double point = SymbolInfoDouble(pSymbol,SYMBOL_POINT);
    double takeProfit = openPrice + (pProfitPoints * point);

    long digits = SymbolInfoInteger(pSymbol,SYMBOL_DIGITS);
    takeProfit = NormalizeDouble(takeProfit,(int)digits);

    return(takeProfit);
}
```

The code for a sell stop loss and take profit calculation are similar. In the event that an opening price is not specified, we use the current Bid price. The stop loss and take profit calculations are reversed relative to the buy order calculations:

```
double SellTakeProfit(string pSymbol,int pProfitPoints, double pOpenPrice = 0)
{
    if(pProfitPoints <= 0) return(0);

    double openPrice;
    if(pOpenPrice > 0) openPrice = pOpenPrice;
    else openPrice = SymbolInfoDouble(pSymbol,SYMBOL_BID);
```

```
    double point = SymbolInfoDouble(pSymbol,SYMBOL_POINT);
    double takeProfit = openPrice - (pProfitPoints * point);

    long digits = SymbolInfoInteger(pSymbol,SYMBOL_DIGITS);
    takeProfit = NormalizeDouble(takeProfit,(int)digits);

    return(takeProfit);
}
```

The SellStopLoss() function is similar – we just add pProfitPoints to the opening price. You can view these functions in the Trade.mqh include file.

Stop Level

One of the most common errors made by expert advisor programmers and traders is invalid stop prices. A stop loss, take profit or pending order price must be a minimum distance away from the current Bid and Ask prices. This minimum distance is called the *stop level*.

The stop level is retrieved from the server using the SymbolInfoInteger() function with the SYMBOL_TRADE_STOPS_LEVEL parameter. We'll need to multiply this value by the point value of the symbol first. To calculate the minimum stop price for buy take profit, sell stop loss, buy stop and sell limit prices, simply add the stop level to the current Ask price:

```
    double stopLevel = SymbolInfoInteger(_Symbol,SYMBOL_TRADE_STOPS_LEVEL) * _Point;
    double minStopLevel = SymbolInfoDouble(_Symbol,SYMBOL_ASK) + stopLevel;
```

The SymbolInfoInteger() function with the SYMBOL_TRADE_STOPS_LEVEL parameter returns the stop level from the server. The stop level is an integer value, so it must be converted to a price by multiplying it by _Point. This value is stored in the stopLevel variable.

Next, the SymbolInfoDouble() function with the SYMBOL_ASK parameter returns the current Ask price. We add the value of the stopLevel variable to the Ask price to get the minimum stop level. Any buy take profit, sell stop loss, buy stop or sell limit price must be above this value. If not, a TRADE_RETCODE_INVALID_STOPS return code will result.

To calculate the maximum stop price for sell take profit, buy stop loss, sell stop or buy limit prices, simply subtract the stop level from the current Bid price:

```
    double stopLevel = SymbolInfoInteger(_Symbol,SYMBOL_TRADE_STOPS_LEVEL) * _Point;
    double maxStopLevel = SymbolInfoDouble(_Symbol,SYMBOL_BID) - stopLevel;
```

Once you've calculated the stop level, you can compare this to your stop loss, take profit or pending order price to see if it is valid:

```
double stopLevel = SymbolInfoInteger(_Symbol,SYMBOL_TRADE_STOPS_LEVEL) * _Point;
double minStopLevel = SymbolInfoDouble(_Symbol,SYMBOL_ASK) + stopLevel;

if(request.price <= minStopLevel)
{
    Print("Invalid stop price");
}
```

This example compares a pending order price to the minimum stop level above the current Ask price. If the `request.price` variable is less than or equal to `minStopLevel`, a message will print to the log indicating that the price is invalid.

Once you know the minimum or maximum stop level price, you can automatically adjust an invalid price to a valid price, simply by making it greater or less than the relevant stop level.

Creating Stop Verification Functions

Before we attempt to place an order with our newly calculated stop loss or take profit price, we need to verify the price to make sure it's not inside the stop level. We'll create a set of functions to check stop and pending order prices above the Ask price and below the Bid price. The function to use depends on the order type and the type of price that we're checking.

Let's create a function to check prices above the Ask price. This will be used to verify buy take profit, sell stop loss, buy stop and sell limit order prices. If the price is below the stop level price, it will be adjusted so that it is above the stop level, plus or minus a specified number of points.

```
double AdjustAboveStopLevel(string pSymbol, double pPrice, int pPoints = 10)
{
    double currPrice = SymbolInfoDouble(pSymbol,SYMBOL_ASK);
    double point = SymbolInfoDouble(pSymbol,SYMBOL_POINT);
    double stopLevel = SymbolInfoInteger(pSymbol,SYMBOL_TRADE_STOPS_LEVEL) * point;
    double stopPrice = currPrice + stopLevel;
    double addPoints = pPoints * point;

    if(pPrice > stopPrice + addPoints) return(pPrice);
    else
    {
        double newPrice = stopPrice + addPoints;
        Print("Price adjusted above stop level to "+DoubleToString(newPrice));
        return(newPrice);
```

```
      }
   }
```

The `AdjustAboveStopLevel()` function has three parameters: pSymbol, pPrice, which is the stop price to verify, and pPoints, an optional parameter that adds an additional number of points to the stop level. This ensures that slippage will not invalidate a price that is very close to the stop level price.

First we determine the current price by retrieving the Ask price for pSymbol, and storing it in the currPrice variable. Next, we retrieve the symbol's point value and store it in the point variable. We retrieve the stop level for the symbol, and multiply that value by the point variable. The result is stored in the stopLevel variable. We calculate the stop level price by adding currPrice to stopLevel, and storing that value in the stopPrice variable. Next, we convert the pPoints parameter to a price value by multiplying it by the symbol's point value, and storing the result in addPoints.

If our stop price (pPrice), is greater than the stop level price (stopPrice + addPoints), we return the original pPrice value to the program. Otherwise, we need to calculate a new stop price. We declare a variable named newPrice, and set it to stopPrice + addPoints. This ensures that the adjusted stop price is not too close to the stop level price. We print a message to the log indicating that the price has been adjusted. Finally, we return the adjusted price to the program.

Next, we'll create a function to check stop prices below the Bid price. This will be used to verify sell stop, buy limit, buy stop loss and sell take profit prices. The code is similar to the AdjustAboveStopLevel() function above:

```
double AdjustBelowStopLevel(string pSymbol, double pPrice, int pPoints = 10)
{
    double currPrice = SymbolInfoDouble(pSymbol,SYMBOL_BID);
    double point = SymbolInfoDouble(pSymbol,SYMBOL_POINT);
    double stopLevel = SymbolInfoInteger(pSymbol,SYMBOL_TRADE_STOPS_LEVEL) * point;
    double stopPrice = currPrice - stopLevel;
    double addPoints = pPoints * point;

    if(pPrice < stopPrice - addPoints) return(pPrice);
    else
    {
        double newPrice = stopPrice - addPoints;
        Print("Price adjusted below stop level to "+DoubleToString(newPrice));
        return(newPrice);
    }
}
```

The changes are highlighted in bold. We assign the current Bid price to the currPrice variable. The stopPrice variable is calculated by subtracting stopLevel from currPrice. If the pPrice parameter is less than stopPrice - addPoints, the original pPrice value is returned to the program. Otherwise, we calculate a new price by assigning the result of stopPrice - addPoints to the newPrice variable. A message is printed to the log, and the newPrice variable is returned to the program.

The above functions will automatically adjust an invalid price. But what if you just want to check if a price is valid without adjusting it? We'll use the CheckAboveStopLevel() and CheckBelowStopLevel() functions. These functions return a boolean value of true or false, depending on whether the price is valid or not.

Here is the code for the CheckAboveStopLevel() function:

```
bool CheckAboveStopLevel(string pSymbol, double pPrice, int pPoints = 10)
{
    double currPrice = SymbolInfoDouble(pSymbol,SYMBOL_ASK);
    double point = SymbolInfoDouble(pSymbol,SYMBOL_POINT);
    double stopLevel = SymbolInfoInteger(pSymbol,SYMBOL_TRADE_STOPS_LEVEL) * point;
    double stopPrice = currPrice + stopLevel;
    double addPoints = pPoints * point;

    if(pPrice >= stopPrice + addPoints) return(true);
    else return(false);
}
```

Thus function is very similar to the AdjustAboveStopLevel() function. The differences are highlighted in bold. Instead of adjusting the pPrice variable relative to the stop level price, we simply return a value of true if the price is valid, or false if it is not. This allows the programmer to specify other actions if a price is invalid.

The CheckBelowStopLevel() function is similar, and all of the stop verification functions in this chapter, can be viewed in the \MQL5\Include\Mql5Book\Trade.mqh file.

Using The Stop Calculation and Verification Functions

Now that we've created functions to calculate a fixed stop loss and take profit price, as well as functions to verify prices, let's demonstrate how we will use these in our expert advisor programs.

For a market order, the stop loss and take profit will be calculated after the order has been placed. First we will retrieve the opening price for the current position. Then the stop loss and take profit will be calculated relative to the opening price. The calculated stop loss and take profit prices will be verified, and finally the order will be modified with the new stop loss and/or take profit price.

Let's refer back to our simple expert advisor program. We'll replace the stop loss and take profit calculation with our stop calculation functions. The resulting prices will be checked against the stop level and adjusted accordingly:

```
// Open buy market order
if(close[0] > ma[0] && glBuyPlaced == false
    && (positionType != POSITION_TYPE_BUY || openPosition == false))
{
    glBuyPlaced = Trade.Buy(_Symbol,TradeVolume);

    // Modify SL/TP
    if(glBuyPlaced == true)
    {
        request.action = TRADE_ACTION_SLTP;

        do Sleep(100); while(PositionSelect(_Symbol) == false);
        double positionOpenPrice = PositionGetDouble(POSITION_PRICE_OPEN);

        double buyStopLoss = BuyStopLoss(_Symbol,StopLoss,positionOpenPrice);
        if(buyStopLoss > 0) request.sl = AdjustBelowStopLevel(_Symbol,buyStopLoss);

        double buyTakeProfit = BuyTakeProfit(_Symbol,TakeProfit,positionOpenPrice);
        if(buyTakeProfit > 0) request.tp = AdjustAboveStopLevel(_Symbol,buyTakeProfit);

        if(request.sl > 0 && request.tp > 0) OrderSend(request,result);

        glSellPlaced = false;
    }
}

// Open sell market order
else if(close[0] < ma[0] && glSellPlaced == false && positionType != POSITION_TYPE_SELL)
{
    glSellPlaced = Trade.Sell(_Symbol,TradeVolume);

    // Modify SL/TP
    if(glSellPlaced == true)
    {
        request.action = TRADE_ACTION_SLTP;

        do Sleep(100); while(PositionSelect(_Symbol) == false);
        double positionOpenPrice = PositionGetDouble(POSITION_PRICE_OPEN);

        double sellStopLoss = SellStopLoss(_Symbol,StopLoss,positionOpenPrice);
        if(sellStopLoss > 0) request.sl = AdjustAboveStopLevel(_Symbol,sellStopLoss);
```

```
                double sellTakeProfit = SellTakeProfit(_Symbol,TakeProfit,positionOpenPrice);
                if(sellTakeProfit > 0) request.tp = AdjustBelowStopLevel(_Symbol,sellTakeProfit);

                if(request.sl > 0 && request.tp > 0) OrderSend(request,result);

                glBuyPlaced = false;
            }
        }
```

The changes are highlighted in bold. First, we calculate the stop loss and take profit prices using our stop calculation functions. Then we use our stop verification functions to adjust the price if necessary. The verified price is assigned to the relevant request variable.

Let's take a closer look at the buy stop loss and take profit calculations:

```
        double buyStopLoss = BuyStopLoss(_Symbol,StopLoss,positionOpenPrice);
        if(buyStopLoss > 0) request.sl = AdjustBelowStopLevel(_Symbol,buyStopLoss);

        double buyTakeProfit = BuyTakeProfit(_Symbol,TakeProfit,positionOpenPrice);
        if(buyTakeProfit > 0) request.tp = AdjustAboveStopLevel(_Symbol,buyTakeProfit);
```

We use the BuyStopLoss() function to calculate the stop loss relative to positionOpenPrice. The result is assigned to the buyStopLoss variable. If the value of buyStopLoss is greater than zero, we pass the buyStopLoss value to the AdjustBelowStopLevel() function. The result is assigned to the result.sl variable. The same is done for the take profit, using the BuyTakeProfit() and AdjustAboveStopLevel() functions.

The examples above will automatically adjust the stop loss or take profit price if it is invalid. But what if you simply want to check if the price is valid or not? The example below checks the stop loss price without modifying it:

```
    if(StopLoss > 0)
    {
        double buyStopLoss = BuyStopLoss(_Symbol,StopLoss,positionOpenPrice);

        if(CheckBelowStopLevel(_Symbol,buyStopLoss) == false)
        {
            Alert("Buy stop loss price is invalid!");
        }
        else if(buyStopLoss > 0) request.sl = buyStopLoss;
    }
```

The `CheckBelowStopLevel()` function is used to check whether the `buyStopLoss` price is valid. If the function returns `false`, an alert is shown to the user and no more action is taken. Otherwise, if `buyStopLoss` is greater than zero, the value of `buyStopLoss` is assigned to `request.sl`.

Using A Dynamic Stop Loss

The examples in this chapter use a fixed stop loss value. There are other ways of determining a stop loss price, such as using an indicator value or a technical support/resistance level. When using an absolute price for a stop loss or take profit, it is necessary to verify it before adding it to the current position. We can easily do this using our stop verification functions.

In the example below, the variable `stopLossPrice` will hold the tentative price that we wish to use as a stop loss for a buy position. We will verify it using the `AdjustBelowStopLevel()` function, ensuring that it is a minimum distance from the order opening price. The `MinStopLoss` input variable allows the user to enforce a minimum stop loss distance:

```
// Input Variables
input int MinStopLoss = 100;

// OnTick() event handler
double stopLossPrice = LowestLow(_Symbol,_Period,8);
request.sl = AdjustBelowStopLevel(_Symbol,stopLossPrice,MinStopLoss);
```

The `LowestLow()` function retrieves the lowest low of the last 8 bars, and assigns the result to `stopLossPrice`. We will cover this function in Chapter 16. We use the `AdjustBelowStopLevel()` function to verify the value of `stopLossPrice`, and ensure that the distance between the current price and the stop loss price is at least 100 points. The verified price is saved to the `result.sl` variable.

In summary, if you need to add a stop loss or take profit price to a position, or you need to open a pending order, be sure to verify the price first. Invalid settings or prices that are too close to the current Bid or Ask price can result in "invalid stop" errors. These can be easily avoided by building price verification into your expert advisors.

Chapter 12 - Handling, Modifying & Closing Positions

Position Information Functions

We will often need to know the status of the currently opened position. We may need to know what the position type is (buy or sell), whether or not the position is currently in profit, and what the current stop loss, take profit or volume is.

We use the `PositionSelect()` function, along with the `PositionGetDouble()`, `PositionGetInteger()` and `PositionGetString()` functions to retrieve information about the current position. Here's an example of the code we've been using to retrieve the current position type:

```
bool openPosition = PositionSelect(_Symbol);
long positionType = PositionGetInteger(POSITION_TYPE);
```

The `PositionSelect()` function selects the position for the current chart symbol. Once the position has been selected, we can use the `PositionGet...()` functions to retrieve information about the position. The above example uses `PositionGetInteger()` with the `POSITION_TYPE` parameter to return the position type. You can view all of the position property constants for all three of the `PositionGet...()` functions in the *MQL5 Reference* under *Standard Constants... > Trade Constants > Position Properties*.

The problem with retrieving position information in MQL5 is remembering which `PositionGet..()` function to use along with the correct position property constant. We're going to create a set of easy-to-remember functions that will retrieve information about the current position with a single function call.

Let's demonstrate with a function to retrieve a position's type. The `PositionType()` function selects the current position for the specified symbol. It will then return the position type constant:

```
long PositionType(string pSymbol = NULL)
{
    if(pSymbol == NULL) pSymbol = _Symbol;
    bool select = PositionSelect(pSymbol);
    if(select == true) return(PositionGetInteger(POSITION_TYPE));
    else return(WRONG_VALUE);
}
```

The pSymbol parameter is optional – if it is not specified, the function will use the current chart symbol. The `PositionSelect()` function selects the position for the specified symbol, and return a boolean value to the select variable. If select is true, the `PositionGetInteger()` function retrieves the position type and returns it to the program. If no position is open, the function returns the `WRONG_VALUE` constant, or -1.

Here's another function that returns the opening price of the position. This function is very similar to the one above, except it uses the PositionGetDouble() function with the POSITION_PRICE_OPEN parameter:

```
double PositionOpenPrice(string pSymbol = NULL)
{
    if(pSymbol == NULL) pSymbol = _Symbol;
    bool select = PositionSelect(pSymbol);
    if(select == true) return(PositionGetDouble(POSITION_PRICE_OPEN));
    else return(WRONG_VALUE);
}
```

In all, we have ten functions that return information about the current position, including the volume, opening time, stop loss, take profit, comment, current profit and more. These functions can be viewed in the \MQL5\Include\Mql5Book\Trade.mqh file.

Let's modify our simple expert advisor with our position information functions:

```
// Current position information
long positionType = PositionType();

// Open buy market order
if(close[0] > ma[0] && glBuyPlaced == false && positionType != POSITION_TYPE_BUY)
{
    glBuyPlaced = Trade.Buy(_Symbol,TradeVolume);

    // Modify SL/TP
    if(glBuyPlaced == true)
    {
        request.action = TRADE_ACTION_SLTP;

        do Sleep(100); while(PositionSelect(_Symbol) == false);
        double positionOpenPrice = PositionOpenPrice();

        double buyStopLoss = BuyStopLoss(_Symbol,StopLoss,positionOpenPrice);
        if(buyStopLoss > 0) request.sl = AdjustBelowStopLevel(_Symbol,buyStopLoss);

        double buyTakeProfit = BuyTakeProfit(_Symbol,TakeProfit,positionOpenPrice);
        if(buyTakeProfit > 0) request.tp = AdjustAboveStopLevel(_Symbol,buyTakeProfit);

        if(request.sl > 0 && request.tp > 0) OrderSend(request,result);

        glSellPlaced = false;
    }
}
```

We are using a single function, `PositionType()`, to return the current position type. If no position is open, the function will return `WRONG_VALUE`. Because of this, we no longer need to check the output of the `PositionSelect()` function, so we've edited the order opening condition.

Once the order is placed, we check the value of the `glBuyPlaced` variable. If `glBuyPlaced` is `true`, we proceed with modifying the order. The `PositionOpenPrice()` function has replaced the `PositionGetDouble()` function for retrieving the position opening price. Since we are retrieving information for the current chart symbol, it is not necessary to pass a parameter to any of these functions.

Creating a Position Modification Function

In the previous chapter, we used the `OrderSend()` function to add a stop loss and take profit to a position. We can easily create a function to modify a position, with the same error handling and retry features as our other functions. The `ModifyPosition()` function will be a public function in our `CTrade` class. It has three parameters: `pSymbol` is the symbol of the position to modify, `pStop` is the stop loss price, and `pProfit` is the take profit price:

```
class CTrade
{
    public:
        bool ModifyPosition(string pSymbol, double pStop, double pProfit = 0);
}
```

The `pProfit` parameter is optional. Most likely, you will be modifying the stop loss of an order, but not always the take profit. Here is the body of our `ModifyPosition()` function. Nearly all of the code in this function should already be familiar to you:

```
bool CTrade::ModifyPosition(string pSymbol, double pStop, double pProfit=0)
{
    request.action = TRADE_ACTION_SLTP;
    request.symbol = pSymbol;
    request.sl = pStop;
    request.tp = pProfit;

    // Order loop
    int retryCount = 0;
    int checkCode = 0;
```

```
      do
      {
          OrderSend(request,result);
          checkCode = CheckReturnCode(result.retcode);

          if(checkCode == CHECK_RETCODE_OK) break;
          else if(checkCode == CHECK_RETCODE_ERROR)
          {
              string errDesc = TradeServerReturnCodeDescription(result.retcode);
              Alert("Modify position: Error ",result.retcode," - ",errDesc);
              break;
          }
          else
          {
              Print("Server error detected, retrying...");
              Sleep(RETRY_DELAY);
              retryCount++;
          }
      }
      while(retryCount < MAX_RETRIES);

      if(retryCount >= MAX_RETRIES)
      {
          string errDesc = TradeServerReturnCodeDescription(result.retcode);
          Alert("Max retries exceeded: Error ",result.retcode," - ",errDesc);
      }

      string errDesc = TradeServerReturnCodeDescription(result.retcode);

      Print("Modify position: ",result.retcode," - ",errDesc,", SL: ",request.sl,", TP:",
          request.tp,",Bid:",SymbolInfoDouble(pSymbol,SYMBOL_BID),", Ask: ",
          SymbolInfoDouble(pSymbol,SYMBOL_ASK),", Stop Level: ",
          SymbolInfoInteger(pSymbol,SYMBOL_TRADE_STOPS_LEVEL));

      if(checkCode == CHECK_RETCODE_OK)
      {
          Comment("Position modified on ",pSymbol,", SL: ",request.sl,", TP: ",request.tp);
          return(true);
      }
      else return(false);
  }
```

Here is how we use our ModifyPosition() function in an expert advisor program. After placing a market order, we calculate and verify the stop loss and take profit prices. Then we call the ModifyPosition() function to modify the open position:

```
// Open buy market order
if(close[0] > ma[0] && glBuyPlaced == false && positionType != POSITION_TYPE_BUY)
{
    glBuyPlaced = Trade.Buy(_Symbol,TradeVolume);

    // Modify SL/TP
    if(glBuyPlaced == true)
    {
        do Sleep(100); while(PositionSelect(_Symbol) == false);
        double positionOpenPrice = PositionOpenPrice();

        double buyStopLoss = BuyStopLoss(_Symbol,StopLoss,positionOpenPrice);
        if(buyStopLoss > 0) buyStopLoss = AdjustBelowStopLevel(_Symbol,buyStopLoss);

        double buyTakeProfit = BuyTakeProfit(_Symbol,TakeProfit,positionOpenPrice);
        if(buyTakeProfit > 0) buyTakeProfit = AdjustAboveStopLevel(_Symbol,buyTakeProfit);

        if(buyStopLoss > 0 || buyTakeProfit > 0)
            Trade.ModifyPosition(_Symbol,buyStopLoss,buyTakeProfit);

        glSellPlaced = false;
    }
}
```

We've replaced the `request.sl` and `request.tp` variables with the `buyStopLoss` and `buyTakeProfit` variables. Before modifying the position, we check to see if the `buyStopLoss` or `buyTakeProfit` variables are greater than zero. If so, the `ModifyPosition()` function of our `CTrade` class will be called to modify the stop loss and take profit of the current position. The above changes can be viewed in the file `\MQL5\Experts\Mql5Book\Simple Expert Advisor with Functions.mq5`

Closing Positions

As you may recall from Chapter 10, when a market order is opened, we first check to see if there is a position currently open in the opposite direction. If so, we increase the lot size of our order to close out the current position, resulting in a position in the opposite direction. However, sometimes you may wish to close a position before opening an order in the opposite direction. We're going to create a function to close an open position. You can close out part or all of a position, but we will not reverse the direction of an open position.

The process of closing a position is the same as opening one. We specify `TRADE_ACTION_DEAL` as the trade action, and fill out the `symbol`, `type`, `volume` and `price` variables of an `MqlTradeRequest` object. For our position closing function, we will need to determine the volume and direction of the current position. We'll need to ensure that the requested close volume is not greater than the current position volume. To close the position, we'll need to place an order in the opposite direction of the current position.

The Close() function is a public function in our CTrade class. It has three parameters – the symbol of the position to close, the close volume (optional), and an order comment (optional).

```
class CTrade
{
    public:
        bool Close(string pSymbol, double pVolume = 0, string pComment = NULL);
}
```

Let's go through the body of our Close() function. First, we fill out the request variables. We specify the trade action and the symbol. Then we we retrieve some information on the current position:

```
bool CTrade::Close(string pSymbol, double pVolume=0.000000, string pComment=NULL)
{
    request.action = TRADE_ACTION_DEAL;
    request.symbol = pSymbol;

    double closeLots = 0;
    long openType = WRONG_VALUE;
    long posID = 0;

    if(PositionSelect(pSymbol) == true)
    {
        closeLots = PositionGetDouble(POSITION_VOLUME);
        openType = PositionGetInteger(POSITION_TYPE);
        posID = PositionGetInteger(POSITION_IDENTIFIER);
        request.sl = PositionGetDouble(POSITION_SL);
        request.tp = PositionGetDouble(POSITION_TP);
    }
    else return(false);
```

We declare three variables – closeLots, openType and posID, and initialize them to a neutral value. The PositionSelect() function selects the currently opened position on the specified symbol. If there is a position open, PositionSelect() returns true. If not, PositionSelect() returns false, and we exit the function.

If a position is currently open, we assign the current position's volume to the closeLots variable, the position type (buy or sell) to openType, and the position ID to posID. The position ID is a unique identifier assigned to each open position. It generally corresponds to the order number that established the position. We will use this in the order comment. We'll also retrieve the stop loss and take profit of the current position and assign them to the request.sl and request.tp variables. This prevents the stop loss and/or take profit from being modified from their current values.

Next, we need to determine the close volume for the position. We check to see if a value has been specified for the pVolume parameter, and whether it is valid:

```
if(pVolume > closeLots || pVolume <= 0) request.volume = closeLots;
else request.volume = pVolume;
```

If the value of pVolume is greater than the volume of the current position (closeLots), or if pVolume has not been specified (less than or equal to zero), then request.volume is assigned the value of closeLots. This closes out the entire position. Otherwise, if a close volume has been specified with pVolume, then request.volume is assigned the value of pVolume. This will partially close out the position.

Now we're going to enter our order loop. Before closing the position, we must determine the order type and the closing price:

```
int retryCount = 0;
int checkCode = 0;

do
{
    if(openType == POSITION_TYPE_BUY)
    {
        request.type = ORDER_TYPE_SELL;
        request.price = SymbolInfoDouble(pSymbol,SYMBOL_BID);
    }
    else if(openType == POSITION_TYPE_SELL)
    {
        request.type = ORDER_TYPE_BUY;
        request.price = SymbolInfoDouble(pSymbol,SYMBOL_ASK);
    }

    OrderSend(request,result);
```

The code highlighted in bold determines the new order type and price. If the currently opened position is a buy position (POSITION_TYPE_BUY), the order type is set to ORDER_TYPE_SELL and the order price is set to the current Bid price. If the current position is a sell position, the type is set to ORDER_TYPE_BUY and the price is set to the current Ask price. The OrderSend() function then closes part or all of the current position.

The remaining code in the function takes care of the error handling and order retry features:

```
checkCode = CheckReturnCode(result.retcode);

if(checkCode == CHECK_RETCODE_OK) break;
```

```
        else if(checkCode == CHECK_RETCODE_ERROR)
        {
            string errDesc = TradeServerReturnCodeDescription(result.retcode);
            Alert("Close position: Error ",result.retcode," - ",errDesc);
            break;
        }
        else
        {
            Print("Server error detected, retrying...");
            Sleep(RETRY_DELAY);
            retryCount++;
        }
    }
    while(retryCount < MAX_RETRIES);

    if(retryCount >= MAX_RETRIES)
    {
        string errDesc = TradeServerReturnCodeDescription(result.retcode);
        Alert("Max retries exceeded: Error ",result.retcode," - ",errDesc);
    }

    string posType;
    if(openType == POSITION_TYPE_BUY) posType = "Buy";
    else if(openType == POSITION_TYPE_SELL) posType = "Sell";

    string errDesc = TradeServerReturnCodeDescription(result.retcode);
    Print("Close ",posType," position #",result.deal,": ",result.retcode," - ",errDesc,",
        Volume: ",result.volume,", Price: ",result.price,", Bid: ",result.bid,",
        Ask: ",result.ask);

    if(checkCode == CHECK_RETCODE_OK)
    {
        Comment(posType," position closed on ",pSymbol," at ",result.price);
        return(true);
    }
    else return(false);
```

Here is how we would use our Close() function in an expert advisor. For example, in our simple expert advisor, we want to close the order if the current close price crosses the moving average. The code to close an order will go in our expert advisor just after we retrieve the current position type, but before the order opening conditions:

```
    long positionType = PositionType();
```

```
if(close[0] < ma[0] && positionType == POSITION_TYPE_BUY)
{
    Trade.Close(_Symbol);
}

else if(close[0] > ma[0] && positionType == POSITION_TYPE_SELL)
{
    Trade.Close(_Symbol);
}
```

For simplicity's sake, we separated the buy and sell close conditions. If the current close price is less than the current moving average value, and a buy position is open, we close out the current position. The same is true if the close price is above the moving average and a sell position is currently open.

You can use the Close() function to close out part of a position. Here's a simplified example of how we can close out half of the current position:

```
double posVolume = PositionVolume();
double closeVolume = posVolume / 2;

Trade.Close(_Symbol,closeVolume);
```

The PositionVolume() function will retrieve the volume of the current position, and assign the result to posVolume. We divide posVolume by 2 to calculate half of the position, and assign the result to closeVolume. We use closeVolume as the second parameter of the Close() function, effectively closing out half of the position.

If you were to close out part of the position using this method, make sure that your closing conditions are very specific. Otherwise, the program will continue to close out half of the position over and over. Later on in the book, we will examine the use of pending orders to scale out of positions.

Chapter 13 - Pending Orders

A pending order is a request to open a trade at a specified price. The requested trade price must be a minimum distance away from the current Bid or Ask price, as determined by the stop level. Once the pending order's opening price is hit, a deal is made and the trade becomes part of the current position.

Along with the order price and volume, an optional stop loss price, take profit price and order expiration time can be specified. There are several expiration types for pending orders. *GTC (Good Til Canceled)* means that the order will not expire. *Today* means that the order will expire at the end of the trading day. *Specified* requires the trader to specify an expiration time. At the specified date and time, the order will automatically expire.

There are three types of pending orders: *stop*, *limit* and *stop limit*. Combined with the buy and sell order types, there are a total of six types of pending orders. Stop and limit orders differ in where the order price is located relative to the current price. The stop limit order type combines the two.

A *buy stop* order is placed above the current price. The deal is made when the Ask price is greater than or equal to the order opening price. A *sell stop* order is placed below the current price. The deal is made when the Bid price is less than or equal to the order opening price. A stop order is placed with the expectation that the price will continue moving in the direction of profit.

A *buy limit* order is placed below the current price. The deal is made when the Ask price is less than or equal to the order opening price. A *sell limit* order is placed above the current price. The deal is made when the Bid price is greater than or equal to the order opening price. A limit order is placed with the expectation that the price will reverse near the limit order price and continue in the direction of profit.

A stop limit order places a limit order when a stop order price is reached. This requires the trader to input two prices, a stop order price and a limit order price. A *buy stop limit* order places a buy limit order below the current price when the Ask price is greater than or equal to the stop order price. A *sell stop limit* order places a sell limit order above the current price when the Bid price is less than or equal to the stop order price.

Since a sell order can be used to close a buy position, and vice versa, it is possible to use pending orders as stop loss and take profit orders. A stop loss or take profit price that is placed on a position will close out the entire position when the price is reached. But a pending order can be used to close out part of a position, or even to reverse a position, when the pending order is triggered.

For example, we have a buy position open for 1 lot on EURUSD at 1.34500. If we place a sell stop order 500 points below at 1.34000, we can close out all or part of the position at this price. If we place a sell stop order for 2 lots at 1.34000, the position will effectively reverse from a net long position of 1 lot to a net sell position of 1 lot.

We can use limit orders to scale out of a profitable position. Using the example above, we could place sell limit orders for 0.5 lots each at 1.35000 and 1.35500, scaling out of our position at 500 and 1000 points respectively. We'll talk more about scaling out of positions later in this chapter.

The OpenPending() Function

Just as we did for market orders, we'll create a function for placing pending orders. The same principles we discussed in Chapter 10 apply here as well. Here is the OpenPending() function declaration in the CTrade class declaration:

```
class CTrade
{
    private:
        MqlTradeRequest request;
        bool OpenPending(string pSymbol, ENUM_ORDER_TYPE pType, double pVolume,
            double pPrice, double pStop = 0, double pProfit = 0, double pStopLimit = 0,
            datetime pExpiration = 0, string pComment = NULL);

    public:
        MqlTradeResult result;
};
```

The OpenPending() function has two additional parameters. pStopLimit is the stop limit price of the order, and pExpiration is the expiration time of the order. Both parameters are optional, with a default value of 0. The other parameters are identical to the OpenPosition() parameters, which we covered on page 98. We've declared the OpenPending() function as private, as we will be creating public functions to access it.

Let's go over the body of the OpenPending() function. First we will fill the request object variables with our function parameters:

```
bool CTrade::OpenPending(string pSymbol, ENUM_ORDER_TYPE pType, double pVolume,
    double pPrice, double pStop = 0, double pProfit = 0, double pStopLimit - 0,
    datetime pExpiration = 0, string pComment = NULL)
{
    request.action = TRADE_ACTION_PENDING;
    request.symbol = pSymbol;
    request.type = pType;
    request.sl = pStop;
    request.tp = pProfit;
    request.comment = pComment;
    request.price = pPrice;
    request.volume = pVolume;
    request.stoplimit = pStopLimit;
```

The TRADE_ACTION_PENDING constant indicates that we are placing a pending order. The remaining request variables are assigned the parameters that are passed into the function. Next, we'll need to determine the expiration time, if any:

```
if(pExpiration > 0)
{
    request.expiration = pExpiration;
    request.type_time = ORDER_TIME_SPECIFIED;
}
else request.type_time = ORDER_TIME_GTC;
```

If the pExpiration parameter has been specified, the value of pExpiration is assigned to the request.expiration variable, and the request.type_time variable is set to ORDER_TIME_SPECIFIED, which indicates that an expiration time has been specified. If pExpiration has not been specified, or has a value of 0, then request.type_time is set to ORDER_TIME_GTC, which indicates that the order does not expire.

Next, we'll place the pending order. Here is the order placement code, with the error handling code and retry on error:

```
// Order loop
int retryCount = 0;
int checkCode = 0;

do
{
    OrderSend(request,result);
    checkCode = CheckReturnCode(result.retcode);

    if(checkCode == CHECK_RETCODE_OK) break;
    else if(checkCode == CHECK_RETCODE_ERROR)
    {
        string errDesc = TradeServerReturnCodeDescription(result.retcode);
        Alert("Open pending order: Error ",result.retcode," - ",errDesc);
        break;
    }
    else
    {
        Print("Server error detected, retrying...");
        Sleep(RETRY_DELAY);
        retryCount++;
    }
}
while(retryCount < MAX_RETRIES);
```

This is similar to the code in the OpenPosition() function, except that we don't have to check for the current Bid or Ask price. Here is the remaining code in the OpenPending() function:

```
if(retryCount >= MAX_RETRIES)
{
    string errDesc = TradeServerReturnCodeDescription(result.retcode);
    Alert("Max retries exceeded: Error ",result.retcode," - ",errDesc);
}

string orderType = CheckOrderType(pType);
string errDesc = TradeServerReturnCodeDescription(result.retcode);

Print("Open ",orderType," order #",result.order,": ",result.retcode," - ",errDesc,
    ", Volume: ",result.volume,", Price: ",request.price,
    ", Bid: ",SymbolInfoDouble(pSymbol,SYMBOL_BID),
    ", Ask: ",SymbolInfoDouble(pSymbol,SYMBOL_ASK),
    ", SL: ",request.sl,", TP: ",request.tp,", Stop Limit: ",request.stoplimit,
    ", Expiration: ",request.expiration);

if(checkCode == CHECK_RETCODE_OK)
{
    Comment(orderType," order opened at ",request.price," on ",pSymbol);
    return(true);
}
else return(false);
```

As before, the function displays an error if retryCount has exceeded MAX_RETRIES. A string description of the order type is retrieved using the CheckOrderType() function, and the return code description is retrieved using the TradeServerReturnCodeDescription() function.

Next, we print information about the order to the log. We use a combination of request and result variables, since the result variables do not contain much information for pending orders. The SymbolInfoDouble() function is used to retrieve the current Bid and Ask price. Finally, we return a value of true if the order was successful, and false if it was not.

You can view the entire OpenPending() function in the \MQL5\Include\Mql5Book\Trade.mqh file.

Using The OpenPending() Function

As we did for the OpenPosition() function, we will create several helper functions to access our private OpenPending() function. Each function will open an order of the specified type:

```
class CTrade
{
    public:
        bool BuyStop(string pSymbol, double pVolume, double pPrice, double pStop = 0,
            double pProfit = 0, datetime pExpiration = 0, string pComment = NULL);
        bool SellStop(string pSymbol, double pVolume, double pPrice, double pStop = 0,
            double pProfit = 0, datetime pExpiration = 0, string pComment = NULL);
        bool BuyLimit(string pSymbol, double pVolume, double pPrice, double pStop = 0,
            double pProfit = 0, datetime pExpiration = 0, string pComment = NULL);
        bool SellLimit(string pSymbol, double pVolume, double pPrice, double pStop = 0,
            double pProfit = 0, datetime pExpiration = 0, string pComment = NULL);

        bool BuyStopLimit(string pSymbol, double pVolume, double pPrice, double pStop = 0,
            double pProfit = 0, double pStopLimit = 0, datetime pExpiration = 0,
            string pComment = NULL);
        bool SellStopLimit(string pSymbol, double pVolume, double pPrice, double pStop = 0,
            double pProfit = 0,  double pStopLimit = 0, datetime pExpiration = 0,
            string pComment = NULL);
};
```

Note that the stop limit order functions contain the pStopLimit parameter, while the other functions do not. Here's the body of the BuyStop() function. The function simply calls the OpenPending() function, passing the the function parameters through to OpenPending(), and specifying the ORDER_TYPE_BUY_STOP constant as the second parameter . The return value of OpenPending() is then returned to the program:

```
bool CTrade::BuyStop(string pSymbol, double pVolume, double pPrice, double pStop = 0,
    double pProfit = 0, datetime pExpiration = 0, string pComment = NULL)
{
    bool success = OpenPending(pSymbol,ORDER_TYPE_BUY_STOP,pVolume,pPrice,pStop,pProfit,0,
        pExpiration,pComment);
    return(success);
}
```

The other stop and limit order functions are identical – save for the order type passed to the OpenPending() function. Here is the sell stop limit order function, which contains the pStopLimit parameter:

```
bool CTrade::SellStopLimit(string pSymbol, double pVolume, double pPrice,
    double pStop = 0, double pProfit = 0, double pStopLimit = 0,
    datetime pExpiration = 0, string pComment = NULL)
{
    bool success = OpenPending(pSymbol,ORDER_TYPE_SELL_STOP_LIMIT,pVolume,pPrice,pStop,
        pProfit,pStopLimit,pExpiration,pComment);
    return(success);
}
```

You can view these functions in the \MQL5\Include\Mq15Book\Trade.mqh file. We will address the usage of these functions later in the chapter.

Handling Pending Orders

When working with pending orders, you will often need to retrieve information about the current orders. Since there can be multiple pending orders open per symbol, it is necessary to get an accurate count of the number of pending orders currently open.

To process the pending order pool, we use a for loop along with the OrderGetTicket() function to select each order in the order pool:

```
for(int i = 0; i < OrdersTotal(); i++)
{
    ulong ticket = OrderGetTicket(i);
    Print(ticket);
}
```

The for loop uses the integer variable i as the incrementor. It is initialized to 0, since the order pool index starts at 0. The OrdersTotal() function returns the number of pending orders currently open. Since the order pool index begins at 0, the maximum value of i needs to be one less than OrdersTotal(). An index of 0 is the oldest order in the pool. We will start at 0 and increment by one as long as i is less than OrdersTotal().

The OrderGetTicket() function selects the order with the order pool index indicated by the i variable. We can then use the OrderGetDouble(), OrderGetInteger() or OrderGetString() functions to retrieve information about the current order. The OrderGetTicket() function also returns the ticket number of the selected order. In the example above, we assign the order ticket to the ticket variable. The ticket number is printed to the log, and the loop repeats.

Now that we know how to loop through the current order pool, we can get an accurate count of the number of orders that are currently open by type. We're going to create a class to hold our order counting function, as well as the variables that hold our order counts and ticket numbers. We'll call this class CPending. The CPending class and all related functions in this chapter will be stored in the \MQL5\Include\Mq15Book\Pending.mqh file:

```
class CPending
{
    private:
        void OrderCount(string pSymbol);
        int BuyLimitCount, SellLimitCount, BuyStopCount, SellStopCount,
            BuyStopLimitCount, SellStopLimitCount, TotalPendingCount;
        ulong PendingTickets[];
```

```
    };
```

The OrderCount() function of our CPending class will iterate through the order pool and count the number of current orders. The integer variables BuyLimitCount, SellLimitCount, etc. will store the order counts, and the PendingTickets[] array will hold the ticket numbers of the current orders. All of these members are private – we will create public functions to access this information.

Here is the body of the OrderCount() function:

```
void CPending::OrderCount(string pSymbol)
{
    BuyLimitCount = 0; SellLimitCount = 0; BuyStopCount = 0; SellStopCount = 0;
    BuyStopLimitCount = 0; SellStopLimitCount = 0; TotalPendingCount = 0;
    ArrayFree(PendingTickets);

    for(int i = 0; i < OrdersTotal(); i++)
    {
        ulong ticket = OrderGetTicket(i);
        if(OrderGetString(ORDER_SYMBOL) == pSymbol)
        {
            long type = OrderGetInteger(ORDER_TYPE);

            switch((int)type)
            {
                case ORDER_TYPE_BUY_STOP:
                BuyStopCount++; break;

                case ORDER_TYPE_SELL_STOP:
                SellStopCount++; break;

                case ORDER_TYPE_BUY_LIMIT:
                BuyLimitCount++; break;

                case ORDER_TYPE_SELL_LIMIT:
                SellLimitCount++; break;

                case ORDER_TYPE_BUY_STOP_LIMIT:
                BuyStopLimitCount++; break;

                case ORDER_TYPE_SELL_STOP_LIMIT:
                SellStopLimitCount++; break;
            }

            TotalPendingCount++;

            ArrayResize(PendingTickets,TotalPendingCount);
```

145

```
                PendingTickets[ArraySize(PendingTickets)-1] = ticket;
            }
        }
    }
```

The first thing we do in the OrderCount() function is to initialize all of the order count variables to zero. You can place more than one expression per line, as long as each expression is terminated by a semicolon. The ArrayFree() function resets the PendingTickets[] array and clears its contents.

The for loop initialization and the OrderGetTicket() function have already been explained. The OrderGetString() function with the ORDER_SYMBOL parameter retrieves the symbol of the currently selected order and compares it to the pSymbol parameter. If the symbol does not match, we continue to the next order in the pool. Otherwise, we process the currently selected order.

The OrderGetInteger() function with the ORDER_TYPE parameter retrieves the order type for the currently selected order, and stores it in the type variable. The switch operator compares the type variable to a list of order types specified with case operators. Note the (int) inside the switch operator – this casts the value of the type variable to a integer to avoid a type conversion warning. When the correct order type is matched, the relevant count variable is incremented, and the break operator exits the switch block.

The TotalPendingCount variable is incremented for every order for the current symbol, regardless of type. The ArrayResize() function resizes the PendingTickets[] array to match the current number of orders indicated by TotalPendingCount. Finally, the currently selected order ticket is stored in the highest index of the array.

The result of the OrderCount() function is that the relevant count variables are filled with the number of open pending orders of each type for the selected symbol. The TotalPendingCount variable tallies all open orders for the selected symbol. Finally, the PendingTickets[] array contains the ticket numbers of all open pending orders for the selected symbol.

Now we'll need to create public functions to access our counter variables and the PendingTickets[] array. Here are the public members of our CPending class:

```
class CPending
{
    public:
        int BuyLimit(string pSymbol);
        int SellLimit(string pSymbol);
        int BuyStop(string pSymbol);
        int SellStop(string pSymbol);
        int BuyStopLimit(string pSymbol);
        int SellStopLimit(string pSymbol);
        int TotalPending(string pSymbol);
```

```
        void GetTickets(string pSymbol, ulong &pTickets[]);
    };
```

The seven functions with the `int` return type return the count for the specified order type. The `GetTickets()` function copies the `PendingTickets[]` array into a second array that the programmer will then process.

Let's take a look at the function body for the `BuyLimit()` function. All seven of these functions call the private `OrderCount()` function. After the function has run, the appropriate count variable is returned to the program:

```
    int CPending::BuyLimit(string pSymbol)
    {
        OrderCount(pSymbol);
        return(BuyLimitCount);
    }
```

The `BuyLimit()` function returns the number of buy limit orders that are currently open on the symbol specified by pSymbol. The remaining six count functions are similar. The only difference is the count variable that is returned by the function. You can view these functions in the `\MQL5\Include\Mql5Book\Pending.mqh` file.

Now let's examine the `GetTickets()` function. This will call the `OrderCount()` function and then copy the `PendingTickets[]` array to a second array passed to the function by reference:

```
    void CPending::GetTickets(string pSymbol,ulong &pTickets[])
    {
        OrderCount(pSymbol);
        ArrayCopy(pTickets,PendingTickets);
        return;
    }
```

The ampersand (&) before the `pTickets[]` parameter indicates that this is an array passed by reference. The array will be modified by the function, and those modifications will be present throughout the rest of the program. The `ArrayCopy()` function copies the `PendingTickets[]` array to the array specified by the pTickets parameter. Here is how we would use the `GetTickets()` function in our program:

```
    // Global variables
    CPending Pending;

    // OnTick() event handler
    ulong tickets[];
```

```
        Pending.GetTickets(_Symbol,tickets);

        for(int i = 0; i < ArraySize(tickets); i++)
        {
            ulong ticket = tickets[i];
            OrderSelect(ticket);

            long orderType = OrderGetInteger(ORDER_TYPE);
            double orderVolume = OrderGetDouble(ORDER_VOLUME_CURRENT);
            double orderOpenPrice = OrderGetDouble(ORDER_PRICE_OPEN);
            double orderSL = OrderGetDouble(ORDER_SL);
            double orderTP = OrderGetDouble(ORDER_TP);

            Print("Ticket:"+ticket+", Type:"+orderType+", Volume:"+orderVolume+",
                Price:"+orderOpenPrice+", SL:"+orderSL+", TP:"+orderTP);
        }
```

First, we declare an object named Pending based on the CPending class at the top of the program. The remainder of the code belongs in the OnTick() event handler, or a function called from it.

The tickets[] array will hold the pending ticket numbers. The GetTickets() function fills the tickets[] array with the ticket numbers of all of the unfilled pending orders for the current chart symbol. A for loop is used to iterate through the ticket numbers in the tickets[] array. The iterator variable i starts at 0. The maximum value of i is determined by the ArraySize() function, which returns the number of elements in the tickets[] array.

Inside the for loop, we assign the value of tickets[i] to the ticket variable. The ticket variable is passed to the OrderSelect() function, which selects the order for further processing. The OrderGetInteger(), OrderGetDouble() and OrderGetString() functions can now be used to retrieve information about the order.

We use the OrderGetInteger() and OrderGetDouble() functions to retrieve information about the currently selected order, including the order type, volume, opening price, stop loss and take profit. Finally, we print this information to the log.

When iterating through the pending order pool in this manner, you will be retrieving information about each order and using that information to make decisions, such as whether to modify or close an order.

Order Information Functions

Just like the position information functions in the last chapter, we're going to create a set of easy-to-remember functions to retrieve order information. Instead of using the OrderGet...() functions, we will create short functions to retrieve this information using only a ticket number.

Let's start with the order type. The OrderGetInteger() function with the ORDER_TYPE parameter returns an order type constant from the ENUM_ORDER_TYPE enumeration. The order must be selected first using the OrderSelect() function. The function below will retrieve the order type using only the ticket number:

```
long OrderType(ulong pTicket)
{
    bool select = OrderSelect(pTicket);
    if(select == true) return(OrderGetInteger(ORDER_TYPE));
    else return(WRONG_VALUE);
}
```

The OrderSelect() function selects the order indicated by the ticket number passed into the pTicket parameter. If the order does not exist, the function returns WRONG_VALUE, or -1. Otherwise, the order type is retrieved with the OrderGetInteger() function and returned to the program.

Let's look at another function that uses the OrderGetDouble() function. This function will return the current volume of the order:

```
double OrderVolume(ulong pTicket)
{
    bool select = OrderSelect(pTicket);
    if(select == true) return(OrderGetDouble(ORDER_VOLUME_CURRENT));
    else return(WRONG_VALUE);
}
```

The OrderGetDouble() function returns the current volume of the order if the ticket number selected by OrderSelect() is valid. Finally, let's look at a function that uses OrderGetString():

```
string OrderComment(ulong pTicket)
{
    bool select = OrderSelect(pTicket);
    if(select == true) return(OrderGetString(ORDER_COMMENT));
    else return(NULL);
}
```

This function returns the order comment. If the order ticket passed to the OrderSelect() function is not valid, then a value of NULL is returned.

There are several more functions that use the OrderSelect() and OrderGet...() functions. You can view them in the \MQL5\Include\Mql5Book\Pending.mqh file. The parameters for the OrderGet...() functions can be viewed in the *MQL5 Reference* under *Standard Constants... > Trade Constants > Order Properties*.

Let's use the order information functions we've defined in the `Pending.mqh` file in the code example from page 147:

```
ulong tickets[];

Pending.GetTickets(_Symbol,tickets);

for(int i = 0; i < ArraySize(tickets); i++)
{
    ulong ticket = tickets[i];

    long orderType = OrderType(ticket);
    double orderVolume = OrderVolume(ticket);
    double orderOpenPrice = OrderOpenPrice(ticket);
    double orderSL = OrderStopLoss(ticket);
    double orderTP = OrderTakeProfit(ticket);

    Print("Ticket:"+ticket+", Type:"+orderType+", Volume:"+orderVolume+",
        Price:"+orderOpenPrice+", SL:"+orderSL+", TP:"+orderTP);
}
```

We've replaced the `OrderGet...()` functions with the order information functions that we've defined. We've also eliminated the `OrderSelect()` function, as it is no longer necessary.

To summarize, we've created the `CPending` class with seven public order counting functions (`BuyLimit()`, `SellLimit()`, etc.) that will return the number of open pending orders of that type for the specified symbol. The `GetTickets()` function will return an array that contains the ticket numbers of all pending orders currently open on the specified symbol. Using the array returned by the `GetTickets()` function, we can retrieve the ticket numbers of the open pending orders. With the ticket number, we can retrieve information about the order using the order information functions such as `OrderType()`, `OrderOpenPrice()` or `OrderStopLoss()`.

Modifying Pending Orders

It may be necessary to modify the opening price, stop loss, take profit or expiration time of a pending order. To do this, we use the `TRADE_ACTION_MODIFY` action with the `OrderSend()` function. We'll need to specify the ticket number, the order opening price, the stop loss, take profit, and the expiration time and type.

When modifying a pending order, it is necessary to specify the current value of any price that will not be changed. For example, if you are changing the opening price of a pending order, and the order currently has a stop loss and take profit price, then you will need to retrieve the current stop loss and take profit prices and pass them to the `OrderSend()` function.

Let's demonstrate a simple pending order modification. In this example, we will be changing the opening price of a pending order. The stop loss and take profit will not be changed. No expiration time was placed with the order. We'll assume that the variable newPrice holds the new pending order price:

```
double newPrice;

ulong tickets[];
Pending.GetTickets(_Symbol,tickets);

for(int i = 0; i < ArraySize(tickets); i++)
{
    ulong ticket = tickets[i];

    request.action = TRADE_ACTION_MODIFY;
    request.order = ticket;
    request.price = newPrice;
    request.sl = OrderStopLoss(ticket);
    request.tp = OrderTakeProfit(ticket);
    request.expiration = 0;
    request.type_time = ORDER_TIME_GTC;

    OrderSend(request,result);
}
```

You'll recognize the GetTickets() function and the for loop from the previous section. We'll assume that there is a single pending order open on the current chart symbol, and this code will modify the opening price to the value stored in newPrice.

The TRADE_ACTION_MODIFY constant identifies this as a pending order modification. When modifying an order, we must specify an order ticket using the request.order variable. Any changes to the price, stop loss, take profit or expiration are assigned to the appropriate variables. If there are no changes, then we must assign the current values to those variables.

Since the order opening price is being changed, we assign the value of the newPrice variable to request.price. We use our OrderStopLoss() and OrderTakeProfit() functions to retrieve the current stop loss and take profit prices, and assign those prices to the request.sl and request.tp variables. This ensures that the stop loss and take profit prices will not be modified. For completeness, we specify a value of 0 for request.expiration, and set request.type_time to ORDER_TIME_GTC, indicating that the order does not expire. The OrderSend() function sends the updated pending order price to the server for modification. The stop loss, take profit and expiration time remain unchanged.

Here's another example where we'll modify the stop loss and take profit prices of a pending order. The order opening price will remain unchanged. The stop loss will be adjusted 500 points below the order opening price, and the take profit will be set to zero:

```
// Global variables
input int StopLoss = 500;

// OnTick() event handler
ulong tickets[];
Pending.GetTickets(_Symbol,tickets);

for(int i = 0; i < ArraySize(tickets); i++)
{
    ulong ticket = tickets[i];

    request.action = TRADE_ACTION_MODIFY;
    request.order = ticket;
    request.price = OrderOpenPrice(ticket);
    request.sl = OrderOpenPrice(ticket) - (StopLoss * _Point);
    request.tp = 0;
    request.expiration = 0;
    request.type_time = ORDER_TIME_GTC;

    OrderSend(request,result);
}
```

The lines in bold indicate the changes from the previous example. The request.price variable is set to the current order opening price. The request.sl variable is set to the order opening price, minus the number of points indicated in the StopLoss variable. The result.tp variable is set to 0, indicating that there will be no take profit on the modified order. If there is currently a take profit price on the order, it will be reset to 0.

The ModifyPending() Function

The ModifyPending() function will modify the opening price, stop loss, take profit or expiration time on an order. The order ticket, price, stop loss and take profit are the required parameters. If the price will not be changed, a value of 0 will be passed to the pPrice parameter. If the stop loss, take profit or expiration time are set and will not be changed, then it will be necessary to pass the current values to the ModifyPending() function:

Here is the ModifyPending() function declaration in the CTrade class declaration:

```
class CTrade
{
    public:
        bool ModifyPending(ulong pTicket, double pPrice, double pStop, double pProfit,
            datetime pExpiration = 0);
};
```

The function is `public`, which means that we will be calling it directly. Here is the first part of the
`ModifyPending()` function, where we set the request variables:

```
bool CTrade::ModifyPending(ulong pTicket, double pPrice, double pStop, double pProfit,
    datetime pExpiration = 0)
{
    request.action = TRADE_ACTION_MODIFY;
    request.order = pTicket;
    request.sl = pStop;
    request.tp = pProfit;

    OrderSelect(pTicket);

    if(pPrice > 0) request.price = pPrice;
    else request.price = OrderGetDouble(ORDER_PRICE_OPEN);

    if(pExpiration > 0)
    {
        request.expiration = pExpiration;
        request.type_time = ORDER_TIME_SPECIFIED;
    }
    else request.type_time = ORDER_TIME_GTC;
```

The trade action is set to `TRADE_ACTION_MODIFY`, and the `pTicket`, `pStop` and `pProfit` parameter values are
assigned to the appropriate request variables. Next, we use the `OrderSelect()` function to select the order
ticket indicated by `pTicket`. If the `pPrice` parameter is greater than zero, we assign the value of `pPrice` to
`request.price`. Otherwise, we retrieve the current open price and assign that value to `request.price`.

If the value of `pExpiration` is greater than zero, we assign the new order expiration time to
`request.expiration`, and set `request.type_time` to `ORDER_TIME_SPECIFIED`. Otherwise, we set
`request.type_time` to `ORDER_TIME_GTC`, which indicates that the order will not have an expiration time.

The rest of the function contains our order modification and error handling code:

```
    int retryCount = 0;
    int checkCode = 0;
```

```
        do
        {
            OrderSend(request,result);

            checkCode = CheckReturnCode(result.retcode);

            if(checkCode == CHECK_RETCODE_OK) break;
            else if(checkCode == CHECK_RETCODE_ERROR)
            {
                string errDesc = TradeServerReturnCodeDescription(result.retcode);
                Alert("Modify pending order: Error ",result.retcode," - ",errDesc);
                break;
            }
            else
            {
                Print("Server error detected, retrying...");
                Sleep(RETRY_DELAY);
                retryCount++;
            }
        }
        while(retryCount < MAX_RETRIES);

        if(retryCount >= MAX_RETRIES)
        {
            string errDesc = TradeServerReturnCodeDescription(result.retcode);
            Alert("Max retries exceeded: Error ",result.retcode," - ",errDesc);
        }

        OrderSelect(pTicket);
        string errDesc = TradeServerReturnCodeDescription(result.retcode);

        Print("Modify pending order #",pTicket,": ",result.retcode," - ",errDesc,
            ", Price: ",OrderGetDouble(ORDER_PRICE_OPEN),", SL: ",request.sl,
            ", TP: ",request.tp,", Expiration: ",request.expiration);

        if(checkCode == CHECK_RETCODE_OK)
        {
            Comment("Pending order ",pTicket," modified,",
                " Price: ",OrderGetDouble(ORDER_PRICE_OPEN),", SL: ",request.sl,
                ", TP: ",request.tp);
            return(true);
        }
        else return(false);
}
```

Here's how we would use our `ModifyPending()` function in an expert advisor program. This example will modify the order opening price, but leave the stop loss and take profit alone:

```
double newPrice;
ulong ticket;

double curSL = OrderStopLoss(ticket);
double curTP = OrderTakeProfit(ticket);

Trade.ModifyPending(ticket,newPrice,curSL,curTP);
```

The `newPrice` variable will hold the new order opening price, while the `ticket` variable contains the order ticket number. We'll assume they both contain valid values. We use the `OrderStopLoss()` and `OrderTakeProfit()` functions to retrieve the current stop loss and take profit values for the specified order ticket, and store those values in `curSL` and `curTP` respectively. The parameters are passed to the `ModifyPending()` function, and the order is updated with the new pending order price.

Here's a second example where we modify the stop loss and take profit, but leave the order price alone:

```
double newSL, newTP;
ulong ticket;

Trade.ModifyPending(ticket,0,newSL,newTP);
```

We'll assume that the `newSL` and `newTP` variables hold valid stop loss and take profit prices. In the `ModifyPending()` function call, we use a 0 for the `pPrice` parameter to indicate that the order opening price will not be changed.

In both of the examples above, the `pExpiration` parameter uses the default value of 0. If an expiration time has been specified with the order, you will need to pass the expiration time to the `ModifyPending()` function when modifying the order.

Deleting Pending Orders

An unfilled pending order can be deleted by assigning the `TRADE_ACTION_REMOVE` constant to the `request.action` variable. The only required parameter is the ticket number of the order to delete:

```
request.action = TRADE_ACTION_MODIFY;
request.order = ticket;

OrderSend(request,result);
```

The above code will delete the pending order that matches the `ticket` variable. Note that once a pending order is filled, it becomes part of the position and must be closed using the position closing methods in the previous chapter.

We'll create a function to delete a pending order, with the same error handling and retry code as the previous function. Here is the function declaration in the `CTrade` class declaration:

```
class CTrade
{
    public:
        bool Delete(ulong pTicket);
}
```

And here is the function itself. The `Delete()` function requires only one parameter – the ticket number of the pending order to delete:

```
bool CTrade::Delete(ulong pTicket)
{
    request.action = TRADE_ACTION_REMOVE;
    request.order = pTicket;

    // Order loop
    int retryCount = 0;
    int checkCode = 0;

    do
    {
        OrderSend(request,result);
        checkCode = CheckReturnCode(result.retcode);

        if(checkCode == CHECK_RETCODE_OK) break;

        else if(checkCode == CHECK_RETCODE_ERROR)
        {
            string errDesc = TradeServerReturnCodeDescription(result.retcode);
            Alert("Delete order: Error ",result.retcode," - ",errDesc);
            break;
        }
        else
        {
            Print("Server error detected, retrying...");
            Sleep(RETRY_DELAY);
            retryCount++;
        }
```

```
    }
    while(retryCount < MAX_RETRIES);

    if(retryCount >= MAX_RETRIES)
    {
        string errDesc = TradeServerReturnCodeDescription(result.retcode);
        Alert("Max retries exceeded: Error ",result.retcode," - ",errDesc);
    }

    string errDesc = TradeServerReturnCodeDescription(result.retcode);
    Print("Delete order #",pTicket,": ",result.retcode," - ",errDesc);

    if(checkCode == CHECK_RETCODE_OK)
    {
        Comment("Pending order ",pTicket," deleted");
        return(true);
    }
    else return(false);
}
```

To use the `Delete()` function, simply pass the ticket number of the order to delete to the `pTicket` parameter:

```
ulong tickets[];
Pending.GetTickets(_Symbol,tickets);

for(int i = 0; i < ArraySize(tickets); i++)
{
    ulong ticket = tickets[i];
    Trade.Delete(ticket);
}
```

This example will delete every pending order that is open on the current chart.

Creating A Pending Order Expert Advisor

We're going to create a simple expert advisor that places pending orders. This strategy is meant to be used on a H4 or higher chart. On the open of a new bar, two pending stop orders are placed a specified number of points above and below the high and low of the previous bar. At the open of the next bar, any unfilled pending orders are deleted, and new pending orders are placed. Any opened position will continue until it hits a stop loss or take profit price.

```
#include <Mql5Book\Trade.mqh>
CTrade Trade;
```

```
#include <Mql5Book\Pending.mqh>
CPending Pending;

// Input variables
input int AddPoints = 100;
input double TradeVolume=0.1;
input int StopLoss=1000;
input int TakeProfit=1000;

// Global variables
bool glBuyPlaced, glSellPlaced;
datetime glLastBarTime;


// OnTick() event handler
void OnTick()
{
    // Time and price data
    MqlRates rates[];
    ArraySetAsSeries(rates,true);
    int copy = CopyRates(_Symbol,_Period,0,3,rates);

    // Check for new bar
    bool newBar = false;
    if(glLastBarTime != rates[0].time)
    {
        if(glLastBarTime > 0) newBar = true;
        glLastBarTime = rates[0].time;
    }

    // Place pending order on open of new bar
    if(newBar == true)
    {
        // Get pending order tickets
        ulong tickets[];
        Pending.GetTickets(_Symbol,tickets);
        int numTickets = ArraySize(tickets);

        // Close any open pending orders
        if(Pending.TotalPending(_Symbol) > 0)
        {
            for(int i = 0; i < numTickets; i++)
            {
                Trade.Delete(tickets[i]);
            }
        }
```

```
            // Open pending buy stop order
            double orderPrice = rates[1].high + (AddPoints * _Point);
            orderPrice = AdjustAboveStopLevel(_Symbol,orderPrice);

            double stopLoss = BuyStopLoss(_Symbol,StopLoss,orderPrice);
            double takeProfit = BuyTakeProfit(_Symbol,TakeProfit,orderPrice);

            Trade.BuyStop(_Symbol,TradeVolume,orderPrice,stopLoss,takeProfit);

            // Open pending sell stop order
            orderPrice = rates[1].low - (AddPoints * _Point);
            orderPrice = AdjustBelowStopLevel(_Symbol,orderPrice);

            stopLoss = SellStopLoss(_Symbol,StopLoss,orderPrice);
            takeProfit = SellTakeProfit(_Symbol,TakeProfit,orderPrice);

            Trade.SellStop(_Symbol,TradeVolume,orderPrice,stopLoss,takeProfit);
        }
    }
```

Let's step through the program:

```
    #include <Mql5Book\Trade.mqh>
    CTrade Trade;

    #include <Mql5Book\Pending.mqh>
    CPending Pending;


    // Input variables
    input int AddPoints = 100;
    input double TradeVolume=0.1;
    input int StopLoss=1000;
    input int TakeProfit=1000;

    // Global variables
    bool glBuyPlaced, glSellPlaced;
    datetime glLastBarTime;
```

First, we include our `Trade.mqh` and `Pending.mqh` files from the `\MQL5\Include\Mql5Book` folder. We create the `Trade` and `Pending` objects based on our `CTrade` and `CPending` classes. We add an input variable named `AddPoints`, which adds or subtracts the specified number of points from the previous bar's high or low price. Input variables to set the trade volume, stop loss and take profit are also included. The global `datetime` variable `glLastBarTime` holds the timestamp of the most recent bar.

```
void OnTick()
{
    // Time and price data
    MqlRates rates[];
    ArraySetAsSeries(rates,true);
    int copy = CopyRates(_Symbol,_Period,0,3,rates);

    // Check for new bar
    bool newBar = false;
    if(glLastBarTime != rates[0].time)
    {
        if(glLastBarTime > 0) newBar = true;
        glLastBarTime = rates[0].time;
    }
```

We use the rates[] array of the MqlRates structure type to hold the high, low and time values of each bar. We will cover the MqlRates structure in Chapter 15. The newBar variable holds a boolean value determining whether a new bar has opened (*i.e.* a change in the current bar's timestamp has occurred). The new bar feature will be covered in Chapter 18.

```
    if(newBar == true)
    {
        // Get pending order tickets
        ulong tickets[];
        Pending.GetTickets(_Symbol,tickets);
        int numTickets = ArraySize(tickets);


        // Close any open pending orders
        if(Pending.TotalPending(_Symbol) > 0)
        {
            for(int i = 0; i < numTickets; i++)
            {
                Trade.Delete(tickets[i]);
            }
        }
    }
```

If the value of the newBar variable is true, indicating that a new bar has opened, we will begin with the order placement code. First, we use the GetTickets() function from our CPending class to retrieve the open order tickets. These are stored in the tickets[] array. The ArraySize() function returns the number of elements in the tickets[] array and stores that value in the numTickets variable. If the number of open orders is greater than zero, as determined by the numTickets variable, we iterate through the order pool using a for loop and delete all open orders using the Trade.Delete() function.

```
// Open pending buy stop order
double orderPrice = rates[1].high + (AddPoints * _Point);
orderPrice = AdjustAboveStopLevel(_Symbol,orderPrice);

double stopLoss = BuyStopLoss(_Symbol,StopLoss,orderPrice);
double takeProfit = BuyTakeProfit(_Symbol,TakeProfit,orderPrice);

Trade.BuyStop(_Symbol,TradeVolume,orderPrice,stopLoss,takeProfit);


// Open pending sell stop order
orderPrice = rates[1].low - (AddPoints * _Point);
orderPrice = AdjustBelowStopLevel(_Symbol,orderPrice);

stopLoss = SellStopLoss(_Symbol,StopLoss,orderPrice);
takeProfit = SellTakeProfit(_Symbol,TakeProfit,orderPrice);

Trade.SellStop(_Symbol,TradeVolume,orderPrice,stopLoss,takeProfit);
```

The orderPrice variable holds the pending order opening price. We add or subtract the AddPoints value (multiplied first by the symbol's _Point value) from the previous bar's high or low price (rates[1].high and rates[1].low). We check and adjust the order price if necessary using the AdjustAboveStopLevel() and AdjustBelowStopLevel() functions. Then we calculate the stop loss and take profit relative to the order opening price. Finally, we place the pending stop orders using the BuyStop() and SellStop() functions of our CTrade class.

You can view the code of this expert advisor in the \Experts\Mq15Book\Pending Expert Advisor.mq5 file.

Using Pending Orders to Scale Out of a Position

If you'd like to scale out of a position at fixed profit or loss levels, the best method is to use pending orders to close out part of a position at a specified price. A position can be closed in profit by using a limit order, while a position in loss can be closed using a stop order. To close a buy position in profit, use a sell limit order. To close it in loss, use a sell stop order. To close a sell position in profit, use a buy limit order. To close it in loss, use a buy stop order.

For example, if you want to close out half of a buy position at 500 points of profit and the rest at 1000 points, place a sell limit order 500 points above the position opening price for half of the position's lot size. The take profit price of the position will take care of the rest. Here's an example:

```
// Input variables
input double TradeVolume=0.2;
input int StopLoss=500;
input int TakeProfit1=500;
input int TakeProfit2=1000;

// OnTick() event handler
// Open buy market order
glBuyPlaced = Trade.Buy(_Symbol,TradeVolume);

// Modify SL/TP
if(glBuyPlaced == true)
{
    do Sleep(100); while(PositionSelect(_Symbol) == false);
    double positionOpenPrice = PositionOpenPrice();

    double buyStopLoss = BuyStopLoss(_Symbol,StopLoss,positionOpenPrice);
    if(buyStopLoss > 0) buyStopLoss = AdjustBelowStopLevel(_Symbol,buyStopLoss);

    double buyTakeProfit = BuyTakeProfit(_Symbol,TakeProfit2,positionOpenPrice);
    if(buyTakeProfit > 0) buyTakeProfit = AdjustAboveStopLevel(_Symbol,buyTakeProfit);

    if(buyStopLoss > 0 || buyTakeProfit > 0)
        Trade.ModifyPosition(_Symbol,buyStopLoss,buyTakeProfit);

    glSellPlaced = false;

    // Open partial close order
    double partialClose = positionOpenPrice + (TakeProfit1 * _Point);
    double partialVolume = TradeVolume / 2;

    Trade.SellLimit(_Symbol,partialVolume,partialClose);
}
```

The example above opens a buy position, sets a stop loss and a take profit of 1000 points, and then places a sell limit order – equal to half the lot size of the buy position – 500 points above the opening price of the buy position. We use two input variables for the take profit values. TakeProfit1 determines the price for the sell limit order, and TakeProfit2 is the take profit price of the buy position. The TakeProfit2 variable is passed to the BuyTakeProfit() function to calculate the take profit price of the buy position.

To calculate the sell limit order price, we add the value of TakeProfit1 (multiplied by the _Point variable) to the position opening price (positionOpenPrice), and store the result in the partialClose variable. We calculate the volume of the sell limit order by dividing the TradeVolume input variable by 2, and storing the result in the partialVolume variable. We use the SellLimit() function to open a sell limit order of 0.1 lots, 500 points above the position opening price.

When the sell limit order is triggered, half of the current position will be closed. The remainder of the position will close at the position's take profit price. This method can be used to add any number of partial close levels to a position. Be sure not to set your pending order volume(s) to be greater than the position volume, or else you will open a position in the opposite direction!

Chapter 14 - Trailing Stops

What is a Trailing Stop?

A trailing stop is a stop loss that moves as a position increases in profit. For a buy order, the trailing stop moves up in price as the position gains in profit, and for a sell order, the trailing stop moves down in price as the position gains in profit. A trailing stop never moves in reverse.

The trailing stop typically follows the current price by a specified number of points. For example, if a trailing stop is set to 500 points, then the stop loss begins moving once the current price is at least 500 points away from the stop loss price. We can delay a trailing stop by requiring that a minimum level of profit be reached first. And while a trailing stop typically follows the price point by point, we can trail the stop in larger increments.

Let's examine how to implement a simple trailing stop. To calculate the trailing stop price, we add or subtract the trailing stop in points from the current Bid or Ask price. If the distance between the position's current stop loss and the current price is greater than the trailing stop in points, we modify the position's stop loss to match the trailing stop price.

The code below will add a simple trailing stop to an expert advisor. This code would be placed below the order placement code, near the end of the OnTick() event handler:

```
// Input variables
input int TrailingStop = 500;

// OnTick() event handler
if(PositionSelect(_Symbol) == true && TrailingStop > 0)
{
    request.action = TRADE_ACTION_SLTP;
    request.symbol = _Symbol;

    long posType = PositionGetInteger(POSITION_TYPE);
    double currentStop = PositionGetDouble(POSITION_SL);

    double trailStop = TrailingStop * _Point;
    double trailStopPrice;

    if(posType == POSITION_TYPE_BUY)
    {
        trailStopPrice = SymbolInfoDouble(_Symbol,SYMBOL_BID) - trailStop;
```

```
            if(trailStopPrice > currentStop)
            {
                request.sl = trailStopPrice;
                OrderSend(request,result);
            }
        }
        else if(posType == POSITION_TYPE_SELL)
        {
            trailStopPrice = SymbolInfoDouble(_Symbol,SYMBOL_ASK) + trailStop;
            if(trailStopPrice < currentStop)
            {
                request.sl = trailStopPrice;
                OrderSend(request,result);
            }
        }
    }
```

An input variable named TrailingStop is used to set the trailing stop in points. The default value of 500 sets a trailing stop of 50 pips (0.00500 or 0.500). The PositionSelect() function inside the if operator determines whether there is a position open on the current chart symbol, and selects that position for further processing. If the PositionSelect() function returns true, and the TrailingStop setting is greater than zero, we proceed with checking the trailing stop.

The request.action variable is set to TRADE_ACTION_SLTP, since we are performing a position modification. The request.symbol variable sets the current chart symbol as the position to modify. We retrieve the position type using the PositionGetInteger() function with the POSITION_TYPE parameter and store the result in the posType variable. The current stop loss is retrieved using the PositionGetDouble() function with the POSITION_SL parameter and stored in currentStop. We convert the TrailingStop input variable to a price value by multiplying it by the symbol's point value. We store this value in the trailStop variable. We also declare a variable named trailStopPrice. We will calculate the value of this variable shortly.

An if-else block checks the position type. If the position is a buy position, we calculate the trailing stop price by subtracting trailStop from the current Bid price, and storing the result in the trailStopPrice variable. Then we compare trailStopPrice to the current stop loss, stored in the currentStop variable. If the trailing stop price is greater than the current stop loss price, this indicates that we need to move the stop to the trailing stop price. The request.sl variable is set to trailStopPrice, and the OrderSend() function modifies the stop loss.

For a sell position, the trailing stop price (trailStopPrice) is calculated by adding the trailStop value to the current Ask price. If the trailing stop price is less than the current stop loss price, we modify the position's stop loss to the trailing stop price.

Minimum Profit

Let's add some modifications to our simple trailing stop. For example, maybe you want the trailing stop to kick in only after a minimum amount of profit has been achieved. To do this, we'll add a minimum profit setting to our expert advisor. First we determine the profit of the current position in points. Then we compare this to the minimum profit setting. If the position's current profit in points is greater than the minimum profit, then the trailing stop will activate. The changes are highlighted in bold:

```
// Input variables
input int TrailingStop = 500;
input int MinimumProfit = 200;


// OnTick() event handler
if(PositionSelect(_Symbol) == true && TrailingStop > 0)
{
    request.action = TRADE_ACTION_SLTP;
    request.symbol = _Symbol;

    long posType = PositionGetInteger(POSITION_TYPE);
    double currentStop = PositionGetDouble(POSITION_SL);
    double openPrice = PositionGetDouble(POSITION_PRICE_OPEN);

    double minProfit = MinimumProfit * _Point;
    double trailStop = TrailingStop * _Point;

    double trailStopPrice;
    double currentProfit;

    if(posType == POSITION_TYPE_BUY)
    {
        trailStopPrice = SymbolInfoDouble(_Symbol,SYMBOL_BID) - trailStop;
        currentProfit = SymbolInfoDouble(_Symbol,SYMBOL_BID) - openPrice;
        if(trailStopPrice > currentStop && currentProfit >= minProfit)
        {
            request.sl = trailStopPrice;
            OrderSend(request,result);
        }
    }

    else if(posType == POSITION_TYPE_SELL)
    {
        trailStopPrice = SymbolInfoDouble(_Symbol,SYMBOL_ASK) + trailStop;
        currentProfit = openPrice - SymbolInfoDouble(_Symbol,SYMBOL_ASK);
```

```
            if(trailStopPrice < currentStop && currentProfit >= minProfit)
            {
                request.sl = trailStopPrice;
                OrderSend(request,result);
            }
        }
    }
```

We've added an input variable named MinimumProfit. The default value of 200 means that the minimum profit of the current position must be at least 200 points (0.00200 or 0.200). We retrieve the position opening price using the PositionGetDouble() function with the POSITION_PRICE_OPEN parameter, and store the result in the openPrice variable. We convert the MinimumProfit setting to a price value by multiplying it by the current symbol's _Point value, and storing the result in the minProfit variable. A variable named currentProfit is declared, and will be calculated shortly.

If the current position is a buy position, we calculate the current profit by subtracting the order opening price (openPrice) from the current Bid price, and storing the result in the currentProfit variable. If currentProfit is greater than minProfit, and the current stop loss price is less than the trailing stop price, we modify the stop loss and set it to the trailing stop price.

For a sell position, we calculate the current profit by subtracting the current Ask price from the order opening price. If the current profit is greater than the minimum profit, and the current stop loss price is greater than the trailing stop price, we modify the stop loss.

Stepping A Trailing Stop

One final modification to the trailing stop is to add a step value. The code above will modify the trailing stop on every minor price change in the direction of profit. This can be a little overwhelming for the trade server, so we will enforce a minimum step of 10 points and allow the user to specify a larger step value:

```
// Input variables
input int TrailingStop = 500;
input int MinimumProfit = 200;
input int Step = 10;

// OnTick() event handler
if(PositionSelect(_Symbol) == true && TrailingStop > 0)
{
    request.action = TRADE_ACTION_SLTP;
    request.symbol = _Symbol;

    long posType = PositionGetInteger(POSITION_TYPE);
    double currentStop = PositionGetDouble(POSITION_SL);
```

```
        double openPrice = PositionGetDouble(POSITION_PRICE_OPEN);

        double minProfit = MinimumProfit * _Point;
        if(Step < 10) Step = 10;
        double step = Step * _Point;
        double trailStop = TrailingStop * _Point;

        double trailStopPrice;
        double currentProfit;

        if(posType == POSITION_TYPE_BUY)
        {
            trailStopPrice = SymbolInfoDouble(_Symbol,SYMBOL_BID) - trailStop;
            currentProfit = SymbolInfoDouble(_Symbol,SYMBOL_BID) - openPrice;
            if(trailStopPrice > currentStop + step && currentProfit >= minProfit)
            {
                request.sl = trailStopPrice;
                OrderSend(request,result);
            }
        }
        else if(posType == POSITION_TYPE_SELL)
        {
            trailStopPrice = SymbolInfoDouble(_Symbol,SYMBOL_ASK) + trailStop;
            currentProfit = SymbolInfoDouble(_Symbol,SYMBOL_ASK) + openPrice;
            if(trailStopPrice < currentStop - step && currentProfit >= minProfit)
            {
                request.sl = trailStopPrice;
                OrderSend(request,result);
            }
        }
    }
```

We've added an input variable named Step, with a default value of 10 points. If Step is set to anything less than 10, we will set the value of Step to 10. We' convert Step to a point value by multiplying it by the symbol's _Point value, and storing the result in the variable step. When checking the trailing stop condition, we add or subtract the step value from the currentStop variable. This ensures that the trailing stop moves in 10 point increments.

The CTrailing Class

We're going to create a reusable trailing stop class that is robust and flexible enough for any situation that a trader may require. We will create a new include file for our trailing stop class. The file is named TrailingStops.mqh, and will be located in the \MQL5\Include\Mql5Book folder.

Here are the include directives and class declaration from the top of the TrailingStops.mqh file:

```
#include <errordescription.mqh>
#include "Trade.mqh"

class CTrailing
{
    protected:
        MqlTradeRequest request;

    public:
        MqlTradeResult result;
        bool TrailingStop(string pSymbol, int pTrailPoints, int pMinProfit = 0,
            int pStep = 10);
};
```

We are including the errordescription.mqh file from the \MQL5\Include folder, and the Trade.mqh file from the current folder. The CTrailing class declaration contains the request and result objects that we have covered in previous chapters. Let's take a look at our trailing stop function parameters:

```
bool TrailingStop(string pSymbol, int pTrailPoints, int pMinProfit = 0, int pStep = 10);
```

The pSymbol parameter is the symbol of the position that we are trailing the stop for. pTrailPoints is the trailing stop in points. pMinProfit is the minimum profit in points, with a default value of 0. Finally, pStep is the step value in points. A default value of 10 points ensures that the trailing stop will only update on significant prices moves (a pip or more).

The code for the CTrailing::TrailingStop() function can be viewed in the TrailingStops.mqh file. If you've studied the previous section, it should look very familiar to you. Here's how we would use our CTrailing class in an expert advisor:

```
// #include and object initialization
#include <Mql5Book\TrailingStops.mqh>
CTrailing Trail;

// Input variables
input bool UseTrailingStop = false;
input int TrailingStop = 0;
input int MinimumProfit = 0;
input int Step = 0;
```

```
// OnTick() event handler
// Place after order placement code
if(UseTrailingStop == true && PositionType(_Symbol) != -1)
{
    Trail.TrailingStop(_Symbol,TrailingStop,MinimumProfit,Step);
}
```

We include our TrailingStops.mqh file and initialize the Trail object based on our CTrailing class. The input variables section contains the variables needed for our trailing stop feature. We have a bool variable named UseTrailingStop to turn the trailing stop on and off. TrailingStop sets the trailing stop in points. MinimumProfit is the minimum position profit in points, and Step moves the trailing stop in increments.

Our trailing stop code is placed near the end of the OnTick() event handler. If the UseTrailingStop input variable is true, and our PositionType() function returns a valid position type, the TrailingStop() function of our CTrailing class will be called, and the trailing stop for the current position will be modified if necessary.

Using a Dynamic Trailing Stop

The previous examples used a fixed trailing stop. What if you wanted to trail an indicator, such as a moving average or PSAR? Or perhaps you want to trail the high or low price of a previous bar?

We're going to create another function that will trail the stop loss based on a specified price. If the price is greater (or less) than the current stop loss, the stop loss will be trailed to that price. We will use the same function name as the TrailingStop() function that we defined in the previous section. The only difference will be the function parameters. This is known as *overloading* a function.

Here is the CTrailing class declaration containing both of our trailing stop functions. Notice the difference between the parameters of the two functions. The first TrailingStop() function, described in the previous section, has an int parameter named pTrailPoints. The second TrailingStop() function replaces that with a double parameter named pTrailPrice:

```
class CTrailing
{
    protected:
        MqlTradeRequest request;

    public:
        MqlTradeResult result;

        bool TrailingStop(string pSymbol, int pTrailPoints, int pMinProfit = 0,
            int pStep = 10);
```

```
        bool TrailingStop(string pSymbol, double pTrailPrice, int pMinProfit = 0,
            int pStep = 10);
};
```

The pTrailPrice parameter is the price that we will trail the stop to. If this price meets our minimum profit and step conditions, and it is closer to the current price than the current stop loss, then the stop will be moved to that price.

Here's an example using the *Parabolic Stop and Reverse* indicator. The PSAR is used to set a stop loss that progressively moves closer to the high or low of the current bar. When the PSAR value gets too close, or the trend reverses, the PSAR will reverse direction. If the PSAR price is below the current bar, then we will trail the stop for an open buy position. If the PSAR price is above the most current bar, then we will trail the stop for an open sell position:

```
// Input variables
input bool UseTrailingStop = false;
input int MinimumProfit = 0;
input int Step = 0;

input double SARStep = 0.2;
input double SARMaximum = 0.02;


// OnTick() event handler
double close[];
ArraySetAsSeries(close,true);
CopyClose(_Symbol,0,1,2,close);

// PSAR indicator
double sar[];
ArraySetAsSeries(sar,true);

int sarHandle = iSAR(_Symbol,0,SARStep,SARMaximum);
CopyBuffer(sarHandle,0,1,2,sar);

// Check SAR price vs. Close price
bool sarSignal = false;

if((PositionType(_Symbol) == POSITION_TYPE_BUY && sar[1] < close[1])
    || (PositionType(_Symbol) == POSITION_TYPE_SELL && sar[1] > close[1]))
{
    sarSignal = true;
}
```

```
// Trailing stop
if(UseTrailingStop == true && sarSignal == true)
{
    Trail.TrailingStop(_Symbol,sar[1],MinimumProfit,Step);
}
```

The input variables include the `UseTrailingStop`, `MinimumProfit` and `Step` settings for the trailing stop. (Note that we've omitted the `TrailingStop` variable, as the PSAR price will determine the trailing stop distance). The `SARStep` and `SARMaximum` input variables are the settings for the PSAR indicator. The remaining code belongs in the `OnTick()` event handler, or a function called from it.

The `close[]` array will hold the close price for each bar, while the `sar[]` array holds the PSAR indicator values. Before modifying the trailing stop, we need to check the PSAR price relative to the close price. If the PSAR is below the close price and the current position is a buy – or if the PSAR is above the close price and the current position is a sell – then the `sarSignal` variable is set to true.

If `UseTrailingStop` and `sarSignal` are both `true`, we pass the PSAR value of the most recently closed bar (`sar[1]`) to the `TrailingStop()` function, and the stop loss will be adjusted to the PSAR price if the `MinimumProfit` and `Step` conditions are met. The second parameter of the `TrailingStop()` function must be of type `double`. If the second parameter is an integer value, the compile will assume that we are passing a fixed trailing stop value, and will use the other `TrailingStop()` function instead.

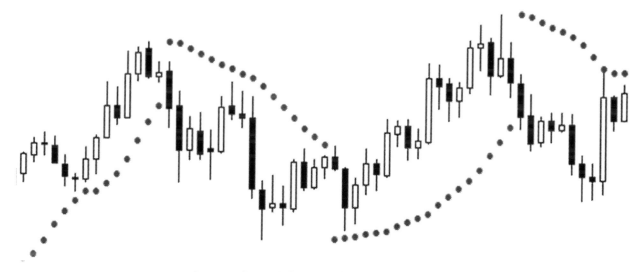

Fig 14.1 – The Parabolic Stop and Reverse (PSAR) indicator.

As long as the PSAR is positioned correctly relative to the current close price, and the minimum profit and/or step conditions are met, the stop loss will be updated to match the PSAR price. You can do this with other indicators as well. Just be sure to check that the indicator value is not above the price if you're trailing a buy position, or vice versa for a sell.

173

Break Even Stop

Sometimes a trader prefers to move the stop loss to the order opening price when a specified amount of profit is reached. The stop loss is moved only once – unlike a trailing stop, which keeps moving the stop as long as the trade increases in profit. This is referred to as a *break even stop*.

The principle behind a break even stop is similar to a trailing stop. First, check to see if the trade has reached a specified minimum profit. If so, check to see if the stop loss is less (or greater) than the position opening price. If so, the stop loss is moved to the order opening price. You can use a break even stop alongside a trailing stop. Just be sure to adjust the minimum profit setting for both stop types so that the trailing stop does not activate before the break even stop.

Here's an example of how to implement a break even stop in code:

```
// Input variables
input bool UseBreakEven = false;
input int BreakEven = 0;
input int LockProfit = 0;


// OnTick() event handler
MqlTradeRequest request;
MqlTradeResult result;
ZeroMemory(request);

// Break even stop
if(UseBreakEven == true && PositionSelect(_Symbol) == true && BreakEven > 0)
{
    request.action = TRADE_ACTION_SLTP;
    request.symbol = _Symbol;
    request.tp = 0;

    long posType = PositionGetInteger(POSITION_TYPE);
    double currentStop = PositionGetDouble(POSITION_SL);
    double openPrice = PositionGetDouble(POSITION_PRICE_OPEN);

    if(posType == POSITION_TYPE_BUY)
    {
        double currentPrice = SymbolInfoDouble(_Symbol,SYMBOL_BID);
        double breakEvenPrice = openPrice + (LockProfit * _Point);
        double currentProfit = currentPrice - openPrice;
```

```
        if(currentStop < breakEvenPrice && currentProfit >= BreakEven * _Point)
        {
            request.sl = breakEvenPrice;
            OrderSend(request,result);
        }
    }
    else if(posType == POSITION_TYPE_SELL)
    {
        double currentPrice = SymbolInfoDouble(_Symbol,SYMBOL_ASK);
        double breakEvenPrice = openPrice - (LockProfit * _Point);
        double currentProfit = openPrice - currentPrice;
        if(currentStop > breakEvenPrice && currentProfit >= BreakEven * _Point)
        {
            request.sl = breakEvenPrice;
            OrderSend(request,result);
        }
    }
}
```

The BreakEven input parameter is the number of pips of profit required for the stop to be moved to the break even price. The LockProfit parameter adds or subtracts the specified number of points to the break even price. So for example, if you want to move the stop loss to break even + 50 points, simply set LockProfit to 50.

The break even stop code goes near the end of the OnTick() event handler, after the order placement code. If the UseBreakEven input parameter is true, BreakEven is greater than zero, and there is a position currently open, we will check for a break even stop condition.

We retrieve the current position's type, stop loss and opening price, and store these values in the variables posType, currentStop and openPrice respectively. If the current position is a buy position, we retrieve the current Bid price and store the value in currentPrice. Then we calculate the break even price by adding LockProfit (multiplied by _Point) to the openPrice value, and storing the result in breakEvenPrice. Next, we calculate the current position profit by subtracting the position open price (openPrice) from the Bid (currentPrice), and storing the result in currentProfit.

Finally, we check for the break even condition. If the current stop loss (currentStop) is less than the break even price (breakEvenPrice), and the current position profit (currentProfit) is greater than BreakEven (multiplied by _Point), then we move the stop loss to the break even price.

The BreakEven() Function

We've added a BreakEven() function to our CTrailing class. Here is the function declaration:

```
bool BreakEven(string pSymbol, int pBreakEven, int pLockProfit = 0);
```

The pSymbol and pBreakEven parameters are required. The pLockProfit parameter is optional. Here's how we would use our BreakEven() function in an expert advisor:

```
#include <Mql5Book/TrailingStops.mqh>
CTrailing Trail;

// Input variables
input bool UseBreakEven = false;
input int BreakEven = 0;
input int LockProfit = 0;


// OnTick() event handler
if(UseBreakEven == true && PositionType(_Symbol) != -1)
{
    Trail.BreakEven(_Symbol,BreakEven,LockProfit);
}
```

The break even code goes near the end of the OnTick() event handler. All we need to do is check that UseBreakEven is set to true, and that a position is currently open. We use our PositionType() function to check for an open position. The BreakEven() function checks the rest.

You can view the code for the BreakEven() function in the \MQL5\Include\Mql5Book\TrailingStops.mqh file.

Chapter 15 - Money Management & Trade Sizing

Up to this point, we've been using an input variable named `TradeVolume` to specify order volume. Programming an expert advisor offers the opportunity to use automated money management techniques that can manage your risk and grow or shrink your trade size as your account balance changes. We'll examine techniques for automatically managing trade sizes, as well as verifying trade volumes for correctness.

Verifying Trade Volume

Before passing a trade volume to the `OrderSend()` function, we should check first to see if it is valid. Most Forex brokers allow trade sizes as small as 0.01 lots, but some brokers have a higher minimum trade size or do not use micro lots.

We verify the trade size by checking it against the minimum and maximum trade volumes allowed by the broker, as well as ensuring that it conforms to the broker's step value. Here's an example of how we would check the trade volume for correctness:

```
// Input variables
input double TradeVolume = 0.12;


// OnTick() event handler
double minVolume = SymbolInfoDouble(_Symbol,SYMBOL_VOLUME_MIN);
double maxVolume = SymbolInfoDouble(_Symbol,SYMBOL_VOLUME_MAX);
double stepVolume = SymbolInfoDouble(_Symbol,SYMBOL_VOLUME_STEP);

double tradeSize;
if(TradeVolume < minVolume) tradeSize = minVolume;
else if(TradeVolume > maxVolume) tradeSize = maxVolume;
else tradeSize = MathRound(TradeVolume / stepVolume) * stepVolume;

if(stepVolume >= 0.1) tradeSize = NormalizeDouble(tradeSize,1);
else tradeSize = NormalizeDouble(tradeSize,2);
```

The `TradeVolume` input variable holds our trade size. The code below it goes in the `OnTick()` event handler before any order is placed. It will usually be placed in a function, so it can be reused over and over again.

The `SymbolInfoDouble()` function retrieves information about the specified symbol from the trade server. In the example above, we use `SymbolInfoDouble()` to retrieve the minimum trade volume, the maximum trade volume, and the step size. For Forex brokers, the step size is generally 0.01 or 0.1. You can view the

SymbolInfo...() parameter constants in the *MQL5 Reference* under *Standard Constants... > Environment State > Symbol Properties*.

Next, we declare a variable named tradeSize, which will hold our verified trade volume. We check TradeVolume against the minimum volume. If TradeVolume is less than the minimum volume, we adjust it to the minimum volume size. We do the same for the maximum volume. Then we check TradeVolume against the step size.

We divide TradeVolume by the step size (stepVolume), round the result to the nearest integer using MathRound(), then multiply by the step size again. If the original trade volume conforms to the step size, this calculation will have no effect. Otherwise, the trade volume will be rounded to the nearest valid step size. In the example above, if stepVolume is 0.1 and TradeVolume is 0.12, the value of TradeVolume would be rounded to 0.1. Finally, we will normalize the trade volume to the number of digits in the step size.

Let's create a function that we can use to verify and automatically adjust the trade volume if necessary. We're going to create a new include file to hold all of the trade volume and money management related functions that we're going to create in this chapter. The include file is named MoneyManagement.mqh, and will be located in the \MQL5\Include\Mq15Book folder.

Here is our trade volume verification function, located in the MoneyManagement.mqh include file:

```
double VerifyVolume(string pSymbol,double pVolume)
{
    double minVolume = SymbolInfoDouble(pSymbol,SYMBOL_VOLUME_MIN);
    double maxVolume = SymbolInfoDouble(pSymbol,SYMBOL_VOLUME_MAX);
    double stepVolume = SymbolInfoDouble(pSymbol,SYMBOL_VOLUME_STEP);

    double tradeSize;
    if(pVolume < minVolume) tradeSize = minVolume;
    else if(pVolume > maxVolume) tradeSize = maxVolume;
    else tradeSize = MathRound(pVolume / stepVolume) * stepVolume;

    if(stepVolume >= 0.1) tradeSize = NormalizeDouble(tradeSize,1);
    else tradeSize = NormalizeDouble(tradeSize,2);

    return(tradeSize);
}
```

The pSymbol parameter is the trade symbol, and pVolume is the trade volume to verify. This function will return the adjusted trade volume to the program.

Money Management

Money management is a method of optimally adjusting position size according to risk. Most traders use the same fixed trade volume for every trade. This can result in trades that are too large or too small for the amount of money that is being risked.

To calculate an optimal trade size, we will use the distance of the stop loss price from the trade entry price as well as a percentage of the current balance to determine the maximum risk per trade. A good guideline is to limit your risk per trade to 2-3% of your current balance. If for some reason we cannot calculate a trade volume (*i.e.* a stop loss or percentage has not been specified), we will fall back to a specified fixed trade volume.

Let's create a function for our money management routine. The function will go in the MoneyManagement.mqh include file, and will be named MoneyManagement():

```
#define MAX_PERCENT 10

double MoneyManagement(string pSymbol, double pFixedVol, double pPercent, int pStopPoints)
{
    double tradeSize;

    if(pPercent > 0 && pStopPoints > 0)
    {
        if(pPercent > MAX_PERCENT) pPercent = MAX_PERCENT;

        double margin = AccountInfoDouble(ACCOUNT_BALANCE) * (pPercent / 100);
        double tickSize = SymbolInfoDouble(pSymbol,SYMBOL_TRADE_TICK_VALUE);

        tradeSize = (margin / pStopPoints) / tickSize;
        tradeSize = VerifyVolume(pSymbol,tradeSize);

        return(tradeSize);
    }
    else
    {
        tradeSize = pFixedVol;
        tradeSize = VerifyVolume(pSymbol,tradeSize);

        return(tradeSize);
    }
}
```

The pSymbol parameter is the trade symbol, pFixedVol is the default trade volume, pPercent is the percentage of the current balance to use, and pStopPoints is the stop loss distance in points.

The tradeSize variable will hold our calculated trade volume. First, we check to see if pPercent and pStopPoints are both greater than zero. If not, then we cannot calculate the trade volume, and will fall back on the default trade volume specified by pFixedVol.

If pPercent and pStopPoints are valid, then we will proceed with calculating the trade volume. First, we compare pPercent to the maximum volume. As mentioned before, it is recommended to limit your risk to no more than 2-3% of your balance. The MAX_PERCENT constant, defined at the top of our MoneyManagement.mqh file, specifies a maximum risk of 10 percent. If pPercent exceeds this, then it will be adjusted to no more than 10 percent.

Next, we calculate the amount of margin to risk. We retrieve the account balance using the AccountInfoDouble() function with the ACCOUNT_BALANCE parameter. We multiply this by pPercent (divided by 100 to obtain a fractional value), and store the result in the margin variable. Then we retrieve the tick size of the symbol from the trade server using the SymbolInfoDouble() function with the SYMBOL_TRADE_TICK_VALUE parameter, and store the result in the tickSize variable. The *tick size* is the amount of profit or loss represented by a single point move.

To calculate our trade volume, we divide the margin to risk (margin) by the stop loss in points (pStopLoss), and divide that result by tickSize. Then we pass our calculated trade volume to the VerifyVolume() function. The verified result is returned to the program.

Let's clarify this with an example: We want to place an order risking no more than 2% of our account balance of $5000. The initial stop loss will be placed 500 points away from the order opening price. The symbol is EURUSD and we're using mini lots, so the tick size will be $1 per point. 2% of $5000 is $100, so this value will be saved in the margin variable. The value of the tickSize variable will be $1.

$100 divided by 500 points is 0.2. Every point of movement will equal approximately $0.20 of profit or loss. 0.2 divided by $1 equals 0.2, so our trade volume will be 0.2 lots. If this trade of 0.2 lots hits its initial stop loss 500 points away, the loss will be approximately $100. If the stop loss distance is 200 points away, the trade volume will be 0.5 lots, but the maximum loss is still $100.

Here's an example of how we can use our money management function in an expert advisor:

```
// Include directive
#include <Mq15Book/MoneyManagement.mqh>

// Input variables
input double RiskPercent = 2;
input double FixedVolume = 0.1;
input int StopLoss = 500;
```

```
// OnTick() event handler
double tradeSize = MoneyManagement(_Symbol,FixedVolume,RiskPercent,StopLoss);
```

To use our money management function, we need to include the MoneyManagement.mqh file in our expert advisor. The RiskPercent input variable is our trade risk as a percentage of the current trade balance. If you do not want to use money management, set this to zero. FixedVolume is the fixed trade volume to use if RiskPercent or StopLoss is zero.

The tradeSize variable will hold our calculated trade volume. The MoneyManagement() function will take the specified input variables and return the calculated and verified trade volume. We can then pass the tradeSize variable to one of our order placement functions as defined in the previous chapters.

The examples above assume a fixed stop loss that is specified by an input variable. What if you want to use a dynamic stop loss price, such as an indicator value or a support/resistance price? We will need to calculate the distance between the desired order opening price (either a pending order price, or the current Bid or Ask price) and the desired stop loss price.

For example, we want to open a buy position. The current Ask price is 1.39426, and the stop loss price we want to use is 1.38600. The difference between the two is 826 points. We'll create a function that will determine the difference in points between the desired opening price and the stop loss price:

```
double StopPriceToPoints(string pSymbol, double pStopPrice, double pOrderPrice)
{
    double stopDiff = MathAbs(pStopPrice - pOrderPrice);
    double getPoint = SymbolInfoDouble(pSymbol,SYMBOL_POINT);
    double priceToPoint = stopDiff / getPoint;
    return(priceToPoint);
}
```

The pStopPrice parameter is our desired stop loss price, and pOrderPrice is our desired order opening price. First, the function calculates the difference between pStopPrice and pOrderPrice, and returns the absolute value using the MathAbs() function. We store the result in the stopDiff variable. Next we retrieve the symbol's point value and store it in the variable getPoint. Finally, we divide stopDiff by getPoint to find the stop loss distance in points.

Here's an example of how we can do this in code. We'll assume that the stopLossPrice variable is equal to 1.38600, and that the current Ask price is 1.39426:

```
double stopLossPrice = 1.38600;
double currentPrice = SymbolInfoDouble(_Symbol,SYMBOL_ASK);
double stopLossDistance = StopPriceToPoints(_Symbol,stopLossPrice,currentPrice)
double tradeSize = MoneyManagement(_Symbol,FixedVolume,RiskPercent,stopLossDistance);
```

The `stopLossPrice` variable contains our desired stop loss price of 1.38600, while the `currentPrice` variable holds the current Ask price of 1.39426. The `stopLossDistance` variable will hold the return value of the `StopPriceToPoints()` function, which is 826. We then pass `stopLossDistance` as the last parameter of the `MoneyManagement()` function. Assuming a `RiskPercent` value of 2% and a balance of $5000 using standard lots, the trade volume will be 0.08 lots.

As long as you have specified an initial stop loss, the `MoneyManagement()` function can be used to limit your trade risk to a specified percentage of your account balance. You can even use a dynamic stop loss by using the `StopPriceToPoints()` function to calculate the stop loss in points. As your account balance grows or shrinks, the trade size will increase or decrease accordingly.

Chapter 16 - Bar and Price Data

In MQL4, we use predefined arrays such as `Close[]` and `Time[]` for bar data, and the predefined variables `Bid` and `Ask` to access the current prices. MQL5 lacks these predefined arrays and variables, but we can create easy methods for accessing this data. We'll examine the various ways to access bar and price data in MQL5, and create classes and functions to make working with prices easy.

Accessing Current Prices

Earlier in this book, we used the `SymbolInfoDouble()` function to retrieve the current Bid and Ask prices. The `SymbolInfo...()` functions require you to specify the symbol to retrieve the information for, as well as a value from one of the `ENUM_SYMBOL_INFO_...` enumerations. Here is how to retrieve the current Bid and Ask price using `SymbolInfoDouble()`:

```
double ask = SymbolInfoDouble(_Symbol,SYMBOL_ASK);
double bid = SymbolInfoDouble(_Symbol,SYMBOL_BID);
```

The `ask` and `bid` variables hold the current Bid and Ask prices for the current chart symbol.

But remembering which `SymbolInfo...()` function to use, along with the correct `ENUM_SYMBOL_INFO_...` identifier can be troublesome. We'll create two quick functions to retrieve the current Bid and Ask prices:

```
double Ask(string pSymbol=NULL)
{
    if(pSymbol == NULL) pSymbol = _Symbol;
    return(SymbolInfoDouble(pSymbol,SYMBOL_ASK));
}

double Bid(string pSymbol=NULL)
{
    if(pSymbol == NULL) pSymbol = _Symbol;
    return(SymbolInfoDouble(pSymbol,SYMBOL_BID));
}
```

Both function contain one parameter, pSymbol, with a default value of NULL. The constant NULL refers to an empty string. If no symbol is specified for the pSymbol parameter, the function will use the current chart symbol (_Symbol). The specified symbol is passed to the `SymbolInfoDouble()` function, and the result is returned to the program.

Let's rewrite our previous code example with our new functions:

```
double ask = Ask();
double bid = Bid();
```

Both functions return the current Bid or Ask price for the current chart symbol.

The MqlTick Structure

Another method of retrieving the current prices is to use the SymbolInfoTick() function and an object of the MqlTick structure type. MqlTick is a structure containing variables to hold the current bid, ask, time, volume and last deal prices:

```
struct MqlTick
{
    datetime    time;         // Time of the last prices update
    double      bid;          // Current Bid price
    double      ask;          // Current Ask price
    double      last;         // Price of the last deal (Last)
    ulong       volume;       // Volume for the current Last price
};
```

The information above is from the *MQL5 Reference*. To use the MqlTick structure to retrieve the current prices, first create an object using MqlTick as the type. Then, pass the object to the SymbolInfoTick() function. Here is the function definition for SymbolInfoTick() from the *MQL5 Reference*:

```
bool SymbolInfoTick(string symbol, MqlTick& tick);
```

The tick parameter is an MqlTick object passed by reference. The member variables of the object are filled with the most recent price data. Here's an example of how we can use SymbolInfoTick() and MqlTick to retrieve the current prices:

```
MqlTick price;
SymbolInfoTick(_Symbol,price);

double ask = price.ask;
double bid = price.bid;
datetime time = price.time;
```

We declare an object named price, using MqlTick as the type. We pass the price object to the SymbolInfoTick() function, specifying the current chart symbol for the first parameter. The function returns the price object with the member variables filled with the current price and time information. The examples below that show the current Ask and Bid prices, as well as the most recent server time, being retrieved using the member variables of the `price` object.

It's up to you whether you want to use `SymbolInfoTick()` to retrieve the current price information. The `Bid()` and `Ask()` functions that we defined earlier in the chapter are a lot easier though.

Bar Data

As mentioned at the beginning of the chapter, MQL4 has predefined arrays that hold the open, close, high, low, time and volume data for each bar on the chart. In MQL5, we will have to create and fill those arrays ourselves. There are several Copy...() functions we can use to retrieve bar data. Let's begin with `CopyRates()`.

CopyRates() and the MqlRates Structure

`MqlRates` is a structure that contains variables that hold price, time, volume and spread information for each bar. It is used as an array type. Here is the structure definition for `MqlRates` from the *MQL5 Reference:*

```
struct MqlRates
{
    datetime time;          // Period start time
    double   open;          // Open price
    double   high;          // The highest price of the period
    double   low;           // The lowest price of the period
    double   close;         // Close price
    long     tick_volume;   // Tick volume
    int      spread;        // Spread
    long     real_volume;   // Trade volume
};
```

To use the `MqlRates` structure, we declare an array object of type `MqlRates` and pass the object to the `CopyRates()` function to fill the array with data. There are several variants of the `CopyRates()` function, but we will only concern ourselves with the first one, which requires us to specify a start position and the number of bars of data to copy:

```
int CopyRates(
    string           symbol_name,    // symbol name
    ENUM_TIMEFRAMES  timeframe,      // period
    int              start_pos,      // start position
    int              count,          // data count to copy
    MqlRates         rates_array[]   // target array to copy
    );
```

185

The `symbol_name` parameter is the chart symbol to use, `timeframe` is the chart period to use, `start_pos` is the index of the starting bar (0 is the most recent bar), `count` is the number of bars to copy into the array, and `rates_array[]` is our MqlRates object.

Let's demonstrate how to use MqlRates and CopyRates() to copy bar data into an array object. We will typically only need data for the most recent bars – three is a good number.

```
MqlRates bar[];
ArraySetAsSeries(bar,true);
CopyRates(_Symbol,_Period,0,3,bar);

double open = bar[1].open;
double close = bar[1].close;
```

First we declare the array object bar[], using MqlRates as the type. Next, we use the ArraySetAsSeries() function to index the bar[] array for a price series. For a series array, the most recent element is indexed at 0. As we increase the array index, we move back in time. A non-series array would be the opposite of this. It is important to always use the ArraySetAsSeries() function to set an array as series before you copy price or indicator data to it.

Next, we call the CopyRates() function. We use the current chart symbol (_Symbol) and period (_Period). We start copying at index 0, or the most recent bar. We will copy 3 bars worth of data. The last parameter is the name of our bar[] array, which will hold our bar data.

To access the bar data, we reference the bar[] array with the appropriate index inside the brackets. We then use the dot (.) operator to access the member variables of the array object. For example, to retrieve the close price of the last bar, we use bar[1].close.

We can simplify this a bit by creating a class that will retrieve the bar data for us. We will name the class CBars. This class, and the other functions that we'll create in this chapter, will go in a new include file named Price.mqh, located in the \MQL5\Include\Mql5Book\ folder. Here is the class declaration for CBars:

```
class CBars
{
    public:
        MqlRates bar[];
        CBars(void);
        void Update(string pSymbol, ENUM_TIMEFRAMES pPeriod);
};
```

All of the members of the CBars class will be public. The bar[] array will hold our price data. The CBars(void) function is our class constructor, a function that runs automatically every time an object is created. Here is the constructor for the CBars class:

```
CBars::CBars(void)
{
    ArraySetAsSeries(bar,true);
}
```

The CBars class constructor sets the bar[] array as a series array. This is done automatically anytime we create an object based on the class. The Update() function calls the CopyRates() function and fills the bar[] array with data. Here is the function declaration for CBars::Update():

```
#define MAX_BARS 100

void CBars::Update(string pSymbol,ENUM_TIMEFRAMES pPeriod)
{
    CopyRates(pSymbol,pPeriod,0,MAX_BARS,bar);
}
```

At least once in the OnTick() event handler of our program, we will call the Update() function to fill the bar[] array with the most recent data. The MAX_BARS constant defines the number of bars worth of data to copy whenever we call the Update() function. We've set it to 100 bars.

Now we'll need to add a few user-friendly functions to retrieve the prices. Here is a function that will retrieve the close price for the indicated bar:

```
double CBars::Close(int pShift=0)
{
    return(bar[pShift].close);
}
```

The function simply retrieves the value of bar[].close for the specified index value. The default value for the pShift parameter is 0, so if no parameter is passed to the function, it will retrieve the price for the current bar.

We have several more functions to retrieve the high, low, open, time and volume information. Here is the complete CBars function declaration with all of the necessary functions:

```
class CBars
{
    public:
        MqlRates bar[];
        CBars(void);
        void Update(string pSymbol, ENUM_TIMEFRAMES pPeriod);
        double Close(int pShift);
        double High(int pShift);
        double Low(int pShift);
        double Open(int pShift);
        datetime Time(int pShift);
        long TickVolume(int pShift);
        long Volume(int pShift);
};
```

Note that our function names correspond to each of the variables in the MqlRates structure. Let's demonstrate how we can use the CBars class in an expert advisor. First we'll need to create an object based on the CBars class. Then the Update() function will need to be called before we can access the price data. Finally, we use either the price retrieval functions or the bar[] array to retrieve the prices:

```
// Include directives
#include <Mql5Book/Price.mqh>
CBars Price;


// OnTick() event handler
Price.Update(_Symbol,_Period);

double close = Price.Close();
double alsoClose = Price.bar[0].close;        // Same value as close variable
```

We include the Price.mqh file and create an object named Price, based on our CBars class. In the OnTick() event handler, before we access any price data, we call the Price.Update() function to retrieve the bar data for the current chart symbol and period.

Next, we illustrate two ways of accessing the price data. The easiest way is to use the price retrieval functions that we defined in the CBars class. The close variable contains the current bar's close price, and is retrieved using the Price.Close() function. The alsoClose variable also contains the current bar's close price, and is retrieved using the bar[] array with the close member variable.

The file \MQL5\Experts\Mql5Book\Simple Expert Advisor with Functions.mq5 has been updated to use the CBars function to access the close price.

Other Copy...() Functions

If you just need to copy a single data series into an array, you can use one of the following functions instead:

- **double CopyClose()** - Copies the close prices only.

- **double CopyOpen()** - Copies the open prices only.

- **double CopyHigh()** - Copies the high prices only.

- **double CopyLow()** - Copies the low prices only.

- **datetime CopyTime()** - Copies the timestamp of each bar.

- **long CopyTickVolume()** - Copies the tick volume of each bar.

- **long CopyRealVolume()** - Copies the trade volume of each bar.

- **int CopySpread()** - Copies the spread values of each bar.

These work similar to the CopyRates() function. First, declare an array of the appropriate type. The type required for each function is listed above before the function name. Next, set it as a series array using ArraySetAsSeries(). Then use the appropriate Copy..() function to copy data into the array.

We'll demonstrate using the CopyClose() function. Here is the function definition for CopyClose():

```
int CopyClose(
    string          symbol_name,      // symbol name
    ENUM_TIMEFRAMES timeframe,        // period
    int             start_pos,        // start position
    int             count,            // data count to copy
    double          close_array[]     // target array to copy
    );
```

The parameters are nearly identical to CopyRates(). There are several variants of the function that allow you to specify start and end dates as well. You can view these in the *MQL5 Reference* under *Timeseries and Indicator Access*. Here's an example of the usage of the CopyClose() function:

```
double close[];
ArraySetAsSeries(close,true);

CopyClose(_Symbol,_Period,0,3,close);

double currentClose = close[0];
```

We declare an array of type `double` named `close[]` that will hold our close prices. Next, we set it as a series array using `ArraySetAsSeries()`. Finally, the `CopyClose()` function copies three bars worth of data into the `close[]` array. To retrieve the current bar's value, we reference the zero index of the `close[]` array.

The other `Copy...()` functions work the same, except that the array type will differ. Refer to the *MQL5 Reference* for details. If you only need a single price series, then these functions may work better for you. We will be using the `CBars` class that we created in the previous section for the remainder of this book.

Highest and Lowest Prices

Sometimes you may need to determine the highest or lowest value of a price series. For example, you may want to place a stop loss for a buy order at the lowest low of the last *X* bars. In MQL4, the functions `iHighest()` and `iLowest()` performed these duties for us. In MQL5, we'll need to do a bit more work.

Assuming that you have your price data already copied into an array, the `ArrayMaximum()` and `ArrayMinimum()` functions can be used to find the highest or lowest value of a price series. Here's how we can find the lowest low of the last 10 bars:

```
double low[];
ArraySetAsSeries(low,true);

CopyLow(_Symbol,_Period,0,100,low);

int minIdx = ArrayMinimum(low,0,10);
double lowest = low[minIdx];
```

First we declare the `low[]` array that will hold our price data. We set the array as series, and use the `CopyLow()` functions to copy 100 bars of low price data for the current chart symbol and period into our `low[]` array.

The `ArrayMinimum()` function takes as its first parameter the array to search. The second parameter is the starting position, and the third is the number of bars to search. Starting at the current bar, we look back 10 bars to find the lowest low. The `ArrayMinimum()` function returns the index value of the bar with the lowest low. We save this value in the `minIdx` variable. A call to `low[minIdx]` will return the lowest low price located by the `ArrayMinimum()` function.

You can use `ArrayMinimum()` or `ArrayMaximum()` on any one-dimensional numeric array. Most commonly, we will be searching for the highest high and lowest low of the last *X* bars. We can create some simple functions that will return the highest high or lowest low of a specified bar range:

```
double HighestHigh(string pSymbol, ENUM_TIMEFRAMES pPeriod, int pBars, int pStart = 0)
{
    double high[];
    ArraySetAsSeries(high,true);

    int copied = CopyHigh(pSymbol,pPeriod,pStart,pBars,high);
    if(copied == -1) return(copied);

    int maxIdx = ArrayMaximum(high);
    double highest = high[maxIdx];

    return(highest);
}
```

This function returns the highest high price for the specified bar range. The `pSymbol` parameter is the symbol to use, and `pPeriod` is the chart period to use. The `pBars` parameter is the number of bars to search, and `pStart` is the start location. The default value of `pStart` is 0, which is the current bar.

We declare the `high[]` array and set it as series, and then use the `CopyHigh()` function to copy the high prices into our array. The `pStart` parameter determines where we start copying the data from, while the `pBars` parameter determines the amount of data in our array. Note the line after the `CopyHigh()` function – if the copying fails for some reason, we return a -1 to the calling program to indicate an error.

When we call the `ArrayMaximum()` function, we only need to specify the array name, since it already contains all of the data that we need to search. The index of the array that contains the highest high is saved to the `maxIdx` variable. We then use `high[maxIdx]` to retrieve the highest high and return that to the calling program.

There is also a `LowestLow()` function that operates identically to the `HighestHigh()` function above. Both functions can be viewed in the `\MQL5\Include\Mql5Book\Price.mqh` include file.

Price-Based Trading Signals

You will frequently use the close, high or low price of a bar as part of an order opening condition, or to calculate a stop loss, take profit or pending order price. Typically, we work with the prices of the two most recent bars.

For example, if you have a trading system where you need to check the close price against an indicator line, you will retrieve the price of the most recently closed bar and compare it to the indicator value of the same bar. Our simple expert advisor that we created earlier in the book compared the close price of the current bar to the current moving average value:

```
if(close[0] > ma[0] && glBuyPlaced == false
    && (positionType != POSITION_TYPE_BUY || openPosition == false))
{
    // Open buy position
}
```

But perhaps you want to wait until the bar closes before opening the order. In that case, we will need to check the moving average and close values of the previous bar. The array index of the current bar is 0, so the index of the previous bar would be 1:

```
if(close[1] > ma[1] && glBuyPlaced == false
    && (positionType != POSITION_TYPE_BUY || openPosition == false))
{
    // Open buy position
}
```

We could define our order opening condition even more explicitly by making sure that the close price crossed the moving average within the last bar. One way of doing this is to check if the previous bar's close price was below the moving average value:

```
if(close[1] > ma[1] && close[2] <= ma[2]
    && (positionType != POSITION_TYPE_BUY || openPosition == false))
{
    // Open buy position
}
```

Because a buy position will only open if the close price is greater than the moving average for the most current bar, and the close price was less than the moving average for the previous bar, we no longer need to check the value of the glBuyPlaced variable. This works best if you have a trading condition that always indicates either a bullish or bearish trading signal at all times.

Candle Patterns

Another use of price data is to detect candle patterns. Many traders use Japanese candlestick patterns such as the doji, engulfing, harami, hammers/shooting stars, and so forth. We use price data to identify these patterns on a chart.

Let's take the engulfing pattern, for example. An engulfing pattern is a reversal pattern where the body of a candle is longer than the body of the previous candle, and the direction is reversed. For example, you may see an engulfing candle at the bottom of a downtrend. The previous candle will be bearish, while the most recent candle will be

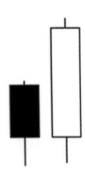

Fig 16.1 – Bullish Engulfing candle.

bullish. The open of the most recent candle will be roughly equal to the close of the previous candle, and the close of the most recent candle will be above the previous candle's open.

When trading a candle pattern, we will look for a confirmation candle in the direction of the anticipated trend. In the case of our engulfing bullish reversal pattern, we are looking for a bullish candle following our bullish engulfing candle.

Let's express this as a trading condition. Assuming that we have two arrays, close[] and open[], filled with price data, here's how we would locate a bullish engulfing pattern in an expert advisor:

```
if(close[3] < open[3] && close[2] > open[3] && close[1] > open[1])
{
    Print("Bullish engulfing reversal pattern detected");
}
```

We start three candles back with the bearish candle. The condition close[3] < open[3] means that the candle is bearish – in other words, the close was lower than the open. Next, we check the engulfing candle. The open price of a candle is usually identical (or very close) to the close price of the previous candle, so we won't bother checking the open of the engulfing candle. The important thing to check is whether the close is greater than the previous bar's open, or close[2] > open[3]. If so, then we have an engulfing candle.

Finally, if close[1] > open[1], then the most recent candle is bullish. If all three candles match the condition, then a message prints to the log indicating that a bullish engulfing pattern was detected on the chart. Of course, you could open a buy position as well.

By comparing the open and close values of a bar, you can determine whether a candle is bullish or bearish. You can also detect candle patterns by examining the open, high, low and close values of consecutive candles.

Chapter 17 - Using Indicators in Expert Advisors

Nearly every expert advisor uses indicators to generate trading signals. In this chapter, we will examine how to use MetaTrader's built-in indicators in your expert advisors, as well as custom indicators that you can find online or in MetaTrader 5's \MQL5\Indicators\Examples folder. We will create classes to simplify the use of indicators, and examine some common indicator-based trading signals.

Single Buffer Indicators

Earlier in the book, we used a moving average indicator in our simple expert advisor. Here is the code to add the moving average indicator to an expert advisor:

```
// Input variables
input int MAPeriod = 10;
input int MAShift = 0;
input ENUM_MA_METHOD MAMethod = MODE_EMA;
input ENUM_APPLIED_PRICE MAPrice = PRICE_CLOSE;


// OnTick() event handler
double ma[];
ArraySetAsSeries(ma,true);

int maHandle = iMA(_Symbol,_Period,MAPeriod,MAShift,MAMethod,MAPrice);
CopyBuffer(maHandle,0,0,3,ma);

double currentMA = ma[0];
```

The input variables include four settings to adjust the moving average parameters: MAPeriod adjusts the period of the indicator. MAShift shifts the indicator forward or backward on the chart. MAMethod changes the calculation method of the indicator (simple, exponential, etc.), and MAPrice selects the price series used to calculate the moving average (close, open, etc.).

Fig 17.1 – A 30 period exponential moving average on a daily chart.

195

In the OnTick() event handler, we initialize the ma[] array, which will hold our moving average data. The ArraySetAsSeries() function sets the ma[] array as a series array. The iMA() function takes the input variables and calculates the indicator for the specified symbol and chart period. Every built-in MetaTrader indicator has a similar function. You can view them in the *MQL5 Reference* under *Technical Indicators*.

Here is the function definition for the iMA() indicator:

```
int iMA(
    string              symbol,         // symbol name
    ENUM_TIMEFRAMES     period,         // period
    int                 ma_period,      // averaging period
    int                 ma_shift,       // horizontal shift
    ENUM_MA_METHOD      ma_method,      // smoothing type
    ENUM_APPLIED_PRICE  applied_price   // type of price or handle
    );
```

Every technical indicator function begins with the symbol and period parameters. The remaining parameters depend on the indicator. The moving average indicator has four parameters that can be adjusted. Some indicators have just one or two parameters, and a few have none at all. Here are the input variables for the moving average indicator again:

```
// Input variables
input int MAPeriod = 10;
input int MAShift = 0;
input ENUM_MA_METHOD MAMethod = MODE_EMA;
input ENUM_APPLIED_PRICE MAPrice = PRICE_CLOSE;
```

Note the type of each parameter. For example, the ma_method parameter of the iMA() function uses the ENUM_MA_METHOD type. Therefore, the corresponding input parameter must be of the same type. In this case, the MAMethod input variable uses the ENUM_MA_METHOD type, so this is the value that we will pass to the ma_method parameter.

By looking at the function declaration for the specific technical indicator function you need to use, you can determine the input parameters you'll need to add to your expert advisor. Note that the four input variables for the moving average indicator match the parameters for the iMA() function.

The iMA() function, as well as all other indicator functions, returns an indicator *handle*, which is a unique identifier for the indicator. This handle is used for all actions related to the indicator, including copying data and removing the indicator from use.

The `CopyBuffer()` function is used to copy the data from the specified indicator buffer into an array. The array can then be used to access the indicator data. `CopyBuffer()` works similar to the `Copy...()` functions in the previous chapter. Here is the function definition for the `CopyBuffer()` function:

```
int CopyBuffer(
    int         indicator_handle,    // indicator handle
    int         buffer_num,          // indicator buffer number
    int         start_pos,           // start position
    int         count,               // amount of bars to copy
    double      buffer               // target array to copy to
    );
```

The `indicator_handle` parameter accepts the indicator handle that is returned by the `iMA()` or other indicator function. The `buffer_num` parameter is the number of the indicator buffer that you want to copy data from. Most indicators have only one buffer, although some have two, three or more. More on this in a minute. The remaining parameters should be familiar to you. The `start_pos` parameter is the start position to begin copying from, `count` is the number of bars to copy, and `buffer` is the name of the array to copy to.

Let's revisit our moving average indicator example:

```
int maHandle = iMA(_Symbol,_Period,MAPeriod,MAShift,MAMethod,MAPrice);
CopyBuffer(maHandle,0,0,3,ma);

double currentMA = ma[0];
```

The `iMA()` function returns an indicator handle, and saves it to the `maHandle` variable. The `CopyBuffer()` function takes the `maHandle` value as its first parameter. The buffer number is zero, since the moving average has only one line. We start at the most recent bar (index of 0) and copy 3 bars worth of data to the `ma[]` array. The `ma[]` array is now filled with data and ready to use. A call to `ma[0]` will return the moving average value for the current bar.

Let's take a look at a second indicator that only uses a single buffer. The RSI indicator is very popular, and is often used to locate price extremes. Here is the function definition for the RSI indicator:

```
int iRSI(
    string              symbol,         // symbol name
    ENUM_TIMEFRAMES     period,         // period
    int                 ma_period,      // averaging period
    ENUM_APPLIED_PRICE  applied_price   // type of price or handle
    );
```

Just like the iMA() function, the first two parameters are symbol and period. The RSI takes two input parameters, one for the averaging period (ma_period) and another for the price series (applied_price). By the way, any indicator function that has the applied_price parameter can be passed an indicator handle instead, meaning that you can use a price series derived from another indicator.

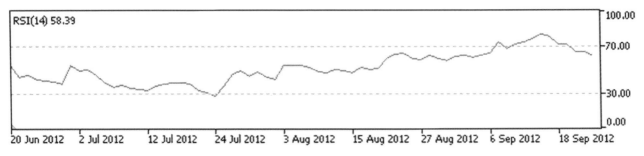

Fig 17.2 – The RSI indicator.

Here's how we would add the RSI indicator to an expert advisor:

```
// Input parameters
input int RSIPeriod = 10;
input ENUM_APPLIED_PRICE RSIPrice = PRICE_CLOSE;


// OnTick() event handler
double rsi[];
ArraySetAsSeries(rsi,true);

int handle = iRSI(_Symbol,_Period,RSIPeriod,RSIPrice);
CopyBuffer(handle,0,0,3,rsi);

double rsi = rsi[0];
double lastRsi = rsi[1];
```

We declare the input variables RSIPeriod and RSIPrice with the appropriate types at the beginning of our program. Inside the OnTick() event handler, we declare the rsi[] array and set it as a series array. We pass our input parameters to the iRSI() function and save the indicator handle to the handle variable. Finally, we pass the handle variable to the CopyBuffer() function and three bars worth of data is copied to the rsi[] array.

The rsi and lastRsi variables are assigned the RSI values for the current bar and the previous bar. You could compare these variables to determine whether the RSI is rising or falling, for example.

Multi-Buffer Indicators

When using indicators with multiple lines (and multiple buffers), we'll need to use several arrays and CopyBuffer() functions to get all of the data into our program. Let's start with the stochastic indicator. The stochastic is an oscillator similar to the RSI. Along with the main stochastic line, a second signal line is also present.

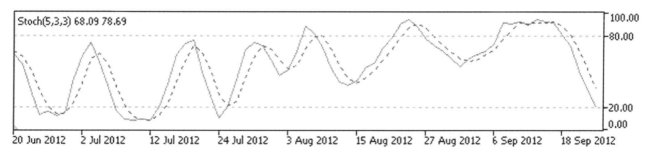

Fig. 17.3 – The stochastic indicator. The red dashed line is the signal line.

Here is how we would add the stochastic indicator to an expert advisor:

```
// Input parameters
input int KPeriod = 10;
input int DPeriod = 3;
input int Slowing = 3;
input ENUM_MA_METHOD StochMethod = MODE_SMA;
input ENUM_STO_PRICE StochPrice = STO_LOWHIGH;


// OnTick() event handler
double main[], signal[];
ArraySetAsSeries(main,true);
ArraySetAsSeries(signal,true);

int handle = iStochastic(_Symbol,_Period,KPeriod,DPeriod,Slowing,StochMethod,StochPrice);
CopyBuffer(handle,0,0,3,main);
CopyBuffer(handle,1,0,3,signal);

double currentStoch = main[0];
double currentSignal = signal[0];
```

The stochastic indicator has five input parameters and two buffers. We declare the arrays main[] and signal[] to hold the stochastic indicator data. Both arrays are set as series arrays using the ArraySetAsSeries() function. The iStochastic() function initializes the indicator and returns the indicator handle to the handle variable. Here is the function definition for iStochastic():

```
int iStochastic(
    string              symbol,          // symbol name
    ENUM_TIMEFRAMES     period,          // period
    int                 Kperiod,         // K-period
    int                 Dperiod,         // D-period
    int                 slowing,         // final smoothing
    ENUM_MA_METHOD      ma_method,       // type of smoothing
    ENUM_STO_PRICE      price_field      // stochastic calculation method
    );
```

Compare the input variables above to the parameters for the iStochastic() function, and note the types for the ma_method and price_field parameters. The ENUM_STO_PRICE enumeration is used to set the calculation method for the stochastic indicator (either *low/high* or *close/close*).

If you look at the iStochastic() entry in the *MQL5 Reference*, you'll see this note in the description:

> **Note**
> The buffer numbers: 0 - MAIN_LINE, 1 – SIGNAL_LINE.

These are the buffer numbers for the two stochastic indicator lines. We pass the buffer number to the buffer_num parameter of the CopyBuffer() function. The CopyBuffer() function will copy the data from that indicator buffer into the specified array. We'll need to do this for each buffer in the indicator:

```
CopyBuffer(handle,0,0,3,main);
CopyBuffer(handle,1,0,3,signal);
```

The buffer numbers are highlighted in bold. The contents of buffer 0 (MAIN_LINE) are copied into the main[] array, and the contents of buffer 1 (SIGNAL_LINE) are copied into the signal[] array. The main[] array holds the values for the main stochastic line (also called the *%K line*), while the signal[] array holds the values for the signal line (also called the *%D line*).

The procedure for adding any multi-buffer indicator is the same. Note the buffer numbers in the *MQL5 Reference* entry for the relevant indicator function. Then declare the appropriate number of arrays, set them as series, initialize the indicator and copy each of the buffers to the corresponding array.

The CIndicator Class

We're going to create a class to simplify the process of adding indicators to a program. We'll start by creating a base class that contains all of the variables and functions shared by every indicator. Then we will create new classes derived from this base class that address the specific needs of each indicator.

All of the built-in indicators that we addressed in the previous section have a few things in common. Every indicator uses at least one array to hold the buffer data. That array needs to be set as a series array. We need a variable to hold the indicator handle. And we need a way to copy the buffer data and access the array. Finally, we need to be able to remove the indicator from our program if necessary.

Our indicator base class will accomplish all of these tasks. We're going to name our base class CIndicator. It will be placed in the \MQL5\Include\Mq15Book\Indicators.mqh include file. This file will be used to hold all of our indicator related classes and functions.

Here is the class declaration for the CIndicator class:

```
class CIndicator
{
    protected:
        int handle;
        double main[];

    public:
        CIndicator(void);
        double Main(int pShift=0);
        void Release();
        virtual int Init() { return(handle); }
};
```

The CIndicator class has two protected variables and four public functions. The protected keyword means that the variable contents are only accessible inside the CIndicator class and in derived classes. The handle variable will contain the indicator handle, and the main[] array will hold the buffer data.

There are four public functions. The CIndicator() function is the class constructor. When an object based on this class is created, the constructor is run automatically. Let's take a look at the CIndicator class constructor:

```
CIndicator::CIndicator(void)
{
    ArraySetAsSeries(main,true);
}
```

The class constructor simply sets the main[] array as a series using the ArraySetAsSeries() function. Every time we create an object based on the CIndicator class, the main[] array is declared and set as a series array.

Next is the `Main()` function:

```
double CIndicator::Main(int pShift=0)
{
    CopyBuffer(handle,0,0,MAX_COUNT,main);
    double value = NormalizeDouble(main[pShift],_Digits);
    return(value);
}
```

Assuming that we already have a valid indicator handle, the `Main()` function copies the buffer data to the `main[]` array, and accesses the data for the bar specified by the `pShift` parameter. Before returning the value, we use the `NormalizeDouble()` function to round the value to the number of significant digits in the symbol price. We'll write a function that will create the indicator handle when we start creating derived classes.

Next, we have the `Release()` function. This function simply releases the indicator from memory if we no longer need it:

```
void CIndicator::Release(void)
{
    IndicatorRelease(handle);
}
```

And finally, the `Init()` function is a virtual function whose functionality will be defined in our derived classes. By declaring the function as `virtual`, we are telling the compiler that the programmer must define the `Init()` function in any derived classes. We'll discuss virtual functions later in the chapter:

```
virtual int Init()
{
    return(handle);
}
```

Derived Classes

The `CIndicator` class will be the basis for derived classes that will be used to initialize and retrieve data from MetaTrader's built-in indicators. Since the implementation of each indicator will be different, we will need to create a separate class for every indicator that we want to use.

Let's start with the moving average indicator. The moving average has just one buffer, so we can create a derived class with a minimum of effort. Here is the class declaration for the `CiMA` class:

```
class CiMA : public CIndicator
{
    public:
        int Init(string pSymbol, ENUM_TIMEFRAMES pTimeframe, int pMAPeriod,
            int pMAShift, ENUM_MA_METHOD pMAMethod, ENUM_APPLIED_PRICE pMAPrice);
};
```

The CiMA class has one public function, Init(), which is used to initialize the indicator. Note the : public CIndicator after the class name. This indicates that the CiMA class is derived from CIndicator. The CiMA class inherits all of the public and protected functions and variables from the CIndicator class.

Remember that the Init() function is declared as a virtual function in CIndicator. This means that any derived classes of CIndicator must implement the Init() function. If the programmer attempts to compile the program without implementing the Init() function, an error will occur.

Here is the function declaration for the CiMA::Init() function:

```
int CiMA::Init(string pSymbol, ENUM_TIMEFRAMES pTimeframe, int pMAPeriod,
    int pMAShift, ENUM_MA_METHOD pMAMethod, ENUM_APPLIED_PRICE pMAPrice)
{
    handle = iMA(pSymbol,pTimeframe,pMAPeriod,pMAShift,pMAMethod,pMAPrice);
    return(handle);
}
```

The Init() class simply calls the iMA() function, and saves the indicator handle to the handle variable that was declared in the CIndicator class. Now all we need to do is access the moving average data using the Main() function that was declared in CIndicator.

Here is how we would use the CiMA class (and its parent class, CIndicator) in an expert advisor:

```
// Create an object based on the CiMA class
#include <Mql5Book\Indicators.mqh>
CiMA MA;

// Input variables
input int MAPeriod = 10;
input ENUM_MA_METHOD MAMethod = 0;
input int MAShift = 0;
input ENUM_APPLIED_PRICE MAPrice = 0;


// OnInit() event handler
MA.Init(_Symbol,_Period,MAPeriod,MAShift,MAMethod,MAPrice);
```

```
// OnTick() event handler
double currentMA = MA.Main();
```

At the top of our expert advisor source code file, we create an object based on the CiMA class. We name this object MA. The input variables necessary for adjusting the moving average settings are also declared near the top of the file.

The Init() function is called from the OnInit() event handler. Remember that OnInit() runs once, when the expert advisor is first initialized. We only need to initialize the indicator once, so placing it in OnInit() will work just fine. You can also place it in the OnTick() event handler with no ill effects.

To retrieve the current bar's moving average value, we simply need to call the Main() function with the bar index as an optional parameter. Since we called Main() without a parameter, it will return the value for the current bar. To retrieve the value for the previous bar, for example, we would call MA.Main(1). The \MQL5\Experts\Mql5Book\Simple Expert Advisor with Functions.mq5 file has been updated with the CiMA class to access the moving average data.

Input variables aside, we can initialize an indicator in just two lines of code: the object declaration at the beginning of the file, and the Init() function to initialize the indicator. We can then access the indicator values using easy-to-remember functions.

Let's create a second indicator class, using an indicator with multiple buffers. We discussed the stochastic indicator earlier in the chapter, which has two buffers. We will need to declare any additional buffer arrays in our class declaration. The class constructor will set the additional arrays as series arrays. Finally, we'll need to add functions to access the additional arrays. Here is the class declaration for the CiStochastic class:

```
class CiStochastic : public CIndicator
{
    private:
        double signal[];

    public:
        int Init(string pSymbol, ENUM_TIMEFRAMES pTimeframe, int pKPeriod, int pDPeriod,
            int pSlowing, ENUM_MA_METHOD pMAMethod, ENUM_STO_PRICE pPrice);
        double Signal(int pShift=0);
        CiStochastic(void);
};
```

Along with the Init() function that was declared as a virtual function in the CIndicator class, the CiStochastic class has a few additional members. A private array named signal[] will hold the indicator values for the signal or %D line. The public Signal() function will be used to access this data. We've also added a class constructor:

```
CiStochastic::CiStochastic(void)
{
    ArraySetAsSeries(signal,true);
}
```

Just like the constructor for the `CIndicator` class, the `CiStochastic` constructor simply sets the `signal[]` array as a series array. We will need to do this for every indicator that has more than one buffer.

Here are the function declarations for the `Init()` and `Signal()` functions:

```
int CiStochastic::Init(string pSymbol, ENUM_TIMEFRAMES pTimeframe, int pKPeriod,
    int pDPeriod, int pSlowing, ENUM_MA_METHOD pMAMethod, ENUM_STO_PRICE pPrice)
{
    handle = iStochastic(pSymbol,pTimeframe,pKPeriod,pDPeriod,pSlowing,pMAMethod,pPrice);
    return(handle);
}

double CiStochastic::Signal(int pShift=0)
{
    CopyBuffer(handle,1,0,MAX_COUNT,signal);
    double value = NormalizeDouble(signal[pShift],_Digits);
    return(value);
}
```

The `Init()` function passes the input parameters to the `iStochastic()` function and saves the indicator handle to the `handle` variable. The `Signal()` function copies the data from buffer 1 of the stochastic indicator to the `signal[]` array and returns the value for the specified bar. We will need to add a similar function for every additional indicator buffer in our multi-buffer indicator classes.

We add the stochastic indicator to our expert advisor the same way we added the moving average – declare an object, initialize the indicator, and access the indicator data:

```
// Create an object based on the CiStochastic class
#include <Mql5Book\Indicators.mqh>
CiStochastic Stoch;

// Input variables
input int KPeriod = 10;
input int DPeriod = 3;
input int Slowing = 3;
input ENUM_MA_METHOD StochMethod = MODE_SMA;
input ENUM_STO_PRICE StochPrice = STO_LOWHIGH;
```

```
// OnInit() event handler
Stoch.Init(_Symbol,_Period,KPeriod,DPeriod,Slowing,StochMethod,StochPrice);


// OnTick() event handler
double currentStoch = Stoch.Main();
double currentSignal = Stoch.Signal();
```

We added the stochastic indicator to our expert advisor using only a few lines of code. We declared an object based on the CiStochastic class named Stoch. We initialized the indicator in the OnInit() event handler using Init(). And we have two functions, Main() and Signal(), to retrieve the indicator data. The currentStoch and currentSignal variables contain the *%K* and *%D* line values for the current bar.

Object Initialization

To sharpen your understanding of how derived classes work, let's walk through the creation of our CiStochastic object. First, we initialize the object:

```
CiStochastic Stoch;
```

The program initializes the protected and public members of the CIndicator class. The variables and objects listed below will be part of the CiStochastic class, and the public members can be accessed through the Stoch object:

```
class CIndicator
{
    protected:
        int handle;
        double main[];

    public:
        CIndicator(void);
        double Main(int pShift=0);
        void Release();
};
```

Next, the CIndicator class constructor executes. The main[] array is set as a series array:

```
CIndicator::CIndicator(void)
{
    ArraySetAsSeries(main,true);
}
```

The `CiStochastic` class members are initialized next:

```
class CiStochastic : public CIndicator
{
    private:
        double signal[];

    public:
        int Init(string pSymbol, ENUM_TIMEFRAMES pTimeframe, int pKPeriod, int pDPeriod,
            int pSlowing, ENUM_MA_METHOD pMAMethod, ENUM_STO_PRICE pPrice);
        double Signal(int pShift=0);
        CiStochastic(void);
};
```

Then, the class constructor for the `CiStochastic` class executes. The `signal[]` array is set as a series array:

```
CiStochastic::CiStochastic(void)
{
    ArraySetAsSeries(signal,true);
}
```

The `Stoch` object is ready to use. The `handle` variable, as well as the `main[]` and `signal[]` arrays, are protected or private members that are not accessible to the programmer. We interact with these members using our public functions, `Init()`, `Main()`, `Signal()` and `Release()`.

The `\MQL5\Include\Mql5Book\Indicators.mqh` file contains classes for the most popular built-in indicators for MetaTrader 5. If you need to create a class for an indicator that is not listed, you can do so using the techniques listed in this chapter.

Custom Indicators

You can also use custom indicators in your expert advisors. To use a custom indicator, you will need to determine the number of buffers in the indicator, as well as their usage. You will also need to determine the names and types of the indicator parameters.

You can download custom indicators online through the MQL5 Codebase, the MQL5 Market, or from MetaTrader-related forums and websites. It will be much easier to work with a custom indicator if you have the MQ5 file for it. Even if you only have the EX5, it is still possible to use the indicator in your project, though it will take a bit more detective work.

Let's use one of the custom indicators that come standard with MetaTrader 5. The *Custom Indicators* tree in the *Navigator* window has an *Examples* subtree containing custom indicator examples of many built-in

MetaTrader indicators, as well as a few extras. We'll use the BB custom indicator, which plots Bollinger Bands on the chart.

When examining a custom indicator, open the Data window (*Ctrl+D*) to see how many lines are plotted on the chart, as well as the labels that are assigned to them, if any. The BB indicator has three lines, which are labeled *Middle*, *Upper* and *Lower*.

Fig. 17.4 – The BB custom indicator.

Open the \Indicators\Examples\BB.mq5 file in MetaEditor. We need to find out how many buffers or plots the indicator uses, as well as the relevant buffer numbers. Look in the OnInit() event handler for the SetIndexBuffer() functions. This assigns the arrays defined in the program to specific indicator buffer numbers:

```
SetIndexBuffer(0,ExtMLBuffer);
SetIndexBuffer(1,ExtTLBuffer);
SetIndexBuffer(2,ExtBLBuffer);
SetIndexBuffer(3,ExtStdDevBuffer,INDICATOR_CALCULATIONS);
```

The first parameter of the SetIndexBuffer() function is the buffer number. The indicator has three lines, but the code shows four buffers! Note the INDICATOR_CALCULATIONS parameter for buffer 3. This indicates that this buffer is used for internal calculations only. We'll need to do a bit more searching to figure out what each buffer does.

Look just below it in the file and you'll see three PlotIndexSetString() functions. These are used to set the labels in the data window:

```
PlotIndexSetString(0,PLOT_LABEL,"Bands("+string(ExtBandsPeriod)+") Middle");
PlotIndexSetString(1,PLOT_LABEL,"Bands("+string(ExtBandsPeriod)+") Upper");
PlotIndexSetString(2,PLOT_LABEL,"Bands("+string(ExtBandsPeriod)+") Lower");
```

From these, we can infer that buffer 0 is the middle line, buffer 1 is the upper band, and buffer 2 is the lower band. Now that we know our buffer numbers, let's figure out the input parameters for the Bollinger Bands indicator. We can find the input variables right near the top of the file:

```
input int     InpBandsPeriod=20;        // Period
input int     InpBandsShift=0;          // Shift
input double  InpBandsDeviations=2.0;   // Deviation
```

We have three input parameters – two `int` variables for the period and shift, and a `double` variable for the deviation. Feel free to copy and paste the input variables from the custom indicator file to your expert advisor file. You can change the names of the input variables in your program if you wish.

The iCustom() Function

The `iCustom()` function works similarly to the built-in indicator functions examined previously in this chapter. Here is the function definition from the *MQL5 Reference*:

```
int  iCustom(
   string            symbol,     // symbol name
   ENUM_TIMEFRAMES   period,     // period
   string            name        // folder/custom indicator_name
   ...                           // list of indicator input parameters
   );
```

Just like the other technical indicator functions, the `iCustom()` parameters begin with `symbol` and `period`. The `name` parameter is for the indicator name, minus the file extension. The indicator file must be located in the `\MQL5\Indicators` folder. If the file is located in a subfolder, then the subfolder name must precede the indicator name, separated by a double slash (\\). For example, the BB indicator is located in the `\MQL5\Indicators\Examples` folder. So the value for the `name` parameter would be `"Examples\\BB"`. (Remember that the double slash (\\) is the escape character for a backslash!)

The ... in the `iCustom()` function definition is where the input parameters for the custom indicator go. The BB custom indicator has three input parameters. We need to pass those parameters to the `iCustom()` function in the order that they appear in the indicator file:

```
input int     InpBandsPeriod=20;         // Period
input int     InpBandsShift=0;           // Shift
input double  InpBandsDeviations=2.0;    // Deviation
```

We would need to pass three parameters of type `int`, `int` and `double` to the `iCustom()` function. Here's an example of how we would use the `iCustom()` function to add the BB indicator to an expert advisor:

```
// Input variables
input int BandsPeriod = 20;         // Period
input int BandsShift = 0;           // Shift
input double BandsDeviation = 2;    // Deviation
```

```
// OnTick() event handler
double upper[], lower[], middle[];
ArraySetAsSeries(upper,true);
ArraySetAsSeries(lower,true);
ArraySetAsSeries(middle,true);

int bbHandle = iCustom(_Symbol,_Period,"Examples\\BB",BandsPeriod,BandsShift,BandsDeviation);

CopyBuffer(bbHandle,0,0,3,middle);
CopyBuffer(bbHandle,1,0,3,upper);
CopyBuffer(bbHandle,2,0,3,lower);

double bbMid = middle[0];
double bbUp = upper[0];
double bbLow = lower[0];
```

The input variables are presented in the order that they appear in the BB indicator file. We've renamed them to BandsPeriod, BandsShift, and BandsDeviation. Next, we declare the three arrays that we will use to hold the indicator data (upper[], lower[] and middle[]), and set them as series arrays. The iCustom() function initializes the BB indicator and returns our indicator handle, saving it in the bbHandle variable. Note that we use "Examples\\BB" for the name parameter in the iCustom() function, since the BB indicator is located in the \Indicators\Examples subfolder.

Note the BandsPeriod, BandsShift, and BandsDeviation parameters in the iCustom() function call. You must pass all of the input parameters of the custom indicator in the order that they appear to the iCustom() function. The parameters must also be of the appropriate data type – the majority of indicators use either int, double or string types. If you do not wish to add an input variable for a particular custom indicator parameter, then simply pass a default value. For example, if you don't plan on ever changing the BandsShift parameter for the BB indicator, then simply substitute 0 for BandsShift in the iCustom() function call.

Finally, we use the CopyBuffer() function to copy the data from the indicator buffers to our arrays. If you do not plan on using an indicator line, then you do not need to copy data for it. For example, if you don't plan on using the middle line of the BB indicator, then simply omit the middle[] array and the ArraySetAsSeries() and CopyBuffer() functions that reference it.

You can add any custom indicator to your expert advisor using the procedure above. First, note the buffer numbers for the corresponding lines/plots in the custom indicator that you wish to use. Next, note the input parameter names and their types. Add the input parameters to your expert advisor, renaming or omitting them as you wish. Pass the input parameters (or appropriate default values) to the iCustom() function along with the indicator name. Finally, use the CopyBuffer() function to copy the buffer data to the series array(s) you've prepared.

A Custom Indicator Class?

For the built-in indicators, we have created classes that make adding them to your expert advisors very easy. Unfortunately, the implementation of custom indicators in MQL5 make is difficult to do the same for custom indicators. As you've seen above, the `iCustom()` function allows for a flexible number of input parameters. We cannot do the same when creating classes in MQL5.

There is a second method of adding indicators to an MQL5 program, the `IndicatorCreate()` function, that uses a fixed number of parameters and an object of the `MqlParam` structure type to pass the input parameters. But using this method introduces a greater amount of complexity with no real gain in simplicity or functionality. Therefore, we will not be covering this method in this book.

In summary, if you wish to add custom indicators to your expert advisor, you will need to use the `iCustom()` function to return an indicator handle, and then use the `CopyBuffer()` function to copy the buffer data to your series arrays as described in the previous section.

Indicator-based Trading Signals

Let's examine a few of the ways that indicators can be used to create trading signals. Almost all indicator-based trading signals fall into one of the following categories:

- The relationship between an indicator line and the price.

- The relationship between two or more indicators lines.

- The change or slope of an indicator line between two bars.

- The value of an indicator relative to a fixed value.

The section on *Price-Based Trading Signals* in the previous chapter addressed the first category. A trading signal can be created when the price is above or below an indicator line. In this chapter, we discussed the Bollinger Bands indicator. We can use this indicator as an example of a price/indicator relationship.

The Bollinger Bands can be used to open trades at price extremes – for example, when the price moves outside the bands. We can express these trading conditions like so:

```
if(Price.Close() > bbUpper && PositionType(_Symbol) != POSITION_TYPE_BUY)
{
    // Open buy position
}
```

```
    else if(Price.Close() < bbLower && PositionType(_Symbol) != POSITION_TYPE_SELL)
    {
        // Open sell position
    }
```

We use the Close() function of our CBars class created in the previous chapter to represent the current close price. The bbUpper and bbLower variables represent the upper and lower Bollinger bands respectively. If the current close price is above the upper band and no buy position is currently open, then we would open a buy position. The same is true for a sell if the close is below the lower band.

You can use two or more indicator lines to create a trading signal. For example, the moving average cross is one of the most basic trading strategies around. It uses two moving averages, one fast and one slow. When the fast moving average is above the slow moving average a buy signal is implied, and vice versa for sell.

For example, lets use a 10 period exponential moving average for the fast MA, and a 30 period simple moving average for the slow MA:

```
    if(fastMA > slowMA && PositionType(_Symbol) != POSITION_TYPE_BUY && glBuyPlaced == false)
    {
        // Open buy position
    }

    if(fastMA < slowMA && PositionType(_Symbol) != POSITION_TYPE_SELL && glSellPlaced == false)
    {
        // Open sell position
    }
```

When the 10 EMA (the fastMA variable) is greater than the 30 SMA (the slowMA variable), a buy signal occurs. When the opposite is true, a sell signal occurs.

You can also use indicators of different types, provided they are all drawn in the same window. For example, you may wish to use a moving average with the Bollinger bands in the earlier example instead of the price:

```
    if(ma[1] > bbUpper && PositionType(_Symbol) != POSITION_TYPE_BUY)
    {
        // Open buy position
    }
```

In this example, we check if the moving average value of the previous bar (ma[1]) is greater than the upper bollinger band (bbUpper). If so, a buy signal occurs.

You can also compare two lines of the same indicator, such as the main and signal lines of the stochastic indicator:

```
if(stoch[1] > signal[1] && PositionType(_Symbol) != POSITION_TYPE_BUY)
{
    // Open buy position
}
```

The `stoch[]` array represents the main or *%K* line of the indicator, while the `signal[]` array is the *%D* line. If the *%K* line is greater than the *%D* line, this indicates a bullish condition.

For trending indicators, you may wish to base trading decisions upon the direction in which the indicator is trending. You can do this by checking the indicator value of a recent bar against the value of a previous bar. For example, if we want a buy signal to occur when a moving average is sloping upward, we can compare the value of the most recently closed bar to the value of the previous bar:

```
if(ma[1] > ma[2] && PositionType(_Symbol) != POSITION_TYPE_BUY)
{
    // Open buy position
}
```

This example checks to see if the moving average value of the most recently closed bar (`ma[1]`) is greater than the value of the previous bar (`ma[2]`). If so, the moving average is trending upward, and a buy signal occurs. You can do this with any indicator that trends up or down with the price, including oscillators such as RSI and MACD.

Many indicators, namely oscillators, appear in a separate chart window. They are not plotted according to price, but rather respond to changes in price. The RSI, for example, has a minimum value of 0 and a maximum value of 100. When the RSI value is below 30, that indicates an oversold condition, and when it is above 70, that indicates an overbought condition.

We can check for these overbought and oversold conditions simply by comparing the current RSI value to a fixed value. The example below checks for an oversold condition as part of a buy signal:

```
if(rsi[1] <= 30 && PositionType(_Symbol) != POSITION_TYPE_BUY)
{
    // Open buy position
}
```

If the RSI value of the most recently closed bar is less than or equal to the oversold level of 30, that indicates a buy signal.

Histogram indicators such as the MACD oscillate around a zero line. Ascending values above zero indicate a bullish trend, while descending values below zero indicate bearish price movement. You may wish to base a trading signal around the indicator value relative to zero:

```
if(macd[1] > 0 && PositionType(_Symbol) != POSITION_TYPE_BUY)
{
    // Open buy position
}
```

If the MACD value of the most recently closed bar is greater than zero, then a buy condition is indicated.

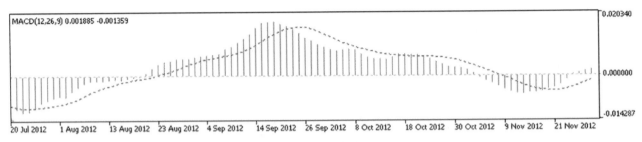

Fig. 17.5 – The MACD indicator.

You may come up with more elaborate indicator conditions than these. But nearly all indicator-based trading conditions are a combination of relationships between indicator readings and/or prices. To combine multiple price and indicator conditions for a trading signal, simply use boolean AND or OR operations between the expressions:

```
if(Price.Close() < bbLower && (rsi[1] < 30 || stoch[1] < signal[1])
    && PositionType(_Symbol) != POSITION_TYPE_BUY)
{
    // Open buy position
}
```

In the expression above, if the close price is less than the lower Bollinger band and either the RSI is less than 30, or the stochastic is less than its signal line, we open a buy position. When combining AND and OR operations, use parentheses to establish which expressions will be evaluated first.

Turning Indicators On and Off

In an expert advisor that has multiple indicators, you may wish to turn individual indicators on and off. To do so, we need to add a boolean input variable that will allow the user to deactivate an indicator if necessary. It will also be necessary to modify the trading condition to allow for both on and off states.

For example, let's create an expert advisor that uses the Bollinger Bands and an RSI. If the price is below the lower band and the RSI is in oversold territory (below 30), then we will open a buy position. We will add an input variable to turn the RSI condition on and off:

```
// Input variables
input bool UseRSI = true;



// OnTick() event handler
if(close[1] < lowerBand && ((rsi <= 30 && UseRSI == true) || UseRSI == false)
    && PositionType(_Symbol) != POSITION_TYPE_BUY)
{
    // Open buy position
}
```

In the example above, we add an input variable named UseRSI. This turn the RSI trade condition on and off. Inside the if operator, we check for both true and false states. If UseRSI == true, we check to see if the rsi value is less than 30. If so, and if the other conditions are true, we open a buy position. If UseRSI == false, and the other conditions are true, we also open a buy position.

The parentheses establish the order in which the conditions are evaluated. The inner set of parentheses contain the operation (rsi <= 30 && UseRSI == true). This is evaluated first. If this condition is false, we then evaluate the condition inside the outer set of parentheses, UseRSI == false. Note the OR operator (||) separating both operations. If one of these conditions evaluates as true, then the entire expression inside the parentheses is true.

Remember that the indicator "on" state is inside the innermost set of parentheses, and is evaluated first. The indicator "off" state is inside the outermost set of parentheses, and is separated from the "on" condition by an OR operator (||). Combining AND and OR operations using parentheses to establish order of evaluation allows you to create complex trading conditions. When doing so, be sure to watch your opening and closing parentheses to make sure that you do not leave one out, add one too many, or nest them incorrectly.

Chapter 18 - Working with Time and Date

In this chapter, we'll learn how to work with time and date in MQL5. We'll create a class that will allow us to place orders only on the open of a new bar. We'll also create a class that allows us to implement a fully-featured trade timer in our expert advisors. We will also learn about the *Timer* event, which allows us to carry out actions at a predefined interval.

Trading On New Bar Open

By default, an expert advisor executes on every new incoming *tick*, or change in price. This means that orders will be opened intrabar, unless you program your expert advisor to trade otherwise. We can program our expert advisor to trade only at the open of each new bar by saving the timestamp of the current bar to a static, global or class variable. When the timestamp of the current bar changes, we'll know that a new bar has opened. At this time, we can check for order opening and closing conditions.

When trading on the open of a new bar, we will use the closing price and indicator values of the previous bar when making trade decisions. If you're looking at a chart of historical trades, keep in mind that the trade criteria is based on the previous bar, and not the bar that the trade opened on!

Note that the Strategy Tester has an *Open prices only* execution mode that mimics this behavior. If your strategy only opens and closes orders on the open of a new bar, then you can use *Open prices only* to perform quick and accurate testing of your expert advisor.

The CNewBar Class

Let's create a class that will keep track of the timestamp of the current bar and allow us to determine when a new bar has opened. We'll create this class in a new include file named \MQL5\Include\Mq15Book\Timer.mqh. All of the classes and functions in this chapter will go in this file.

Here is the class declaration for our CNewBar class:

```
class CNewBar
{
    private:
        datetime Time[], LastTime;

    public:
        void CNewBar();
        bool CheckNewBar(string pSymbol, ENUM_TIMEFRAMES pTimeframe);
};
```

We have two private variables in our class. The Time[] array stores the timestamp for the current bar, and the LastTime variable contains the timestamp for the most recently checked bar. Note that we declared both variables on the same line, since they share the same type. We will compare these two values to determine if a new bar has opened. Our class also contains a constructor and the CheckNewBar() function. The class constructor simply sets the Time[] array as a series array:

```
void CNewBar::CNewBar(void)
{
    ArraySetAsSeries(Time,true);
}
```

The CheckNewBar() function is used to check for the open of a new bar. Here is the function declaration:

```
bool CNewBar::CheckNewBar(string pSymbol, ENUM_TIMEFRAMES pTimeframe)
{
    bool firstRun = false, newBar = false;
    CopyTime(pSymbol,pTimeframe,0,2,Time);

    if(LastTime == 0) firstRun = true;

    if(Time[0] > LastTime)
    {
        if(firstRun == false) newBar = true;
        LastTime = Time[0];
    }

    return(newBar);
}
```

The function takes two parameters, the symbol and the period of the chart we are using. We initialize two boolean variables, firstRun and newBar, and explicitly set them to false. The CopyTime() function updates the Time[] array with the timestamp of the most recent bar.

We check the LastTime class variable to see if it has a value assigned to it. The first time this function runs, LastTime will be equal to zero, and we will set the firstRun variable to true. This indicates that we have just attached the expert advisor to the chart. Since we do not want the expert advisor to trade intrabar, this is a necessary check to ensure that we don't attempt to open an order right away.

Next, we check to see if Time[0] > LastTime. If this is the first time we've run this function, then this expression will be true. This expression will also evaluate to true every time a new bar opens. If the timestamp of the current bar has changed, we check to see if firstRun is set to false. If so, we set newBar to true. We update the LastTime variable with the current bar's timestamp, and return the value of newBar to the program.

The execution of CheckNewBar() works like this: When the expert advisor is first attached to a chart, the function will return a value of false because firstRun will be set to true. On each subsequent check of the function, firstRun will always be false. When the current bar's timestamp (Time[0]) is greater than LastTime, we set newBar to true, update the value of LastTime, and return a value of true to the program. This indicates that a new bar has opened, and we can check our trading conditions.

Here is how we would use the CNewBar class in an expert advisor:

```
// Include file and object declaration
#include <Mql5Book\Timer.mqh>
CNewBar NewBar;

// Input variables
input bool TradeOnNewBar = true;

// OnTick() event handler
bool newBar = true;
int barShift = 0;

if(TradeOnNewBar == true)
{
    newBar = NewBar.CheckNewBar(_Symbol,_Period);
    barShift = 1;
}

if(newBar == true)
{
    // Order placement code
}
```

We declare an object based on the CNewBar class named NewBar. The TradeOnNewBar input variable allows us to select between trading on a new bar, or trading on every tick. In the OnTick() event handler, we declare a local bool variable named newBar and initialize it to true, and an int variable named barShift.

If TradeOnNewBar is set to true, we call our CheckNewBar() function and save the return value to the newBar variable. Most of the time, this value will be false. We will also set the value of barShift to 1. If TradeOnNewBar is set to false, then newBar will be true, and barShift will be 0.

If newBar is true, we go ahead and check our order placement conditions. Any code that you want to run only at the open of a new bar will go inside these brackets. This includes all order opening conditions and possibly your closing conditions as well.

When using the CNewBar class to check for the open of a new bar, the barShift variable will be used to set the bar index of any price or indicator values. For example, we'll use the moving average and close price functions that we've defined in previous chapters:

```
double close = Price.Close(barShift);
double ma = MA.Main(barShift);
```

The close and ma variables will be assigned the value for the current bar (barShift = 0) if TradeOnNewBar is set to false, or the value of the previous bar (barShift = 1) if TradeOnNewBar is set to true.

The datetime Type

We addressed the datetime type previously on page 16. The datetime type is used to hold date and time values. In a datetime variable, the date and time is represented as the number of seconds elapsed since January 1, 1970 at midnight. This makes it easy to compare two datetime values, and manipulate them mathematically.

For example, let's say we have two datetime variables, date1 and date2. We know that date1 is equal to July 12, 2012 at 3:00, and date2 is equal to July 14, 2012 at 22:00. If we wanted to know which date is earlier, we can compare the two :

```
datetime date1 = D'2012.07.12 03:00';
datetime date2 = D'2012.07.14 22:00';

if(date1 < date2)
{
    Print("date1 is sooner");              // True
}

else if(date1 > date2)
{
    Print("date2 is sooner");
}
```

The correct result is "date1 is sooner". Another advantage of working with datetime values is that if you want to add or subtract hours, days or any period of time, you can simply add or subtract the appropriate number of seconds to or from the datetime value. For example, we'll add 24 hours to the date1 variable above:

```
datetime addDay = date1 + 86400;          // Result:  2012.07.13 03:00
```

There are 86,400 seconds in a 24 hour period. By adding 86400 to a datetime value, we have advanced the date by exactly 24 hours. The date1 variable now has a value equal to July 13, 2012 at 3:00.

A datetime value is not human-readable, although the MetaTrader 5 terminal will automatically convert datetime values to a readable string constant when printing them to the log. If you need to convert a datetime value to a string for other purposes, the TimeToString() function will convert a datetime variable to a string in the format *yyyy.mm.dd hh:mm*. In this example, we will convert date2 using the TimeToString() function:

```
string convert = TimeToString(date2);
Print(convert);                              // Result: 2012.07.14 22:00
```

The TimeToString() function converts the date2 variable to a string, and saves the result to the convert variable. If we print out the value of convert, it will be 2012.07.14 22:00.

We can create a datetime value by constructing a string in the format *yyyy.mm.dd hh:mm:ss*, and converting it to a datetime variable using the StringToTime() function. For example if we want to convert the string 2012.07.14 22:00 to a datetime value, we pass the string to the StringToTime() function:

```
string dtConst = "2012.07.14 22:00";
datetime dtDate = StringToTime(dtConst);
```

The dtDate variable is assigned a datetime value equivalent to 2012.07.14 22:00. We can also create a datetime constant by enclosing the string in single quotes and prefacing it with a capital D. This datetime constant can be assigned directly to a datetime variable:

```
datetime dtDate = D'2012.07.14 22:00';
```

This method allows for more flexibility when constructing the datetime constant string. For example, you could use *dd.mm.yyyy* as your date format and leave off the time. The datetime constant topic in the *MQL5 Reference* under *Language Basics > Data Types > Integer Types > Datetime Type* has more information on formatting a datetime constant.

Finally, we can use the MqlDateTime structure. This structure allows us to retrieve specific information from a datetime variable, such as the hour or the day of the week.

The MqlDateTime Structure

The `MqlDateTime` structure contains variables that hold information about a `datetime` value. Here is the structure definition from the *MQL5 Reference*:

```
struct MqlDateTime
{
    int year;            // Year
    int mon;             // Month
    int day;             // Day
    int hour;            // Hour
    int min;             // Minutes
    int sec;             // Seconds
    int day_of_week;     // Day of week (0-Sunday, 1-Monday, ... 6-Saturday)
    int day_of_year;     // Day number of the year (January 1st = zero)
};
```

Using the `MqlDateTime` structure, we can retrieve any date or time element from a `datetime` value. We can retrieve the hour, minute or day and assign that value to an integer variable. We can even retrieve the day of the week or the day of the year. We can also assign values to these variables to construct a `datetime` value.

The `TimeToStruct()` function is used to convert a `datetime` value to an object of the `MqlDateTime` type. The first parameter of the function is the `datetime` value to convert. The second parameter is the `MqlDateTime` object to load the values into. Here's an example:

```
datetime dtTime = D'2012.10.15 16:36:23';

MqlDateTime timeStruct;
TimeToStruct(dtTime,timeStruct);

int day = timeStruct.day;
int hour = timeStruct.hour;
int dayOfWeek = timeStruct.day_of_week;
```

First, we construct a `datetime` variable, dtTime, using a `datetime` constant. Next, we declare an object of type `MqlDateTime` named `timeStruct`. We use the `TimeToStruct()` function to convert the `datetime` value in dtTime to the `MqlDateTime` structure. Finally, we show how to retrieve the day, hour and day of week from the `timeStruct` object. The day is 15, the hour is 16, and the dayOfWeek is 1 for Monday.

We can also create an `MqlDateTime` object, assign values to its member variables, and construct a `datetime` value using the `StructToTime()` function. The day_of_week and day_of_year variables are not used when creating a datetime value using an MqlDateTime object. Here's an example of how to create a datetime value using the StructToTime() function:

```
MqlDateTime timeStruct;

timeStruct.year = 2012;
timeStruct.mon = 10;
timeStruct.day = 20;
timeStruct.hour = 2;
timeStruct.min = 30;
timeStruct.sec = 0;

datetime dtTime = StructToTime(timeStruct);
```

Be sure to explicitly assign values to all of the variables of the MqlDateTime object, or else you may not get the results you expect! The StructToTime() function converts the timeStruct object to a datetime value, and stores the result in the dtTime variable. If we print out the dtTime variable, we can see the values that we assigned to the timeStruct object:

```
Print(dtTime);                              // Result: 2012.10.20 02:30:00
```

What happens if you don't assign a value to an MqlDateTime object variable, or if you assign a value that is invalid?

```
MqlDateTime timeStruct;

// Zero for month and day
timeStruct.year = 2012;
timeStruct.mon = 0;
timeStruct.day = 0;

timeStruct.hour = 0;
timeStruct.min = 0;
timeStruct.sec = 0;

datetime dtTime = StructToTime(timeStruct);

Print(TimeToString(dtTime));                // Result: 2012.01.01 00:00


// Invalid month and day
timeStruct.mon = 13;
timeStruct.day = 32;
```

223

```
dtTime = StructToTime(timeStruct);

Print(TimeToString(dtTime));                    // Result: 2012.12.31 00:00
```

The year must be specified, or else the StructToTime() function returns nothing. If the month or day are less than 1, they default to a value of 1. If the month is larger than the maximum value of 12, it defaults to December (12). If the day is larger than the number of days in the month, it either defaults to 31 if there are 31 days in the month, or else the excess value overflows into the following month. Needless to say, you should not overflow the day variable, or else your date may end up several days off. Invalid hour or minute values will default to their minimum and maximum of 0 and 59 respectively.

Creating A Trade Timer Class

Now that we've learned how to create and convert datetime values, we can use this information to create a trade timer class for our expert advisor. We'll need to create datetime values for our start and end times. Since we'll usually be working with times that fall within the current day or week, we'll create a function that will calculate a datetime value for a specified time for the current date. We can then manipulate that value to get a specific date if necessary.

The CreateDateTime() Function

Let's create a function that will create a datetime value for the current date. We'll specify the hour and minute, and the function will return a value for that time for the current date. An MqlDateTime object will be used to create our datetime value.

All of the code in this chapter will go in the \MQL5\Include\Mql5Book\Timer.mqh include file. Here is the code for the CreateDateTime() function:

```
datetime CreateDateTime(int pHour = 0, int pMinute = 0)
{
    MqlDateTime timeStruct;
    TimeToStruct(TimeCurrent(),timeStruct);

    timeStruct.hour = pHour;
    timeStruct.min = pMinute;

    datetime useTime = StructToTime(timeStruct);

    return(useTime);
}
```

First, we create an `MqlDateTime` object named `timeStruct`. We use the `TimeToStruct()` function to fill the member variables with the current date and time using the `TimeCurrent()` function. Next, we assign the `pHour` and `pMinute` parameter values to the `hour` and `min` variables of the `timeStruct` object. Finally, we use `StructToTime()` to construct our new `datetime` value and assign the result to the `useTime` variable. The value of `useTime` is returned to the program.

Once we have a `datetime` value for a specified time, we can easily manipulate this value if necessary. For example, we want our trade timer to start at 20:00 each day. We will stop trading for the day at 8:00 the following day. First, we will use our `CreateDateTime()` function to create `datetime` values for the start and end time:

```
datetime startTime = CreateDateTime(22,0);
datetime endTime = CreateDateTime(8,0);

Print("Start: ",startTime,", End: ",endTime);

// Result: Start: 2012.10.22 22:00:00, End: 2012.10.22 08:00:00
```

The problem here is that our end time is earlier than our start time. Assuming that today is October 22, and we want our timer to start at 20:00, we'll need to advance the end time by 24 hours to get the correct time. You'll recall from earlier in the chapter that 24 hours is equal to 86400 seconds. We can simply add this value to `endTime` to get the correct time.

Instead of having to remember that 86400 seconds equals a day, let's define some constants that we can easily refer to if we need to add or subtract time from a `datetime` variable. These will go at the top of our `Timer.mqh` include file:

```
#define TIME_ADD_MINUTE 60
#define TIME_ADD_HOUR 3600
#define TIME_ADD_DAY   86400
#define TIME_ADD_WEEK 604800
```

Using these constants, we can easily add or subtract the specified time period. Let's add 24 hours to our `endTime` variable:

```
endTime += TIME_ADD_DAY;

Print("Start: ",startTime," End: ",endTime);

// Result: Start: 2012.10.22 22:00:00, End: 2012.10.23 08:00:00
```

Now our start and end times are correct relative to each other.

The CTimer Class

Let's examine the simplest type of trade timer. This timer will take two datetime values and determine whether the current time falls between those values. If so, our trade timer is active and trading can commence. If the current time is outside those values, then our trade timer is inactive, and trades will not be placed.

The CTimer class will hold our timer-related functions. We will start with one function – the CheckTimer() function, which will check two datetime variables to see if trading is allowed. We'll add other class members later:

```
class CTimer
{
    public:
        bool CheckTimer(datetime pStartTime, datetime pEndTime, bool pLocalTime = false);
};
```

Here is the body of the CheckTimer() function:

```
bool CTimer::CheckTimer(datetime pStartTime, datetime pEndTime, bool pLocalTime = false)
{
    if(pStartTime >= pEndTime)
    {
        Alert("Error: Invalid start or end time");
        return(false);
    }

    datetime currentTime;
    if(pLocalTime == true) currentTime = TimeLocal();
    else currentTime = TimeCurrent();

    bool timerOn = false;
    if(currentTime >= pStartTime && currentTime < pEndTime)
    {
        timerOn = true;
    }

    return(timerOn);
}
```

The pStartTime parameter holds the trading start time, while the pEndTime parameter holds the trading end time. The pLocalTime parameter is a boolean value that determines whether we use local or server time.

First, we check to see if pStartTime is greater than or equal to pEndTime. If so, we know that our start and end times are invalid, so we show an error message and exit with a value of false. Otherwise, we continue checking our timer condition.

We declare a datetime variable named currentTime that will hold the current time. If pLocalTime is true, we will use the local computer time. If it is false, we use the server time. The TimeLocal() and TimeCurrent() functions retrieve the current time from the local computer or the server, respectively. Normally, we will use the server time, but it is a simple addition to allow the user to use local time, so we have added the option.

Once the currentTime variable has been assigned the current time, we compare it to our trading start and end times. If currentTime >= pStartTime and currentTime < pEndTime, then the trade timer is active. We will set the timerOn variable to true and return that value to the program.

Let's demonstrate how to create a simple trade timer using CheckTimer(). We'll be using two datetime input variables. The MetaTrader 5 interface makes it easy to input a valid datetime value. We'll set a start and end time, and use the CheckTimer() function to check for a valid trade condition:

```
#include <Mql5Book/Timer.mqh>
CTimer Timer;

input datetime StartTime = D'2012.10.15 08:00';
input datetime EndTime = D'2012.10.19 20:00';



// OnTick() event handler
bool timerOn = Timer.CheckTimer(StartTime,EndTime,false);

if(timerOn == true)
{
    // Order placement code
}
```

First, we include the Timer.mqh file and declare the Timer object, based on our CTimer class. The input variables StartTime and EndTime have a valid start and end time entered. In the OnTick() event handler, we call the CheckTimer() function and pass our StartTime and EndTime input variables to it. (We've passed a value of false for the pLocalTime parameter, meaning that we'll use server time to determine the current time).

If the current time is between the start and end times, the boolean timerOn variable is set to true. When we check our order opening conditions, we check if timerOn is true. If so, we proceed with checking the order conditions.

The problems with using `datetime` input variables to set our start and end times is that they have to be constantly updated. What if you just wanted to trade the same hours each day, for example?

The DailyTimer() Function

Most savvy Forex traders know that certain hours of the day are more conducive to trading. The open of the London session through the end of the New York session is the most active trading period of the day. We can improve the performance of our expert advisors by limiting our trading to these hours.

We'll create a timer that will allow us to trade the same hours each day. We set a start and end hour and minute, and unless we decide to change our trading hours we need not edit it again. Our daily timer operates by the same principles as our simple timer in the last section. We create two `datetime` values using our `CreateDateTime()` function. We compare our start and end times, and increment or decrement them by one day as necessary. If the current time falls between the start and end times, trading is enabled.

Let's add our daily timer function to the `CTimer` class. We're also going to add two private `datetime` variables – `StartTime` and `EndTime` – to the `CTimer` class. These will be used to save our current start and end times, just in case we need to retrieve them elsewhere in our program:

```
class CTimer
{
    private:
        datetime StartTime, EndTime;

    public:
        bool CheckTimer(datetime pStartTime, datetime pEndTime, bool pLocalTime = false);
        bool DailyTimer(int pStartHour, int pStartMinute, int pEndHour, int pEndMinute,
            bool pLocalTime = false);
};
```

Here is the body of our `DailyTimer()` function:

```
bool CTimer::DailyTimer(int pStartHour, int pStartMinute, int pEndHour, int pEndMinute,
    bool pLocalTime = false)
{
    datetime currentTime;
    if(pLocalTime == true) currentTime = TimeLocal();
    else currentTime = TimeCurrent();

    StartTime = CreateDateTime(pStartHour,pStartMinute);
    EndTime = CreateDateTime(pEndHour,pEndMinute);
```

```
        if(EndTime <= StartTime)
        {
            StartTime -= TIME_ADD_DAY;

            if(currentTime > EndTime)
            {
                StartTime += TIME_ADD_DAY;
                EndTime += TIME_ADD_DAY;
            }
        }

        bool timerOn = CheckTimer(StartTime,EndTime,pLocalTime);

        return(timerOn);
    }
```

For this function, we input the start and end hour and minute using the `int` variables pStartHour, pStartMinute, pEndHour and pEndMinute. We also include the pLocalTime parameter for selecting between server and local time. After assigning the current time to the currentTime variable, we call the CreateDateTime() function and pass the pStartHour, pStartMinute, pEndHour and pEndMinute variables. The resulting `datetime` values are stored in StartTime and EndTime respectively.

Next, we determine whether we need to increment or decrement the start and/or end time values. First, we check to see if the EndTime value is less than the StartTime value. If so, we subtract one day from the start time (using the TIME_ADD_DAY constant) so that the value of StartTime is sooner than the value of EndTime. If the value of currentTime is greater than EndTime, the timer has already expired and we need to set it for the next day. We increment both StartTime and EndTime by one day, so that the timer is set for the following day. Finally, we pass the StartTime and EndTime values to the CheckTimer() function, along with our pLocalTime parameter. The result is saved to the timerOn variable, which is returned to the program.

Let's demonstrate how we can use the daily timer in our expert advisor program:

```
#include <Mq15Book/Timer.mqh>
CTimer Timer;

input bool UseTimer = false;
input int StartHour = 0;
input int StartMinute = 0;
input int EndHour = 0;
input int EndMinute = 0;
input bool UseLocalTime = false;
```

```
// OnTick() event handler
bool timerOn = true;
if(UseTimer == true)
{
    timerOn = Timer.DailyTimer(StartHour,StartMinute,EndHour,EndMinute,UseLocalTime);
}

if(timerOn == true)
{
    // Order placement code
}
```

We've added an input variable named UseTimer to turn the timer on and off. We have inputs for start and end hour and minute, as well as for local/server time.

In the OnTick() event handler, we declare a boolean variable named timerOn (not to be confused with the local variable of the same name in our DailyTimer() function!) The value of this variable determines whether we can trade or not. We will initialize it to true. If the UseTimer input variable is set to true, we call the DailyTimer() function. The result of the function is saved to the timerOn variable. If timerOn is true, trading will commence, and if it is false, we will wait until the start of the next trading day.

The PrintTimerMessage() Function

One issue from a user perspective is knowing whether or not trading is enabled by the timer. Let's create a short function that writes a comment to the chart as well as to the log, to inform the user when the timer has started and stopped. The function is named PrintTimerMessage(), and we will make it a private member of the CTimer class. We will also declare a private variable named TimerStarted that will hold our on/off state:

```
class CTimer
{
    private:
        datetime StartTime, EndTime;
        bool TimerStarted;
        void PrintTimerMessage(bool pTimerOn);

    public:
        bool CheckTimer(datetime pStartTime, datetime pEndTime, bool pLocalTime = false);
        bool DailyTimer(int pStartHour, int pStartMinute, int pEndHour, int pEndMinute,
            bool pLocalTime = false);
};
```

Here is the code for the PrintTimerMessage() function:

```
void CTimer::PrintTimerMessage(bool pTimerOn)
{
    if(pTimerOn == true && TimerStarted == false)
    {
        string message = "Timer started";
        Print(message);
        Comment(message);
        TimerStarted = true;
    }
    else if(pTimerOn == false && TimerStarted == true)
    {
        string message = "Timer stopped";
        Print(message);
        Comment(message);
        TimerStarted = false;
    }
}
```

The function type is void, since we do not need this function to return a value. The pTimerOn parameter takes the value of our timerOn variable from the DailyTimer() function. If pTimerOn is true, we check to see if the timer is active and print a message to the log and to the screen.

The TimerStarted variable contains the timer activation state. When the timer is first activated and pTimerOn is true, TimerStarted will be false. We'll print the message "Timer started" to the chart and to the log, and set TimerStarted to true. If pTimerOn is false and TimerStarted is true, we print the message "Timer stopped" to the chart and log, and set TimerStarted to false.

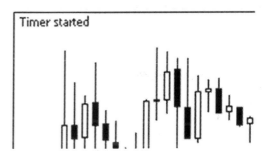

Fig. 18.1 – A chart comment generated by the PrintTimerMessage() function.

Now all we need to do is add this to the end of our DailyTimer() function:

```
bool timerOn = CheckTimer(StartTime,EndTime,pLocalTime);
PrintTimerMessage(timerOn);

return(timerOn);
```

The result is that we will have one message printed to the log when the timer activates, and another when the timer deactivates. The message will also be printed to the comment area of the chart, and will remain there until it is overwritten by another comment.

The BlockTimer() Function

The trade timers we've created so far take a single start and end time. The daily timer is sufficient for most traders, but if you need more flexibility in setting your trade timer, we've created the BlockTimer() function. We call it the "block timer" because the user will set several blocks of time that the expert advisor will be allowed to trade each week. This allows the user to avoid volatile market events such as the non-farm payroll report.

We will specify the days to start and stop trading by using the ENUM_DAY_OF_WEEK enumeration. The user will select the day of the week and specify a start and end hour and minute in the expert advisor inputs. For each block of time, we need a start day, start hour, start minute, end day, end hour and end minute. We'll also need a boolean variable to indicate whether to use that timer block.

A fixed number of timer blocks will need to be specified in the inputs, according to the trader's needs. Five blocks should be enough for most traders. Due to the number of variables required for each timer block, we will create a structure that will hold all of them. We will create an array based on this structure that will hold all of the variables for each timer block. This array will be passed to the BlockTimer() function, which will determine whether trading should be enabled.

Here is the structure that we will define in the Timer.mqh include file. This will be declared on the global scope, at the top of the file:

```
struct TimerBlock
{
    bool enabled;             // Enable or disable timer block
    int start_day;            // Start day (1: Monday... 5: Friday)
    int start_hour;           // Start hour
    int start_min;            // Start minute
    int end_day;              // End day
    int end_hour;             // End hour
    int end_min;              // End minute
};
```

Let's demonstrate how we will use this structure to fill an array object with timer information. First, we will declare the input variables in our expert advisor. We will add two timer blocks, each with the necessary inputs:

```
sinput string Block1;         // Timer Block 1
input bool UseTimer = true;
input ENUM_DAY_OF_WEEK StartDay = 5;
input int StartHour = 8;
input int StartMinute = 0;
input ENUM_DAY_OF_WEEK EndDay = 5;
```

```
input int EndHour = 12;
input int EndMinute = 25;

sinput string Block2;              // Timer Block 2
input bool UseTimer2 = true;
input ENUM_DAY_OF_WEEK StartDay2 = 5;
input int StartHour2 = 13;
input int StartMinute2 = 0;
input ENUM_DAY_OF_WEEK EndDay2 = 5;
input int EndHour2 = 18;
input int EndMinute2 = 0;

input bool UseLocalTime = false;
```

Each timer block has a boolean variable to turn the timer block on and off (UseTimer), a StartDay and EndDay variable of type ENUM_DAY_OF_WEEK, and the StartHour, StartMinute, EndHour and EndMinute integer variables. Note the Block1 and Block2 variables with the sinput modifier. These are static input variables that are used for informational and formatting purposes. The comment following the variable identifier is displayed in the input window in MetaTrader:

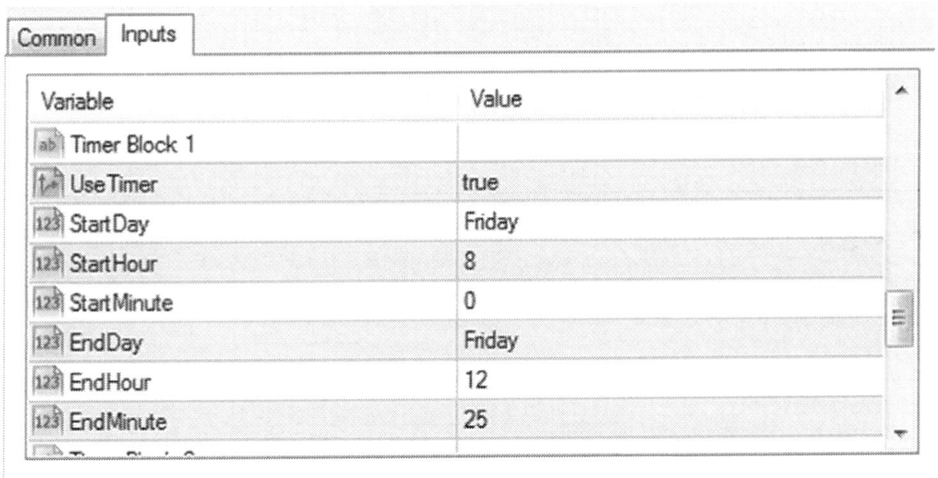

Fig. 18.2 – The block timer inputs as they appear in the expert advisor *Inputs* tab.

Now that we have our input variables declared, we will declare our TimerBlock structure object on the global scope:

```
TimerBlock block[2];
```

This declares an array object named block, with two elements. Next, we need to load our input values into this array. This will take quite a bit of code, but there's no easy way around this. We will copy the input variables into the array inside the OnInit() event handler:

```
// OnInit() event handler
block[0].enabled = UseTimer;
block[0].start_day = StartDay;
block[0].start_hour = StartHour;
block[0].start_min = StartMinute;
block[0].end_day = EndDay;
block[0].end_hour = EndHour;
block[0].end_min = EndMinute;

block[1].enabled = UseTimer2;
block[1].start_day = StartDay2;
block[1].start_hour = StartHour2;
block[1].start_min = StartMinute2;
block[1].end_day = EndDay2;
block[1].end_hour = EndHour2;
block[1].end_min = EndMinute2;
```

All of the input variables from the first timer block are copied into the member variables of the block[] array at element 0. The same is done for the second timer block at element 1. Now that the input values are copied into our block[] array, let's pass them to our timer function. This is the easy part, and it works just like the other timer functions in this chapter:

```
// OnTick() event handler
bool timerOn = true;
if(UseTimer == true)
{
    timerOn = Timer.BlockTimer(block,UseLocalTime);
}
```

Inside the OnTick() event handler, we check the timer state before we check our order conditions. If the current time falls inside one of our timer blocks, the value of timerOn will be set to true. We can then check the order opening conditions and perform any actions that occur when our timer is active.

Let's examine our BlockTimer() function:

```
bool CTimer::BlockTimer(TimerBlock &pBlock[], bool pLocalTime = false)
{
    MqlDateTime today;
    bool timerOn = false;
    int timerCount = ArraySize(pBlock);
```

```
    for(int i = 0; i < timerCount; i++)
    {
        if(pBlock[i].enabled = false) continue;

        StartTime = CreateDateTime(pBlock[i].start_hour, pBlock[i].start_min);
        EndTime = CreateDateTime(pBlock[i].end_hour, pBlock[i].end_min);

        TimeToStruct(StartTime,today);
        int dayShift = pBlock[i].start_day - today.day_of_week;
        if(dayShift != 0) StartTime += TIME_ADD_DAY * dayShift;

        TimeToStruct(EndTime,today);
        dayShift = pBlock[i].end_day - today.day_of_week;
        if(dayShift != 0) EndTime += TIME_ADD_DAY * dayShift;

        timerOn = CheckTimer(StartTime,EndTime,pLocalTime);
        if(timerOn == true) break;
    }

    PrintTimerMessage(timerOn);
    return(timerOn);
}
```

The BlockTimer() function has two parameters: The pBlock[] parameter takes an array object of the TimerBlock structure type passed by reference, and the pLocalTime parameter is a boolean variable that determines whether to use server or local time.

First, we declare the variables that will be used in our function. An MqlDateTime object named today will be used to retrieve the day of the week for the current date. The timerCount variable will hold the size of the pBlock[] array, which we retrieve by using the ArraySize() function. A for loop will be used to process the timer blocks. The number of timer blocks is determined by the timerCount variable. We will calculate the start and end times for each timer block, and determine whether the current time falls within those times. If so, we break out of the loop and return a value of true to the calling program.

Inside the for loop, the first thing we check is the enabled variable of the current timer block. If it is true, we continue calculating the start and end time. We use the CreateDateTime() function to calculate the StartTime and EndTime variables using the start_hour, start_min, end_hour and end_min variables of the pBlock[] object.

Next, we calculate the correct date based on the day of the week indicated for the start and end time. We use TimeToStruct() to convert the StartTime and EndTime values to an MqlDateTime structure. The result is stored in the today object. The today.day_of_week variable will hold the current day of the week. If the current day of the week differs from the start_day or end_day value of the pBlock[] object, we calculate the difference and store it to the dayShift variable. The dayShift variable is multiplied by the TIME_ADD_DAY constant, and added or subtracted from the StartTime or EndTime variables. The result is that StartTime and EndTime are set to the correct time and date relative to the current week.

After the start and end times for the current timer block have been determined, we use the CheckTimer() function to see if the current time falls within the start time and end time of the current timer block. If the function returns true, we break out of the for loop. The PrintTimerMessage() function will print an informative message to the chart and the log, and the value of timerOn is returned to the program.

Programming a flexible trade timer is the most complex thing we've had to do so far. With the timer functions we've defined in this chapter, you should be able to implement a trade timer that is flexible enough for your needs.

Retrieving StartTime and EndTime

A final bit of code to add: If for some reason you need to check the current start or end time that the trade timer is using, use the GetStartTime() and GetEndTime() functions. These functions retrieve the appropriate datetime variable and return it to the program. Since these are very short functions, we can declare the entire function in the class declaration:

```
class CTimer
{
    private:
        datetime StartTime, EndTime;

    public:
        datetime GetStartTime() {return(StartTime);};
        datetime GetEndTime() {return(EndTime);};
};
```

For clarity, we've removed the other functions and variables from the CTimer class for this example. Note the return statement inside the brackets after the function name. This is the function body. The sole purpose of GetStartTime() and GetEndTime() is to return the value of the StartTime or EndTime variable to the program. If you have a short function whose only purpose is to return a value, then you can place the body right in the class declaration.

The OnTimer() Event Handler

So far we've been only been using the OnInit() and OnTick() event handlers in our expert advisors. There are several optional event handlers that can be used for specific purposes. One of those is the OnTimer() event handler, which executes at a predefined time interval.

The OnTick() event handler executes only when a change in price is received from the terminal. The OnTimer() event, on the other hand, can execute every *X* number of seconds. If you want your trading strategy to perform an action at regular intervals, place that code in the OnTimer() event handler.

To use the OnTimer() event handler, we need to set the timer interval using the EventSetTimer() function. This function is typically declared inside the OnInit() event handler or in a class constructor. For example, if we want the expert advisor to perform an action once every 60 seconds, here is how we set the event timer:

```
int OnInit()
{
    EventSetTimer(60);
}
```

This will execute the OnTimer() event handler every 60 seconds, if one exists in your program. The *MQL5 Wizard* can be used to add the OnTimer() event to your source file when creating it, but you can always add it later. The OnTimer() event handler is of type void with no parameters:

```
void OnTimer()
{

}
```

If for some reason you need to stop your event timer, the EventKillTimer() will remove the event timer, and the OnTimer() event handler will no longer run. This is typically declared in the OnDeinit() event handler or a class destructor, although it should work anywhere in the program:

```
EventKillTimer();
```

The EventKillTimer() function takes no parameters, and does not return a value.

Chapter 19 - Putting It All Together

We've spent the better part of this book creating functions and classes that place, close, modify and manage orders. We've added useful features such as trailing stops, money management and trade timers. We've also created classes that allow us to add indicators and work with price data easily. Now we're going to show you how to put it all together in creating a fully-featured and robust expert advisor.

Creating A Template

MetaEditor 5 doesn't allow the use of custom templates like MetaEditor 4 does. So to save time, we will need to create our own template, which we will use when creating our expert advisors. When we create a new expert advisor, we'll simply open this file and save it under a new name.

The template will we'll be using is named `MQL Book Template.mq5`. To prevent this file from being overwritten, navigate to the `\MQL5\Experts\Mql5Book` folder in *Windows Explorer* and locate the `MQL Book Template.mq5` file. Right-click on the file and select *Properties*. Put a check mark in the *Read-only* attribute. When attempting to save a read-only file, MetaEditor will alert you and prompt you to save it to a new file.

Here is our template file. We'll go through it a section at a time. First is our `#include` directives and object declarations:

```
// Trade
#include <Mql5Book\Trade.mqh>
CTrade Trade;

// Price
#include <Mql5Book\Price.mqh>
CBars Price;

// Money management
#include <Mql5Book\MoneyManagement.mqh>

// Trailing stops
#include <Mql5Book\TrailingStops.mqh>
CTrailing Trail;

// Timer
#include <Mql5Book\Timer.mqh>
CTimer Timer;
CNewBar NewBar;
```

```
    // Indicators
    #include <Mq15Book\Indicators.mqh>
```

We include six files from the \MQL5\Include\Mq15Book directory. We've also declared several objects for the classes in those files. The Trade object contains our order placement functions. The Price object is for price data functions. Trail contains the trailing stop functions, and Timer and NewBar contain the trade timer and new bar functions. If you need to add indicators to your expert advisor, you will create indicator objects here, ideally under the #include directive for the Indicators.mqh file.

Next, we have some descriptive properties and our input variables:

```
//+------------------------------------------------------------------+
//| Expert information                                               |
//+------------------------------------------------------------------+

#property copyright "Andrew Young"
#property version   "1.00"
#property description ""
#property link       "http://www.expertadvisorbook.com"


//+------------------------------------------------------------------+
//| Input variables                                                  |
//+------------------------------------------------------------------+

input ulong Slippage = 3;
input bool TradeOnNewBar = true;

sinput string MM;  // Money Management
input bool UseMoneyManagement = true;
input double RiskPercent = 2;
input double FixedVolume = 0.1;

sinput string SL;  // Stop Loss & Take Profit
input int StopLoss = 20;
input int TakeProfit = 0;

sinput string TS;      // Trailing Stop
input bool UseTrailingStop = false;
input int TrailingStop = 0;
input int MinimumProfit = 0;
input int Step = 0;
```

```
   sinput string BE;       // Break Even
   input bool UseBreakEven = false;
   input int BreakEvenProfit = 0;
   input int LockProfit = 0;

   sinput string TI;  // Timer
   input bool UseTimer = false;
   input int StartHour = 0;
   input int StartMinute = 0;
   input int EndHour = 0;
   input int EndMinute = 0;
   input bool UseLocalTime = false;
```

The #property directives describe our program, and will appear in the *Common* tab in the expert advisor *Properties* dialog. The input section includes settings for our most commonly-used features, including money management, trailing and break even stop, and trade timer. The optional features all have boolean input variables to switch the feature on an off. Note the sinput variables – these divide our input variables into clearly defined sections in the *Inputs* window.

Next, we have our global variables and the OnInit() event handler:

```
//+------------------------------------------------------------------+
//| Global variables                                                 |
//+------------------------------------------------------------------+

bool glBuyPlaced, glSellPlaced;


//+------------------------------------------------------------------+
//| Expert initialization function                                   |
//+------------------------------------------------------------------+

int OnInit()
{
    Trade.Deviation(Slippage);
    return(0);
}
```

The glBuyPlaced and glSellPlaced variables keep track of whether a position was previously opened in the specified direction. In most trading systems we only want to open one position on a new trade signal, and not open another one until a trade signal appears in the opposite direction, or a condition occurs where we set either of these variables to false. The OnInit() event handler contains code that will run once when the program is first started. Above, we set the trade slippage.

Next, we're going to examine the OnTick() event handler:

```
//+------------------------------------------------------------------+
//| Expert tick function                                             |
//+------------------------------------------------------------------+

void OnTick()
{
    // Check for new bar
    bool newBar = true;
    int barShift = 0;

    if(TradeOnNewBar == true)
    {
        newBar = NewBar.CheckNewBar(_Symbol,_Period);
        barShift = 1;
    }

    // Timer
    bool timerOn = true;
    if(UseTimer == true)
    {
        timerOn = Timer.DailyTimer(StartHour,StartMinute,EndHour,EndMinute,UseLocalTime);
    }

    // Update prices
    Price.Update(_Symbol,_Period);
```

The first section of code checks for the opening of a new bar. We declare a boolean variable named newBar and initialize it to true. The barShift variable is initialized to zero. If the TradeOnNewBar input variable is set to true, we call the CheckNewBar() function and save the result to newBar, and set the barShift variable to 1. Otherwise, newBar remains set to true, barShift remains zero, and intrabar trading is enabled.

After that is the timer code. We define a boolean variable named timerOn and initialize it to true. If the UseTimer input variable is set to true, we check the DailyTimer() function, and assign the return value to timerOn. Otherwise, the value of timerOn remains true. If we are using bar data in our expert advisor, the Price.Update() function updates the Bar object with price and time data.

Next is our order placement code with our money management feature:

```
// Order placement
if(newBar == true && timerOn == true)
{
    // Money management
    double tradeSize;
    if(UseMoneyManagement == true)
        tradeSize = MoneyManagement(_Symbol,FixedVolume,RiskPercent,StopLoss);
    else tradeSize = VerifyVolume(_Symbol,FixedVolume);

    // Open buy order
    if(PositionType() != POSITION_TYPE_BUY && glBuyPlaced == false)
    {
        glBuyPlaced = Trade.Buy(_Symbol,tradeSize);

        if(glBuyPlaced == true)
        {
            do Sleep(100); while(PositionSelect(_Symbol) == false);
            double openPrice = PositionOpenPrice(_Symbol);

            double buyStop = BuyStopLoss(_Symbol,StopLoss,openPrice);
            if(buyStop > 0) AdjustBelowStopLevel(_Symbol,buyStop);

            double buyProfit = BuyTakeProfit(_Symbol,TakeProfit,openPrice);
            if(buyProfit > 0) AdjustAboveStopLevel(_Symbol,buyProfit);

            if(buyStop > 0 || buyProfit > 0)
                Trade.ModifyPosition(_Symbol,buyStop,buyProfit);
            glSellPlaced = false;
        }
    }
}
```

We check the value of the newBar and timerOn variables to determine whether to check the trading conditions. If both are true, we proceed. The money management code is next. If the UseMoneyManagement input variable is true, we calculate the trade volume and save it to the tradeSize variable. Otherwise, we use the VerifyVolume() function to verify the FixedVolume setting and save the result to the tradeSize variable.

The buy order conditions are next. We've inserted two trade conditions, the position type and the value of glBuyPlaced. The PositionType() function will return the current position type, or -1 if there is no position open. Since we don't want to open an order if a position is already open, we only open an order if no buy position is open. The glBuyPlaced variable determines whether a buy position was previously open for this trade signal. We'll need to add more conditions to this if operator, but this is the minimum for now.

If the trade conditions are true, the Buy() function of the Trade object will place our order and set the glBuyPlaced variable to true if the order was placed successfully. If glBuyPlaced is true, then we proceed to modify the position.

After pausing execution with the Sleep() function and checking for an open position using the PositionSelect() function, we retrieve the position opening price and store that value in the openPrice variable. Next, we call the BuyStopLoss() function and save the value to the buyStop variable. The AdjustBelowStopLevel() function verifies the buyStop price and adjusts it if necessary. The same is done for the buyProfit variable. If buyStop or buyProfit is greater than zero, we call the ModifyPosition() function to add the stop loss and take profit to the buy position. Finally, the glSellPlaced variable is set to false.

The sell order placement code is very similar. Here is is for completeness:

```
// Open sell order
if(PositionType() != POSITION_TYPE_SELL && glSellPlaced == false)
{
    glSellPlaced = Trade.Sell(_Symbol,tradeSize);

    if(glSellPlaced == true)
    {
        do Sleep(100); while(PositionSelect(_Symbol) == false);
        double openPrice = PositionOpenPrice(_Symbol);

        double sellStop = SellStopLoss(_Symbol,StopLoss,openPrice);
        if(sellStop > 0) sellStop = AdjustAboveStopLevel(_Symbol,sellStop);

        double sellProfit = SellTakeProfit(_Symbol,TakeProfit,openPrice);
        if(sellProfit > 0) sellProfit = AdjustBelowStopLevel(_Symbol,sellProfit);

        if(sellStop > 0 || sellProfit > 0)
            Trade.ModifyPosition(_Symbol,sellStop,sellProfit);
        glBuyPlaced = false;
    }
}

} // Order placement end
```

After the sell order placement code, the final closing bracket finishes our order placement block. Remember that anything inside these brackets is only run if a new bar has just opened, the timer is active, or both features are disabled.

Finally, we have the break even and trailing stop code, and the end of the OnTick() event handler:

```
    // Break even
    if(UseBreakEven == true && PositionType(_Symbol) != -1)
    {
        Trail.BreakEven(_Symbol,BreakEvenProfit,LockProfit);
    }

    // Trailing stop
    if(UseTrailingStop == true && PositionType(_Symbol) != -1)
    {
        Trail.TrailingStop(_Symbol,TrailingStop,MinimumProfit,Step);
    }

}   // End of OnTick()
```

We have just created an expert advisor template that includes money management, a trade timer, a new bar check, a trailing stop, break even stop, error handling, price verification and more. Now all we need to do is add our indicators and our order opening and closing conditions.

We're going to create two expert advisors using this template. The first is a moving average cross, which is a trend trading system. The other will use the Bollinger Bands and RSI to create a counter-trend trading system.

Moving Average Cross

The moving average cross uses two moving averages, a fast MA and a slow MA. When the fast MA is greater than the slow MA, we open a buy position. When the fast MA is less than the slow MA, we open a sell position. Only one position is opened in each direction. When the moving averages cross in the opposite direction, we close any currently opened position and reset the glBuyPlaced and glSellPlaced variables.

Fig. 19.1 – The moving average cross system.

First, we need to declare two objects based on the CiMA class – one for the fast MA, and one for the slow MA:

```
#include <MqlBook\Indicators.mqh>
CiMA FastMA;
CiMA SlowMA;
```

The object that will be used for the fast MA is named `FastMA`, and of course, the object for the slow MA is named `SlowMA`. Next, we need to add the settings for the moving averages. The variable names for the fast MA settings are prefixed by "Fast", while those for the slow MA are prefixed by "Slow":

```
sinput string FaMA;            // Fast MA
input int FastMAPeriod = 10;
input ENUM_MA_METHOD FastMAMethod = 0;
input int FastMAShift = 0;
input ENUM_APPLIED_PRICE FastMAPrice = PRICE_CLOSE;

sinput string SlMA;            // Slow MA
input int SlowMAPeriod = 20;
input ENUM_MA_METHOD SlowMAMethod = 0;
input int SlowMAShift = 0;
input ENUM_APPLIED_PRICE SlowMAPrice = PRICE_CLOSE;
```

We have a 10 period SMA and a 20 period SMA set up by default. Next, we need to initialize the indicators. We do this in the `OnInit()` event handler:

```
int OnInit()
{
    FastMA.Init(_Symbol,_Period,FastMAPeriod,FastMAShift,FastMAMethod,FastMAPrice);
    SlowMA.Init(_Symbol,_Period,SlowMAPeriod,SlowMAShift,SlowMAMethod,SlowMAPrice);

    Trade.Deviation(Slippage);

    return(0);
}
```

Now all we need to do is use the `Main()` function of the `FastMA` and `SlowMA` objects to retrieve the moving average values. We do this in the `if` operators that hold the buy and sell order conditions:

```
// Open buy order
if(FastMA.Main(barShift) > SlowMA.Main(barShift) && PositionType() != POSITION_TYPE_BUY
    && glBuyPlaced == false)
{
    glBuyPlaced = Trade.Buy(_Symbol,tradeSize);

    if(glBuyPlaced == true)
    {
        do(Sleep(100)); while(PositionSelect(_Symbol) == false);
        double openPrice = PositionOpenPrice(_Symbol);
```

```
        double buyStop = BuyStopLoss(_Symbol,StopLoss,openPrice);
        if(buyStop > 0) AdjustBelowStopLevel(_Symbol,buyStop);

        double buyProfit = BuyTakeProfit(_Symbol,TakeProfit,openPrice);
        if(buyProfit > 0) AdjustBelowStopLevel(_Symbol,buyProfit);

        if(buyStop > 0 || buyProfit > 0) Trade.ModifyPosition(_Symbol,buyStop,buyProfit);
        glSellPlaced = false;
    }
}
```

If the fast MA is greater than the slow MA, no buy position is currently open, and glBuyPlaced is false, we open a buy order. Note the use of the barShift variable for the Main() function parameter. If TradeOnNewBar is set to true, barShift will always be 1. Therefore, we will be checking the value of the last bar, instead of the current bar. If TradeOnNewBar is set to false, barShift will be zero, and we will check the value of the current bar.

And here is the condition for a sell order:

```
// Open sell order
if(FastMA.Main(barShift) < SlowMA.Main(barShift) && PositionType() != POSITION_TYPE_SELL
    && glSellPlaced == false)
{
    // ...
}
```

That's it! We now have a functioning moving average cross with money management, trailing stop, break even stop and trade timer. You can view the code in the Moving Average Cross.mq5 file in the \MQL5\Experts\Mql5Book folder.

Bands/RSI Counter-trend System

Our second example will use two indicators – the RSI and the Bollinger Bands. This will be a counter-trend system, which means that we will look for price extremes and attempt to trade in the opposite direction. First, we look for the price to move outside of the outer Bollinger bands. Then we look for an overbought or oversold condition on the RSI. For example, if the price moves below the lower Bollinger band and the RSI is below 30, we would open a buy order. If the price is above the upper band and the RSI is above 70, we would open a sell order.

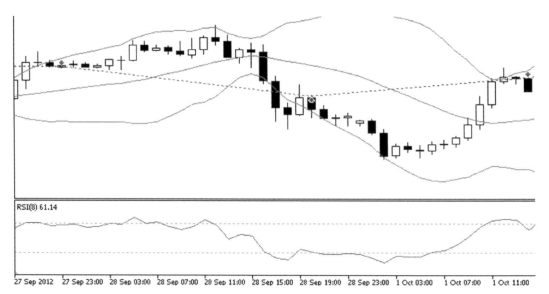

Fig. 19.2 – A counter-trend system using Bollinger Bands and RSI.

Let's start by declaring our indicator objects:

```
#include <Mql5Book\Indicators.mqh>
CiBollinger Bands;
CiRSI RSI;
```

Next, we'll add our input parameters:

```
sinput string BB;       // Bollinger Bands
input int BandsPeriod = 20;
input int BandsShift = 0;
input double BandsDeviation = 2;
input ENUM_APPLIED_PRICE BandsPrice = PRICE_CLOSE;

sinput string RS;  // RSI
input int RSIPeriod = 8;
input ENUM_APPLIED_PRICE RSIPrice = PRICE_CLOSE;
```

We'll add the indicator Init() functions to the OnInit() event handler:

```
int OnInit()
{
    Bands.Init(_Symbol,_Period,BandsPeriod,BandsShift,BandsDeviation,BandsPrice);
    RSI.Init(_Symbol,_Period,RSIPeriod,RSIPrice);
```

```
    Trade.Deviation(Slippage);

    return(0);
}
```

Finally, we'll add our buy and sell order conditions:

```
// Open buy order
if(Bar.Close(barShift) < Bands.Lower(barShift) && RSI.Main(barShift) < 30
    && PositionType() != POSITION_TYPE_BUY && glBuyPlaced == false)
{
    // ...
}

// Open sell order
if(Bar.Close(barShift) > Bands.Upper(barShift) && RSI.Main(barShift) > 70
    && PositionType() != POSITION_TYPE_SELL && glSellPlaced == false)
{
    // ...
}
```

If the close price of the current bar is less than the lower Bollinger band price, and the RSI reading is below 30, we open a buy order. If the close is greater than the upper Bollinger band, and the RSI is above 70, we open a sell order.

When testing this out in the Strategy Tester, we can see that there is room for improvement. For one, the orders usually enter too soon. Instead of waiting for the price to move back inside the bands, the order opens immediately. Secondly, this strategy could benefit by adding to an open position as new trade signals appear in the same direction.

Let's redefine our trading conditions: First, we look for the price to move outside of the bands, accompanied by an overbought or oversold condition on the RSI. Then we wait for the price to move back inside the bands, at which time we open the order.

We'll need to check for the trade condition in two steps. First, we check to see if the close price is outside of the bands and an overbought or oversold RSI condition exists. Then, we check if the price has moved inside the bands. The first set of conditions will need to be checked outside of the normal buy/sell order conditions. Let's create a global variable that will hold the signal value:

```
enum Signal
{
    SIGNAL_BUY,
    SIGNAL_SELL,
    SIGNAL_NONE,
};

Signal glSignal;
```

This is declared on the global scope of the program. We've created an enumeration named Signal with three values: SIGNAL_BUY, SIGNAL_SELL and SIGNAL_NONE. The glSignal global variable will hold one of these values at all times.

In the OnTick() event handler, before the order placement code, we will check for the first set of conditions. These are the same conditions we defined previously:

```
if(Bar.Close(barShift) < Bands.Lower(barShift) && RSI.Main(barShift) < 30)
    glSignal = SIGNAL_BUY;

else if(Bar.Close(barShift) > Bands.Upper(barShift) && RSI.Main(barShift) > 70)
    glSignal = SIGNAL_SELL;
```

If the close price is less than the lower Bollinger band and the RSI is less than 30, we set the value of glSignal to SIGNAL_BUY. This value is retained even when the condition is no longer true. The same is true for the sell condition, in which case we set the value of glSignal to SIGNAL_SELL.

Next, we check the order opening conditions. We check the value of glSignal, and determine whether the close price has recently crossed the upper or lower band:

```
if(glSignal == SIGNAL_BUY && Bar.Close(barShift) > Bands.Lower(barShift)
    && Bar.Close(barShift+1) <= Bands.Lower(barShift+1))
{
    // Open buy position
}
```

First, we check if glSignal contains the value of SIGNAL_BUY. Next, we check to see if the current bar's close price is above the lower band. Finally, we check to see if the previous bar's close price was below the lower band. Note that we add 1 to the barShift value to reference the previous bar.

We make the order opening condition very specific to ensure that our expert advisor will not keep opening orders once the price moves inside the bands. Notice that the PositionType() and glBuyPlaced conditions are gone. As long as the specific order condition is fulfilled, we will allow our expert advisor to open another order in the same direction as our current position.

For completeness, here are the sell conditions:

```
if(glSignal == SIGNAL_SELL && Bar.Close(barShift) < Bands.Upper(barShift)
    && Bar.Close(barShift+1) >= Bands.Upper(barShift+1))
{
    // Open sell position
}
```

One more thing: After we have opened the order and confirm that it has been placed, we reset the value of glSignal to SIGNAL_NONE, to avoid any errant orders:

```
glSignal = SIGNAL_NONE;
```

Now we have a counter-trend trading system that trades exactly according to our wishes. This example shows that it is necessary to be very specific about your trading conditions when programming expert advisors. Your trading method may appear to be obvious at first glance, but it may take a bit more work to get your expert advisor to trade it correctly. You can view the code for this trading system in the file Bands RSI Countertrend.mq5, located in \MQL5\Experts\Mql5Book\.

A Pending Order Template

The template that we created earlier in this chapter is for market orders. Occasionally you may want to program an expert advisor that places pending orders. We will create a template that places pending stop orders instead of market orders.

This file is named MQL Book Pending Template.mq5, and is located in the \MQL5\Experts\Mql5Book folder. We will note the changes over the template file detailed earlier in the chapter:

```
// Pending
#include <MqlBook\Pending.mqh>
CPending Pending;
```

We include the Pending.mqh include file that contains our pending order management functions, and create the Pending object based on the CPending class.

```
    // Open pending buy stop order
    if(PositionType() != POSITION_TYPE_BUY && glBuyPlaced == false)
    {
        double orderPrice = 0;
        orderPrice = AdjustAboveStopLevel(_Symbol,orderPrice);

        double buyStop = BuyStopLoss(_Symbol,StopLoss,orderPrice);
        double buyProfit = BuyTakeProfit(_Symbol,TakeProfit,orderPrice);

        glBuyPlaced = Trade.BuyStop(_Symbol,tradeSize,orderPrice,buyStop,buyProfit);

        if(glBuyPlaced == true)
        {
            glSellPlaced = false;
        }
    }


    // Open pending sell stop order
    if(PositionType() != POSITION_TYPE_SELL && glSellPlaced == false)
    {
        double orderPrice = 0;
        orderPrice = AdjustBelowStopLevel(_Symbol,orderPrice);

        double sellStop = SellStopLoss(_Symbol,StopLoss,orderPrice);
        double sellProfit = SellTakeProfit(_Symbol,TakeProfit,orderPrice);

        glSellPlaced = Trade.SellStop(_Symbol,tradeSize,orderPrice,sellStop,sellProfit);

        if(glSellPlaced == true)
        {
            glBuyPlaced = false;
        }
    }
```

Above is the pending buy and sell order placement code. The orderPrice variable must be filled with the pending order opening price by the programmer. The order price is checked for correctness, the stop loss and take profit are calculated relative to it, and the pending stop order is placed. Finally, the glBuyPlaced or glSellPlaced variable is set to false.

Breakout Trading System

Let's create a pending order trading system using this template. We will create a trading system that finds the highest and lowest price of the last *X* bars. When the trade timer starts, a pending buy stop order will be placed at the highest high and a pending sell stop order will be placed at the lowest low. The stop loss for both orders will be placed at the opposite price. Only one trade in each direction will be placed, and all trades will be closed at the timer end time.

For this strategy, we will remove the new bar check, the trailing stop and the break even features. We will also remove the StopLoss, Slippage and UseTimer settings. Let's start with the #include directives:

```
// Trade
#include <MqlBook\Trade.mqh>
CTrade Trade;

// Price
#include <MqlBook\Price.mqh>

// Money management
#include <MqlBook\MoneyManagement.mqh>

// Timer
#include <MqlBook\Timer.mqh>
CTimer Timer;

// Pending
#include <MqlBook\Pending.mqh>
CPending Pending;
```

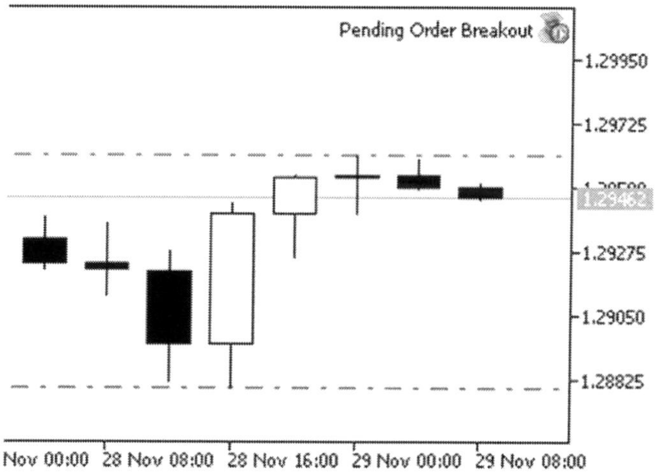

Fig. 19.3 – A pending breakout trading system.

These are the include files and objects that we will need for this strategy. Next, let's examine the input variables:

```
sinput string MM;  // Money Management
input bool UseMoneyManagement = true;
input double RiskPercent = 2;
input double FixedVolume = 0.1;

sinput string TS;  // Trade Settings
input int HighLowBars = 8;
input int TakeProfit = 0;

sinput string TI;  // Timer
input int StartHour = 8;
input int StartMinute = 0;
input int EndHour = 20;
input int EndMinute = 0;
input bool UseLocalTime = false;
```

We added a new input variable named HighLowBars. This is the number of bars that we are going to search (starting from the current bar) to find the highest high and lowest low. We grouped it in with the TakeProfit variable, added a static input variable and labeled the group as "Trade Settings".

Let's skip ahead to the order placement code. We will come back to the timer code later:

```
// Order placement
if(timerOn == true)
{
    // Highest high, lowest low
    double hHigh = HighestHigh(_Symbol,_Period,HighLowBars);
    double lLow = LowestLow(_Symbol,_Period,HighLowBars);

    double diff = (hHigh - lLow) / _Point;

    // Money management
    double tradeSize;
    if(UseMoneyManagement == true)
        tradeSize = MoneyManagement(_Symbol,FixedVolume,RiskPercent,(int)diff);
    else tradeSize = VerifyVolume(_Symbol,FixedVolume);
```

If the trade timer is active, we will start by finding the highest high and lowest low. We use the HighestHigh() and LowestLow() functions that we defined in our Price.mqh include file. The HighLowBars parameter indicates the number of bars to search. The return values are saved in the hHigh and lLow variables, respectively.

Since we are using our money management code, we need to figure out the stop loss in points to be able to calculate the lot size. We do this by subtracting the lowest low (lLow) from the highest high (hHigh) and dividing it by the current symbol's _Point value. The result is saved to the variable diff.

The money management code is the same as the previous expert advisors, except we pass the diff variable as the final parameter to the MoneyManagement() function. The (int) in front of the diff variable simply converts the value of diff to an integer, rounding it off and preventing the "possible loss of data due to type conversion" warning that occurs when we implicitly change data types.

Here is the pending buy and sell stop order code:

```
// Open pending buy stop order
if(Pending.BuyStop(_Symbol) == 0 && glBuyPlaced == false)
{
    double orderPrice = hHigh;
    orderPrice = AdjustAboveStopLevel(_Symbol,orderPrice);
```

```
    double buyStop = lLow;
    double buyProfit = BuyTakeProfit(_Symbol,TakeProfit,orderPrice);

    glBuyPlaced = Trade.BuyStop(_Symbol,tradeSize,orderPrice,buyStop,buyProfit);
}

// Open pending sell stop order
if(Pending.SellStop(_Symbol) == 0 && glSellPlaced == false)
{
    double orderPrice = lLow;
    orderPrice = AdjustBelowStopLevel(_Symbol,orderPrice);

    double sellStop = hHigh;
    double sellProfit = SellTakeProfit(_Symbol,TakeProfit,orderPrice);

    glSellPlaced = Trade.SellStop(_Symbol,tradeSize,orderPrice,sellStop,sellProfit);
}
```

Let's look at the buy stop order code first. If the `Pending.BuyStop()` function returns zero – indicating that no pending orders are open – and the `glBuyPlaced` variable is `false`, we proceed with placing the order. The `orderPrice` variable is assigned the value of `hHigh`. This is our order opening price. We check it using the `AdjustAboveStopLevel()` function to make sure it is not too close to the current price. The `buyStop` variable is set to `lLow`, which is our stop loss. The take profit is calculated, if it has been specified. The `Trade.BuyStop()` function places our pending order, and if it is successful, the `glBuyPlaced` variable is set to true.

When the trade timer is first activated for the day, a buy and sell stop order are placed. No more orders are placed for the day, and all orders are closed at the timer end time. Let's take a look at the timer code. This goes before the order placement code above:

```
// Timer
bool timerOn = Timer.DailyTimer(StartHour,StartMinute,EndHour,EndMinute,UseLocalTime);

if(timerOn == false)
{
    if(PositionSelect(_Symbol) == true) Trade.Close(_Symbol);

    int total = Pending.TotalPending(_Symbol);
    if(total > 0)
    {
        ulong tickets[];
        Pending.GetTickets(_Symbol,tickets);
```

```
            for(int i=0; i<total; i++)
            {
                Trade.Delete(tickets[i]);
            }
        }

        glBuyPlaced = false;
        glSellPlaced = false;
    }
```

First, we declare the timerOn variable, and set it using the DailyTimer() function. If the value of timerOn is false, indicating that the timer is off, we need to close any open orders and reset our glBuyPlaced and glSellPlaced variables. First, we check the output of the PositionSelect() function. If it returns true, we use the Trade.Close() function to close the current position.

Next, we need to check for any open pending orders. The Pending.TotalPending() function returns the number of open pending orders, and saves it to the total variable. If total is greater than zero, we process the pending orders.

We declare a ulong array named tickets[] that holds the ticket numbers of any open pending orders. The Pending.GetTickets() function fills the tickets[] array with the ticket numbers. We iterate through the tickets[] array using a for loop, and delete each open order using the Trade.Delete() function. Finally, we set glBuyPlaced and glSellPlaced to true.

You can view the code for this expert advisor in the \Experts\Mql5Book\Pending Order Breakout.mq5 file. We've just demonstrated how to create several basic strategies using the techniques we've examined in this book. Although some advanced strategies will require a bit more modification to the template file, the basics are there so you can easily implement your strategy without having to code a new strategy from scratch.

Chapter 20 - Tips & Tricks

This chapter covers additional MQL5 features that may be useful in your expert advisor projects. We'll discuss methods to inform users of errors and trade events; work with chart objects in MetaTrader; learn how to read and write to CSV files; work with terminal variables, and learn how to stop execution of an expert advisor and close the trade terminal.

User Information and Interaction

It is sometimes necessary to inform the user of trade actions, errors or other events. This section examines dialog boxes, email and mobile notifications, sound alerts and chart comments.

Alert() Function

If you need to alert the user to an error or other adverse condition, the built-in Alert dialog is ideal. The Alert dialog window shows a running log of alert messages, indicating the time and symbol for each. If sound events are enabled in the *Options* tab of the *Tools* menu, then an alert sound will play when the dialog appears.

The Alert() function is used to show the alert dialog. The Alert() function takes any number of arguments, of any type. We've been using the Alert() function all throughout our include files. For example, here is an Alert() function call when an error occurs in our CTrade::OpenPosition() function in Trade.mqh:

```
Alert("Open market order: Error ",result.retcode," - ",errDesc);
```

This function has several arguments, including strings and an integer variable, all separated by commas.

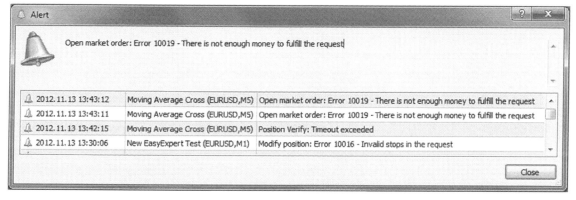

Fig. 20.1 – The *Alert* dialog.

MessageBox() Function

If you prefer something a little more elaborate, or if you need to accept user input, the MessageBox() function allows you to display a standard Windows dialog box with user-defined text, caption, icons and buttons. Here is the definition of the MessageBox() function:

```
int  MessageBox(
   string  text,              // Message text
   string  caption=NULL,      // Title bar caption
   int     flags=0            // Button and icon constants
   );
```

The text parameter is the text to show in the dialog window. The caption parameter is the text to show in the title bar of the dialog window. The flags parameter defines which buttons to show, as well as icons and default buttons. The MessageBox() flags can be viewed in the *MQL5 Reference* under *Standard Constants... > Input/Output Constants > MessageBox*. Here are a few of the most commonly-used button flags:

- **MB_OK** – OK button

- **MB_OKCANCEL** – OK and Cancel buttons

- **MB_YESNO** – Yes and No buttons

- **MB_RETRYCANCEL** – Retry and Cancel buttons

Let's create a simple message box with text, a caption and yes/no buttons. For example, if you want to prompt to user to place an order when a trading signal is received:

```
int place = MessageBox("Place the order?","Confirmation",MB_YESNO);
```

This will create the message box dialog shown to the right.

We can add context to our message box by adding an icon. Since we are prompting the user with a question, we'll use the question mark icon. Here are the flags for the message box icons:

- **MB_ICONERROR** – A red error icon.

- **MB_ICONQUESTION** – A question mark icon.

- **MB_ICONWARNING** – An exclamation/warning icon.

- **MB_ICONINFORMATION** – An information icon.

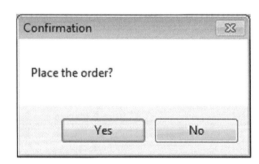

Fig. 20.2 – The *Message Box* dialog.

258

Here is how we would add the question mark icon to our message box. Flags must be separated with a pipe character (|):

```
int place = MessageBox("Place the order?","Confirmation",MB_YESNO|MB_ICONQUESTION);
```

Fig. 20.3 to the right shows the Message Box dialog with the question mark icon.

When presented with the message box, the user will click a button and the box will close. If the message box is a simple information or error message with a single OK button, then we do not need to do anything else. But if the message box has several buttons, we will need to retrieve the value of the button that the user pressed and take appropriate action.

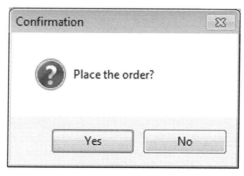

Fig. 20.3 – The *Message Box* dialog with icon.

In the example below, the place integer variable will hold the return value of the MessageBox() function. The return value for the Yes button is IDYES, while the return value for the No button is IDNO. If the user clicked Yes, then we need to proceed to place the order:

```
int place = MessageBox("Place the order?","Confirmation",MB_YESNO|MB_ICONQUESTION);

if(place == IDYES)
{
    // Open position
}
```

You can view additional return value constants for MessageBox() buttons in the *MQL5 Reference* under *Standard Constants... > Input/Output Constants > MessageBox*.

SendMail() Function

If you'd like your expert advisor to send you an email whenever a trade is placed, simply add the SendMail() function to your expert advisor after the order placement has been confirmed. You will need to enable email notifications in MetaTrader under the *Tools* menu > *Options* > *Email* tab. Under the *Email* tab, you will enter your email server information and your email address.

The SendMail() function takes two parameters. The first is the subject of the message, and the second is the message text. For example, if you want to send an email just after a buy position has been opened:

```
#include <Mq15Book\Trade.mqh>

if(PositionSelect(_Symbol) == true)
{
    string subject = "Buy position opened on "+_Symbol;
    string message = "Price: "+PositionOpenPrice()+", SL: "+PositionStopLoss()+",
        TP: "+PositionTakeProfit();
    SendMail(subject,message);
}
```

If the PositionSelect() function returns true, indicating that a position has been successfully opened, we will prepare the subject and message body of the email and pass those string variables to the SendMail() function. An email will be sent to the email address defined in the *Email* tab of the *Tools* menu > *Options* dialog.

Sending Mobile Notifications

A mobile edition of MetaTrader is available for iPhone and Android devices. Your expert advisors can send trade notifications to the mobile MetaTrader terminal on your smartphone by using the SendNotification() function. You will need to configure MetaTrader to send notifications under the *Tools* menu > *Options* > *Notifications* tab. In the *Notifications* tab, you will enter your MetaQuotes ID, which you can retrieve from your mobile version of MetaTrader.

The SendNotification() function takes one parameter, a string indicating the text to send. You can use the SendNotification() function anywhere you would use the SendMail() function. Here's an example:

```
#include <Mq15Book\Trade.mqh>

if(PositionSelect(_Symbol) == true)
{
    string message = "Buy position opened on "+_Symbol+". Price: "+PositionOpenPrice()+",
        SL: "+PositionStopLoss()+",TP: "+PositionTakeProfit();
    SendNotification(message);
}
```

Playing Sound

The PlaySound() function will play a WAV sound file located in the \Sounds directory. This can be used to play an audible alert when a trade is placed, or whenever you want the user's attention. MetaTrader comes with several sound files, but you can find more online.

If you want the user to be able to choose the sound file, use an input string variable to enter the file name:

```
input string SoundFile = "alert.wav";

// ...

PlaySound(SoundFile);
```

Comment() Function

The Comment() function will display text in the top left corner of the chart. This is useful for informing users of actions taken by the expert advisor, such as modifying or closing orders. We've been using the Comment() function throughout our expert advisors to write informative comments to the chart. Here's an example from the CTrade::OpenPosition() function in Trade.mqh:

```
if(checkCode == CHECK_RETCODE_OK)
{
    Comment(orderType," position opened at ",result.price," on ",pSymbol);
    return(true);
}
```

The problem with using chart comments is that all programs have access to this function. So if you have an indicator and an expert advisor that both write comments to the chart using the Comment() function, they will overwrite each other. If you need to display information on the chart that is always present, then consider using chart objects.

Chart Objects

Chart objects consist of lines, technical analysis tools, shapes, arrows, labels and other graphical objects. You can insert objects on a chart using the *Insert* menu > *Objects* submenu. MQL5 has a variety of functions for creating, manipulating and retrieving information from chart objects.

Creating and Modifying Objects

The ObjectCreate() function is used for creating new chart objects. Here is the function definition for ObjectCreate():

```
bool  ObjectCreate(
    long         chart_id,      // chart identifier
    string       name,          // object name
    ENUM_OBJECT  type,          // object type
    sub_window   nwin,          // window index
    datetime     time1,         // time of the first anchor point
```

```
    double        price1,        // price of the first anchor point
    ...
    datetime      timeN=0,       // time of the N-th anchor point
    double        priceN=0,      // price of the N-th anchor point
);
```

The chart_id parameter specifies the chart to create the object on. Since we will always be working with the current chart, chart_id will be 0. The name parameter is the name of the object to create. We will need to reference this name anytime we need to use the object. The type parameter is the type of object to create. It takes a value of the ENUM_OBJECT enumeration type. The object types can be viewed in the *MQL5 Reference* under *Standard Constants... > Objects Constants > Object Types*.

The nwin parameter is the index of the subwindow of the chart. Subwindows are opened by indicators such as RSI and stochastics that display in a separate window. Since we will be creating objects in the main chart window, nwin will be 0. The time1 and price1 parameters are the time and price for the first anchor point of the object. Most objects have one or more anchor points, although some do not use them, or use only one or the other. The first set of anchor points must always be specified, even if they are not used.

If the object uses more than one set of anchor points, they must also be specified. For example, most trend line objects use two anchor points. So in the ObjectCreate() function, a second set of anchor points would be passed to the function. You can view the number of anchor points for each type of object in the MQL5 Reference under *Object Functions > ObjectCreate*.

The ObjectCreate() function will create the object in the location specified. However, we will still need to set the properties of the object. The ObjectSet...() functions are used to set the object's properties. There are three ObjectSet...() functions: ObjectSetInteger(), ObjectSetDouble() and ObjectSetString(). All three functions share the same parameters. Let's look at the function definition of ObjectSetInteger():

```
    bool  ObjectSetInteger(
        long    chart_id,        // chart identifier
        string  name,            // object name
        int     prop_id,         // property
        long    prop_value       // value
    );
```

As discussed previously, chart_id will be 0. The name parameter is the name of the object to modify. The prop_id parameter takes a value of the ENUM_OBJECT_PROPERTY_INTEGER enumeration, which indicates the property to modify. Finally, the prop_value parameter is the value to set. The ENUM_OBJECT_PROPERTY_INTEGER constants can be viewed in the *MQL5 Reference* under *Standard Constants... > Objects Constants > Object Properties*.

As an example, let's create a trend line object and set a few of its properties. The object type for a trend line is OBJ_TREND. Since a trend line has two anchor points, we will need to pass two sets of time and price values. We'll assume that the time1, time2, price1 and price2 variables are filled with the appropriate values:

```
datetime time1, time2;
double price1, price2;

ObjectCreate(0,"Trend",OBJ_TREND,0,time1,price1,time2,price2);
```

This creates a trend line object named "Trend" on the current chart. Next, let's modify a few of the properties of our trend line. We're going to modify the color, the style and the ray right properties:

```
ObjectSetInteger(0,"Trend",OBJPROP_COLOR,clrGreen);
ObjectSetInteger(0,"Trend",OBJPROP_STYLE,STYLE_DASH);
ObjectSetInteger(0,"Trend",OBJPROP_RAY_RIGHT,true);
```

The first ObjectSetInteger() function call adjusts the color property, using the OBJPROP_COLOR constant. The value used is the color constant for green, clrGreen. The second call of the function adjusts the line style, using the OBJPROP_STYLE constant. The value is STYLE_DASH, a constant of the ENUM_LINE_STYLE type. Finally, we use the OBJPROP_RAY_RIGHT constant to set the ray right property to true. The ray right property extends the trend line to the right beyond the second anchor point.

Now we have a green dashed trend line that extends to the right. All of the examples above use integer types to adjust the properties. The type used for each object property constant is listed in the *MQL5 Reference* under *Standard Constants... > Objects Constants > Object Properties*.

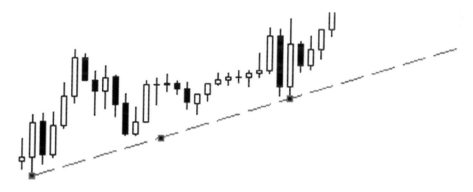

Fig. 20.4 – A trend line object with the color, style and ray right properties set.

If you need to move an object, the ObjectMove() function allows you to adjust one of the anchor points of an object. Here is the function definition for ObjectMove():

```
bool  ObjectMove(
    long       chart_id,        // chart identifier
    string     name,            // object name
    int        point_index,     // anchor point number
    datetime   time,            // time
    double     price            // price
    );
```

The name parameter is the name of the object to modify. The point_index parameter is the anchor point to modify. Anchor point numbers start at 0, so the first anchor point would be 0, the second would be 1, and so on. The time and price parameters modify the time and price for the specified anchor point.

Retrieving Time and Price From Line Objects

When using line objects such as trend lines or channels, you may need to retrieve the price value of a line at a particular bar. Assuming that we know the timestamp of the bar, we can easily retrieve the price. The ObjectGetValueByTime() function will retrieve the price for a specified time:

```
double  ObjectGetValueByTime(
    long       chart_id,        // chart identifier
    string     name,            // object name
    datetime   time,            // time
    int        line_id          // line number
    );
```

As always, the chart_id is 0 for the current chart. The name parameter is the name of a line object on our chart. The time parameter is the timestamp of a bar that intersects the line. The line_id parameter is for channel objects that have several lines. For a trend line, line_id would be 0.

Using the "Trend" line object we created above, here is how we would retrieve the price for the current bar. We will use the CPrice::Time() function we created earlier in the book:

```
double trendPrice = ObjectGetValueByTime(0,"Trend",Price.Time(),0);
```

The ObjectGetValueByTime() function will return the value of the trend line for the current bar and save the result to the trendPrice variable.

Now, what if you have a price, and you want to know what bar comes closest to that price? The ObjectGetTimeByValue() function will return the timestamp of the bar where a line object intersects a given price:

```
datetime  ObjectGetTimeByValue(
    long    chart_id,      // chart identifier
    string  name,          // object name
    double  value,         // price
    int     line_id        // line number
    );
```

The `value` parameter is the price to search for. The function will return the timestamp of the closest bar where the line intersects the price:

```
datetime trendTime = ObjectGetTimeByValue(0,"Trend",1.265,0);
```

Label and Arrow Objects

Earlier in the chapter, we talked about using the `Comment()` function to write information to the current chart. The *label* object can also be used for this purpose. Unlike chart comments, label objects can be placed anywhere on the chart, and they can use any color or font that you like.

The object type constant for the label object is `OBJ_LABEL`. Label objects do not use anchor points, but rather use the *corner, x-distance* and *y-distance* properties for positioning. Here's an example of the creation and positioning of a label object:

```
ObjectCreate(0,"Label",OBJ_LABEL,0,0,0);

ObjectSetInteger(0,"Label",OBJPROP_CORNER,1);
ObjectSetInteger(0,"Label",OBJPROP_XDISTANCE,20);
ObjectSetInteger(0,"Label",OBJPROP_YDISTANCE,40);
```

We've created a label object named "`Label`" and set the position to the bottom left corner using the `ObjectSetInteger()` function with the `OBJPROP_CORNER` property. The label is 20 pixels from the left border (`OBJPROP_XDISTANCE`) and 40 pixels above the bottom border (`OBJPROP_YDISTANCE`).

Note that the `time` and `price` parameters for the `ObjectCreate()` function are set to 0, since they are not used when creating label objects. The corners are labeled from 0 to 3, starting counter-clockwise from the top-left corner. A value of 1 is the lower-left corner, while 3 would be the upper-right corner. The x-distance and y-distance are set in pixels from the specified corner.

Next, we'll need to set the color, font and text of the label object:

```
        double price = Bid();

        ObjectSetInteger(0,"Label",OBJPROP_COLOR,clrWhite);
        ObjectSetString(0,"Label",OBJPROP_FONT,"Arial");
        ObjectSetInteger(0,"Label",OBJPROP_FONTSIZE,10);
        ObjectSetString(0,"Label",OBJPROP_TEXT,"Bid: "+(string)price);
```

We've set the color of the label object to white, using 10 point Arial font. The text of the label contains the current Bid price. Every time this code is run, the label object will be updated with the current Bid price.

In summary, the label object is ideal for printing useful information to the chart. The object is anchored to the chart window itself, and will not move if the chart is scrolled. The font, color, position and text are fully adjustable.

Fig. 20.5 – The label object.

The last object type we'll examine is the arrow object. You may wish to draw an arrow on the chart when an order is placed. MQL5 defines two arrow object types that are useful for marking buy and sell signals – OBJ_ARROW_BUY and OBJ_ARROW_SELL. Arrow objects use one anchor point – the price and time where the arrow should be placed:

```
        string time = Price.Time();
        double price = Ask();

        ObjectCreate(0,"BuyArrow"+time,OBJ_ARROW_BUY,0,time,price);
```

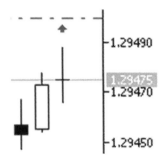

The example above will set a buy arrow object at the current Ask price on the current bar. We append the time of the current bar to the object name so that each arrow we draw will have a unique name. This code would be called after a trade has been placed.

Fig. 20.6 – The *Buy Arrow* object.

Deleting Objects

To delete an object, simply call the ObjectDelete() function and pass the chart_id (usually 0) and the object name:

```
        ObjectDelete(0,"Label");
```

To delete all objects from a chart, use the ObjectsDeleteAll() function. You can choose to delete only objects of a certain type or from certain subwindows. To delete all objects from the current chart, use this call:

```
        ObjectsDeleteAll(0);
```

It is a good idea to call this function from your program's `OnDeinit()` function to ensure that all objects are deleted when a program is removed from the chart.

File Functions

MQL5 has a set of functions for reading and writing to files. You can, for example, create a log of your expert advisor trades, or import/export trading signals to a file. All files must be in the `\MQL5\Experts\Files` folder of your MetaTrader 5 installation.

We will examine how to read and write to a CSV file. A CSV (*comma separated value*) file contains data much like a spreadsheet. You can create and view CSV files in programs such as Microsoft Excel or OpenOffice Calc, as well as any text editor. In this example, our CSV file will record information about trades. We will write the symbol, open price, stop loss, take profit and open time of a trade to each line of the file. We will then read that information back into our program.

The `FileOpen()` function opens files for reading and writing. If the file does not exist, it will be created. Here is the definition of the `FileOpen()` function:

```
int  FileOpen(
    string  file_name,           // File name
    int     open_flags,          // Combination of flags
    short   delimiter='\t'       // Delimiter
    uint    codepage=CP_ACP      // Code page
    );
```

The `file_name` parameter is the name of the file to open in the `\MQL5\Experts\Files` directory. The `open_flags` parameter contains a combination of flags describing the file operations. The file opening flags can be viewed in the *MQL5 Reference* under *Standard Constants... > Input/Output Constants > File Opening Flags*. The `delimiter` parameter is the field delimiter for a CSV file. The default is the tab character, but we will use a comma. The `codepage` parameter will be left at its default.

The `FileOpen()` function returns an integer that will serve as the file handle. Every time we perform an operation on the file, we will need to reference the file handle. For the file opening flags, we will be using a combination of `FILE_READ`, `FILE_WRITE` and `FILE_CSV`.

Writing to a CSV File

The `FileWrite()` function is used to write a line of data to a CSV file. The example below shows how to open a file, write a line of data to it, and then close the file:

```
    string symbol;
    double openPrice, sl, tp;
    datetime openTime;

    // ...

    int fileHandle = FileOpen("Trades.csv",FILE_READ|FILE_WRITE|FILE_CSV,",");
    FileSeek(fileHandle,0,SEEK_END);
    FileWrite(fileHandle,symbol,openPrice,sl,tp,openTime);
    FileClose(fileHandle);
```

The symbol, openPrice, sl, tp and openTime variables will contain the information to write to the file. We'll assume that these variables are filled with the appropriate values. The FileOpen() function creates a file named "Trades.csv". The flags specify read and write privileges to a CSV file. The delimiter will be a comma. The file handle is saved to the fileHandle variable.

You will need to add the FILE_READ flag when using the FILE_WRITE flag, even if you are not reading information from the file, because the FileSeek() function will not work without it. The FileSeek() function moves the file pointer to a specified point in the file. In this example, the pointer is moved to the end of the file. The first parameter of the FileSeek() function is the file handle, the second is the shift in bytes, and the third parameter is the start location. The SEEK_END constant indicates that we will move the file pointer to the end of the file. When opening a file that already has data in it, failing to move the file pointer to the end of the file will result in data being overwritten. Therefore, we always use FileSeek() to locate the end of the file before writing data.

The FileWrite() function writes a line of data to the CSV file. The first parameter is the file handle. The remaining parameters are the data to write to the file, in the order that they appear. Up to 63 additional parameters can be specified, and they can be of any type. The delimiter specified in the FileOpen() function will be placed between each data field in the CSV file, and a new line character (\r\n) will be written at the end of the line.

Finally, the FileClose() function will close the file. Be sure to close a file when you are done using it, or else you may not be able to open it in another program. If you plan on keeping a file open for an extended period of time, or are doing subsequent read/write operations, use the FileFlush() function to write the data to the file without closing it.

Here is what our Trades.csv file will look with several lines of data written to it:

```
EURUSD,1.2345,1.2325,1.2375,2012.11.15 04:17:41
EURUSD,1.2357,1.2337,1.2397,2012.11.15 04:20:04
EURUSD,1.2412,1.2398,1.2432,2012.11.15 04:21:35
```

From left to right, each line contains the trade symbol, opening price, stop loss, take profit and open time, each separated by a comma. After each line is written to the file, a new line is started.

If you need to write several lines of data to a file at once, place the `FileWrite()` function inside a loop, and loop it as many times as you need to. The example below assumes that we have several arrays, each with the same number of elements, that are properly sized and filled with data. (You could also use a structure array for this.) We use a `for` loop to write each line of data to the file:

```
string symbol[];
double openPrice[], sl[], tp[];
datetime openTime[];

// ...

int fileHandle = FileOpen("Trades.csv",FILE_READ|FILE_WRITE|FILE_CSV,",");
FileSeek(fileHandle,0,SEEK_END);

for(int i = 0; i < ArraySize(symbol); i++)
{
    FileWrite(fileHandle,symbol[i],openPrice[i],sl[i],tp[i],openTime[i]);
}

FileClose(fileHandle);
```

We use the `ArraySize()` function on the `symbol[]` array to determine the number of times to run the loop. The `i` increment variable is the array index. If each array has five elements, for example, we write five lines of data to the file.

Reading From a CSV File

Next, we'll examine how to read data from a CSV file. The `FileRead...()` functions are used to read data from a field and convert it to an appropriate type. There are four functions used to read data from a CSV file:

- **FileReadString()** - Reads a `string` from a CSV file.

- **FileReadBool()** - Reads a string from a CSV file and converts it to `bool` type.

- **FileReadDatetime()** - Reads a string from a CSV file in the format *yyyy.mm.dd hh:mm:ss* and converts it to `datetime` type.

- **FileReadNumber()** - Reads a string from a CSV file and converts it to `double` type.

If you are reading an integer from a CSV file using the `FileReadNumber()` function, you will need to convert it to the appropriate type if you need to use it as an integer type in your program.

269

If we examine the fields in our Trades.csv file, we have a string, three double values and a datetime value on each line. We will need to read each field of data from the file using the appropriate function so that it is converted to the correct type. We're going to read the entire contents of the file, line by line, and save the result to a structure array:

```
struct Trades
{
    string symbol;
    double openPrice;
    double sl;
    double tp;
    datetime openTime;
};

Trades trade[];
int i;

int fileHandle = FileOpen("Trades.csv",FILE_READ|FILE_CSV,",");

while(FileIsEnding(fileHandle) == false)
{
    ArrayResize(trade,ArraySize(trade) + 1);

    trade[i].symbol = FileReadString(fileHandle);
    trade[i].openPrice = FileReadNumber(fileHandle);
    trade[i].sl = FileReadNumber(fileHandle);
    trade[i].tp = FileReadNumber(fileHandle);
    trade[i].openTime = FileReadDatetime(fileHandle);

    i++;
}

FileClose(fileHandle);
```

First, we create a structure named Trades to hold the data read from the CSV file. We create an array object named trade[], and initialize the incrementor variable i. We open the Trades.csv file using the FILE_READ and FILE_CSV flags. The while loop will read each line of data from the file, one field at a time.

The FileIsEnding() function returns a value of true if the end of the file has been reached, and false otherwise. As long as the end of the file has not been reached, we continue reading the next line. The ArrayResize() function resizes our trade[] array, one element at a time. We call the ArraySize() function to get the current size of the trade[] array and add 1 to it to increase the size.

The `FileRead...()` functions reads each field of data from the file and converts it to the appropriate type. The result is saved to the appropriate member variable of our `trades[]` array. After the current line has been read, we increment the `i` variable and check the `FileIsEnding()` condition again. After the loop exits, we close the file. We can now access the data read from our CSV file using the `trade[]` array object.

Global Variables

MetaTrader has the ability to save variables to the terminal, which remain even if the terminal is shut down. These are referred to as *Global Variables*. Global Variables that are saved to the terminal are deleted after one month. You can view the Global Variables saved to your terminal by clicking the *Tools* menu > *Global Variables,* or by pressing the F3 key.

Do not confuse the Global Variables of the terminal with variables that we define on the global scope of a program! Global variables in a program are available only to that program, while the Global Variables of the terminal are available to all programs. You can use MetaTrader's Global Variables to save information about your program's state in the event that execution is interrupted.

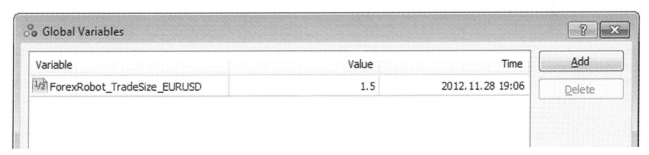

Fig. 20.7 – The *Global Variables* window.

The `GlobalVariableSet()` function is used to save a Global Variable to the terminal. It has two parameters – the `name` of the variable, and the `value` to assign to it. Make sure that you use unique names for your Global Variables. For example, you could use the name of your trading system, followed by the name of the variable and the symbol that it is placed on:

```
string varName = "ForexRobot_TradeSize_"+_Symbol;
// Example: ForexRobot_TradeSize_EURUSD

GlobalVariableSet(varName,1.5);
```

In this example, our Global Variable name is `ForexRobot_TradeSize_EURUSD`. The current symbol is EURUSD, so we will be able to identify our Global Variable based on the symbol we are currently trading. We would save this Global Variable to the terminal any time its value is set or changed.

If our terminal shut down unexpectedly (a computer crash or power failure), we can read the contents of the Global Variable using `GlobalVariableGet()`, and continue where we left off. We would usually do this in our `OnInit()` event handler:

```
// OnInit()
string varName = "ForexRobot_TradeSize_"+_Symbol;
double tradeSize = GlobalVariableGet(varName);
```

To prevent our program from using outdated Global Variables, we will need to delete them if necessary. If we manually remove our expert advisor from the chart, then we need to delete the Global Variable(s) that are currently saved. We do this in the `OnDeinit()` event handler using the `GlobalVariableDel()` function:

```
void OnDeinit(const int reason)
{
    string varName = "ForexRobot_TradeSize_"+_Symbol;
    GlobalVariableDel(varName);
}
```

The `OnDeinit()` event handler is called for many reasons. Obviously, it is called if the program is removed from the chart, the chart is closed, or the terminal is shut down. But it is also called if the input parameters are changed, the period of the chart is changed, or a template is applied. We don't want to delete any Global Variables when this occurs. So it is necessary to check the reason for deinitialization before deleting any Global Variables.

The `reason` parameter of the `OnDeinit()` function contains the reason for deinitialization. You can view the Deinitialization Codes in the *MQL5 Reference* under *Standard Constants... > Named Constants > Uninitalization Reason Codes.* The codes we are concerned with are REASON_CHARTCHANGE, REASON_PARAMETERS, and REASON_TEMPLATE. If the `reason` parameter contains any of these codes, we will not delete the Global Variable:

```
void OnDeinit(const int reason)
{
    if(reason != REASON_CHARTCHANGE && reason != REASON_PARAMETERS
        && reason != REASON_TEMPLATE)
    {
        string varName = "ForexRobot_TradeSize_"+_Symbol;
        GlobalVariableDel(varName);
    }
}
```

Stopping Execution

If you wish to stop the execution of an expert advisor programmatically, use the ExpertRemove() function. Once the current event is finished executing, the expert advisor will stop its operation and remove itself from the chart.

If you wish to close the terminal, the TerminalClose() function will close MetaTrader. The TerminalClose() function takes one parameter, a deinitialization code that will be passed to the OnDeinit() function. When calling the TerminalClose() function, it must be followed by the return operator:

```
TerminalClose(REASON_CLOSE);
return;
```

Chapter 21 - Indicators, Scripts & Libraries

Indicators

In Chapter 17, we examined how to add indicators to our expert advisor programs. MQL5 allows you to create your own custom indicators as well. In this section, we will create a custom indicator that will plot a price channel using the highest high and lowest low of the last *x* bars. This is also referred to as a *Donchian channel*.

Drawing Styles

MQL5 has over a dozen different drawing styles for indicator lines. The drawing style determines how the line will appear in the chart window. Here are a few of the most common drawing styles:

- **DRAW_LINE** – This is the most common drawing style, and consists of a single line of the specified color. The Moving Average, RSI and many other indicators use this drawing style.

- **DRAW_HISTOGRAM** – The histogram drawing style is typically used by oscillators such as the MACD, the OsMA and the Bill Williams' oscillators. It consists of vertical lines oscillating around a zero axis.

- **DRAW_SECTION** – The section drawing style connects prices on non-consecutive bars with an unbroken line. The ZigZag custom indicator that comes with MetaTrader is the typical example of this drawing style.

- **DRAW_ARROW** – The arrow drawing style will draw arrow objects on the chart. The Fractals indicator uses arrow objects to indicate swing highs and lows.

- **DRAW_NONE** – Used for indicator buffers that will not be drawn on the chart.

Each drawing style also has a color variant. The DRAW_COLOR_ drawing styles allows the programmer to vary the color of the indicator line on a bar-by-bar basis. You can view all of the drawing styles with examples in the *MQL5 Reference* under *Custom Indicators > Indicator Styles in Examples*.

The OnCalculate() Event Handler

All indicators require the OnCalculate() event handler. It is the equivalent of the OnStart() event handler for expert advisors, and runs on every incoming tick. There are two variants of the OnCalculate() event handler. The first is for indicators that use a single price series. For example, a moving average indicator allows the user to select a price series to calculate the data on (close, high, low, etc.) The selected price series is passed to the OnCalculate() event handler. Here is the first variant of OnCalculate():

```
    int OnCalculate (const int rates_total,        // size of the price[] array
                     const int prev_calculated,    // bars handled on a previous call
                     const int begin,              // where the significant data start from
                     const double& price[]         // array to calculate
        );
```

The `rates_total` parameter contains the number of bars in the history for the current chart symbol. The `prev_calculated` parameter is the number of bars in the history that have already been calculated previously by the indicator. The first time that `OnCalculate()` runs, `prev_calculated` will be zero. On subsequent runs, `prev_calculated` will be equal to `rates_total`. When a new bar opens, and the value of `rates_total` increases by one, the difference between `rates_total` and `prev_calculated` will be 1, indicating that we need to calculate the most recent bar.

By comparing the value of `rates_total` to `prev_calculated`, we avoid wasting processor time on recalculating bars that have already been calculated. The `begin` parameter is generally not used. The `price[]` array contains the price data that the indicator will use in its calculations. The price series used by the indicator is selected by the user in the *Parameters* tab of the indicator *Properties* window. The *Apply to* drop-down box allows the user to select the price series to use:

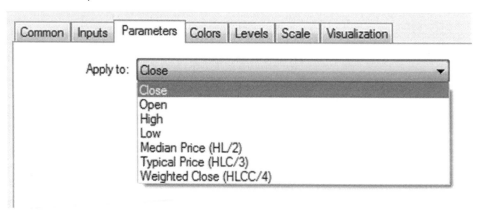

Fig. 21.1 – The *Apply to* drop-down box under the *Parameters* tab of the indicator *Properties* dialog.

The second variant of the `OnCalculate()` event handler adds additional price and time series arrays that can be used in indicator calculations. If your indicator requires multiple price series (such as the high AND low of each bar), then use the second variant of `OnCalculate()`:

```
    int OnCalculate (const int rates_total,        // size of input time series
                     const int prev_calculated,    // bars handled in previous call
                     const datetime& time[],       // Time
                     const double& open[],         // Open
                     const double& high[],         // High
                     const double& low[],          // Low
                     const double& close[],        // Close
```

```
        const long& tick_volume[],   // Tick Volume
        const long& volume[],        // Real Volume
        const int& spread[]          // Spread
    );
```

Our channel indicator will use this variant of the OnCalculate() event handler, since we need to use both the high and low price series.

MQL5 Wizard

The *MQL5 Wizard* can be used to create a starting template for your custom indicator. It is much more convenient to use the wizard to add our event handlers, buffers and lines than it is to add them manually. Open the *MQL5 Wizard* by clicking the *New* button on the MetaEditor toolbar. Select *Custom Indicator* and click *Next* to continue.

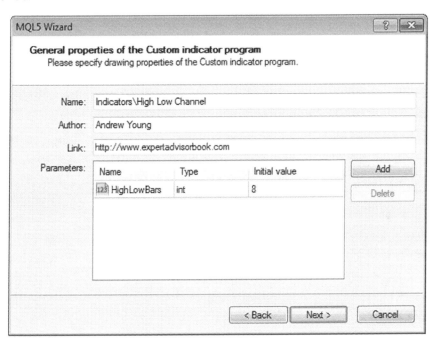

Fig. 21.2 – The custom indicator properties dialog of the *MQL5 Wizard*.

The custom indicators are saved to the \MQL5\Indicators folder by default. You can add input variables on this screen if you wish. In Fig. 21.2, we have added an int input variable named HighLowBars, with a default value of 8.

The next screen allows you to select the event handlers to add to your indicator. The first variant of the OnCalculate() event handler is selected by default. You can add additional event handlers if necessary. For our indicator, we will need to select the second variant of the OnCalculate() event handler. Fig. 21.3 below shows the Event handlers dialog:

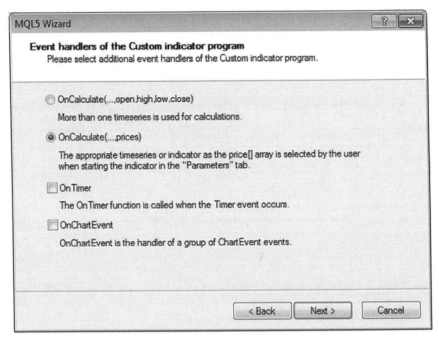

Fig. 21.3 – The event handlers dialog of the *MQL5 Wizard* for custom indicators.

The final screen is where you set the drawing properties of the indicator. If this indicator will be displayed in a separate window (such as an oscillator), check *Indicator in separate window* to add the relevant #property directive to the indicator file. The *Plots* window allows you to add and set the properties for the indicator lines:

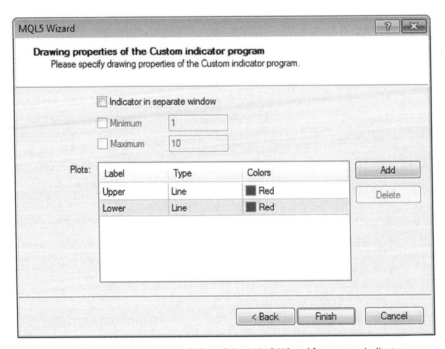

Fig. 21.4 – The drawing properties dialog of the *MQL5 Wizard* for custom indicators.

The *Label* column is the name of the indicator line as it will appear in the *Data Window*. It is also used to create the array buffer name. We have added two indicator lines named Upper and Lower. Double-click on the *Type* column to reveal a drop-down box to select the line's drawing type. We have left our lines set to the *Line* drawing type. Finally, the *Color* column is where you set the color of the indicator line. We have set both lines to Red.

Click *Finish* to close the Wizard and open the indicator template in MetaEditor. Here is what our indicator template look like. We've left out the OnCalculate() event handler for now, and formatted the file for clarity:

```
#property indicator_chart_window
#property indicator_buffers 2
#property indicator_plots   2

//--- plot Upper
#property indicator_label1  "Upper"
#property indicator_type1   DRAW_LINE
#property indicator_color1  clrRed
#property indicator_style1  STYLE_SOLID
#property indicator_width1  1

//--- plot Lower
#property indicator_label2  "Lower"
#property indicator_type2   DRAW_LINE
#property indicator_color2  clrRed
#property indicator_style2  STYLE_SOLID
#property indicator_width2  1

//--- input parameters
input int       HighLowBars=8;

//--- indicator buffers
double          UpperBuffer[];
double          LowerBuffer[];

//+------------------------------------------------------------------+
//| Custom indicator initialization function                         |
//+------------------------------------------------------------------+
int OnInit()
  {
//--- indicator buffers mapping
   SetIndexBuffer(0,UpperBuffer,INDICATOR_DATA);
   SetIndexBuffer(1,LowerBuffer,INDICATOR_DATA);

   return(0);
  }
```

The relevant #property directives have been inserted for our indicator lines. You can view all of the indicator #property directives in the *MQL5 Reference* under *Language Basics > Preprocessor > Program Properties*. Our HighLowBars input variable has been inserted, as well as two arrays for our buffers, UpperBuffer[] and LowerBuffer[]. The SetIndexBuffer() functions in the OnInit() event handler assigns the arrays to the relevant indicator buffers.

Calculating the Indicator

Our indicator calculations are carried out in the OnCalculate() event handler. The OnCalculate() event handler for our indicator is shown below:

```
//+------------------------------------------------------------+
//| Custom indicator iteration function                        |
//+------------------------------------------------------------+
int OnCalculate(const int rates_total,
                const int prev_calculated,
                const datetime &Time[],
                const double &Open[],
                const double &High[],
                const double &Low[],
                const double &Close[],
                const long &TickVolume[],
                const long &Volume[],
                const int &Spread[])
  {
//---

    ArraySetAsSeries(UpperBuffer,true);
    ArraySetAsSeries(LowerBuffer,true);
    ArraySetAsSeries(High,true);
    ArraySetAsSeries(Low,true);

    int bars = rates_total - 1;
    if(prev_calculated > 0) bars = rates_total - (prev_calculated - 1);

    for(int i = bars; i >= 0; i--)
    {
        UpperBuffer[i] = High[ArrayMaximum(High,i,HighLowBars)];
        LowerBuffer[i] = Low[ArrayMinimum(Low,i,HighLowBars)];
    }

//--- return value of prev_calculated for next call
    return(rates_total);
  }
```

None of the arrays in this program are set as series arrays by default. We will need to set them as series arrays using the `ArraySetAsSeries()` function. This is usually optional, but our indicator requires us to access the price data as a series. Both of our indicator buffers, as well as the `High[]` and `Low[]` arrays passed by the `OnCalculate()` event handler will be set as series:

```
ArraySetAsSeries(UpperBuffer,true);
ArraySetAsSeries(LowerBuffer,true);
ArraySetAsSeries(High,true);
ArraySetAsSeries(Low,true);
```

We use a `for` loop to calculate the indicator values for each of the bars on the current chart. We determine the number of bars to process by using the `prev_calculated` and `rates_total` parameters of the `OnCalculate()` event handler. As mentioned earlier, the `rates_total` variable contains the total number of bars on the chart, while `prev_calculated` contains the number of bars calculated by the previous run of the `OnCalculate()` event handler.

For series arrays, the maximum array index is `rates_total` - 1. This refers to the oldest bar on the chart. The most recent bar has an index of zero. When `OnCalculate()` is first run, the value of `prev_calculated` will be zero. If `prev_calculated` is zero, we set the maximum array index to `rates_total` - 1. On subsequent runs, we calculate the maximum array index by subtracting `prev_calculated` from `rates_total`. This ensures that only the most recent bar(s) will be calculated:

```
int bars = rates_total - 1;
if(prev_calculated > 0) bars = rates_total - prev_calculated;
```

The variable `bars` will hold the starting array index. In our `for` loop below, we assign the value of `bars` to our incrementor variable `i`. We will decrement the value of `i` until `i` = 0:

```
for(int i = bars; i >= 0; i--)
{
    // Indicator calculations
}
```

As long as your price and buffer arrays are set as series, the `for` loop above will work for calculating most indicators. The code to calculate the indicator and fill the buffers goes inside the loop.

To calculate the array buffers for our channel indicator, we simply use the `ArrayMaximum()` and `ArrayMinimum()` functions to find the highest and lowest values for the number of bars indicated by `HighLowBars`, relative to the array index indicated by the `i` incrementor variable. The resulting array index is used in the High[] and Low[] arrays to return the highest high and lowest low. The result is saved to the UpperBuffer[] and LowerBuffer[] arrays respectively:

```
for(int i = bars; i >= 0; i--)
{
    UpperBuffer[i] = High[ArrayMaximum(High,i,HighLowBars)];
    LowerBuffer[i] = Low[ArrayMinimum(Low,i,HighLowBars)];
}
```

The last step is to return the value of rates_total and exit the OnCalculate() event handler. This is inserted automatically by the MQL5 Wizard:

```
//--- return value of prev_calculated for next call
    return(rates_total);
}
```

We've just created a simple indicator that takes price data from the OnCalculate() event handler and calculates two indicator lines. This indicator can be used to create trading signals, or as a stop loss for trending positions. We've only touched upon you can do with custom indicators in MQL5. To learn more about custom indicator function, consult the *MQL5 Reference* under *Custom Indicators*.

You can view the source code for this file in \MQL5\Indicators\High Low Channel.mq5.

Fig. 21.5 – The High Low Channel custom indicator.

Scripts

A *script* is a simple MQL5 program that executes once when it is attached to a chart. It consists of a single event handler, the OnStart() event handler. When a script is attached to a chart, the OnStart() event handler executes. Unlike an expert advisor or indicator, a script does not repeat its execution after the OnStart() event handler has finished. The script is automatically detached from a chart after execution.

To create a script, use the *MQL5 Wizard*. All scripts are saved to the \MQL5\Scripts directory. Your new script file will contain an empty OnStart() event handler. There are a couple of #property directives that control the behavior of your script. If your script has input variables, you'll want to use the script_show_inputs property to allow the user to adjust the inputs and verify execution. If your script does not have input variables, the script_show_confirm property displays a confirmation box asking to user whether to execute the script. You'll want to add one of these #property directives to your script.

Here is an empty script file containing several #property directives and the OnStart() event handler:

```
#property copyright "Andrew Young"
#property link       "http://www.expertadvisorbook.com"
#property script_show_confirm

void OnStart()
{

}
```

We're going to create a useful script that can be used to close all open orders and positions on a chart. When attached to a chart, the script will first prompt the user as to whether to execute the script. If so, the script will first close any open position on the current chart symbol. Then it will close any open pending orders.

```
#property copyright "Andrew Young"
#property link       "http://www.expertadvisorbook.com"
#property description "Close the current position and all orders for the current
    chart symbol."

#property script_show_confirm

#include <Mql5Book\Trade.mqh>
CTrade Trade;

#include <Mql5Book\Pending.mqh>
CPending Pending;
```

```
void OnStart()
{
    // Close current position
    if(PositionType(_Symbol) != WRONG_VALUE)
    {
        bool closed = Trade.Close(_Symbol);
        if(closed == true)
        {
            Comment("Position closed on "+_Symbol);
        }
    }

    // Close any open pending orders
    if(Pending.TotalPending(_Symbol) > 0)
    {
        // Get pending order tickets
        ulong tickets[];
        Pending.GetTickets(_Symbol,tickets);
        int numTickets = ArraySize(tickets);

        // Close orders
        for(int i = 0; i < numTickets; i++)
        {
            Trade.Delete(tickets[i]);
        }

        if(Pending.TotalPending(_Symbol) == 0)
        {
            Comment("All pending orders closed on "+_Symbol);
        }
    }
}
```

The #property directives include the copyright, link and description, as well as the
script_show_confirm property. This prompts the user with a confirmation dialog before executing the script.
We've also included our Trade.mqh and Pending.mqh files from the \MQL5\Include\Mq15Book folder and
created objects based on the CTrade and CPending classes.

When the script is executed, the OnStart() event handler runs. We first check the output of the
PositionType() function. If it indicates an open position, we call the Trade.Close() function to close the
current position. A chart comment is shown if the position is closed properly.

Next, we check the Pending.TotalPending() function to see if there are pending orders open. If so, we use
the Pending.GetTickets() function to retrieve the current order tickets, and close them using
Trade.Delete(). If no pending orders are open, then a comment will print to the chart.

This script will close all orders and positions on the current chart symbol. We can modify the program to specify the symbol to close positions and orders for. We'll add an input variable named CloseSymbol. If a value is specified for CloseSymbol, the script will close all orders on the specified symbol. Otherwise, the script will use the current chart symbol:

```
#property script_show_inputs

#include <Mql5Book\Trade.mqh>
CTrade Trade;

#include <Mql5Book\Pending.mqh>
CPending Pending;

input string CloseSymbol = "";

void OnStart()
{
    // Check symbol name
    string useSymbol = CloseSymbol;
    if(CloseSymbol == "") useSymbol = _Symbol;

    // Close current position
    if(PositionType(useSymbol) != WRONG_VALUE)
    {
        bool closed = Trade.Close(useSymbol);
        if(closed == true)
        {
            Comment("Position closed on "+useSymbol);
        }
    }

    // Close any open pending orders
    if(Pending.TotalPending(useSymbol) > 0)
    {
        // Get pending order tickets
        ulong tickets[];
        Pending.GetTickets(useSymbol,tickets);
        int numTickets = ArraySize(tickets);

        // Close orders
        for(int i = 0; i < numTickets; i++)
        {
            Trade.Delete(tickets[i]);
        }
```

```
            if(Pending.TotalPending(useSymbol) == 0)
            {
                Comment("All pending orders closed on "+useSymbol);
            }
        }
    }
}
```

We use the `script_show_inputs` property directive to show the input window to the user before script execution. The user will input a symbol name for `CloseSymbol` and execute the script. If no symbol name has been specified, the program will assign the current chart symbol to the `useSymbol` variable. The `useSymbol` variable is used throughout the script to indicate the symbol to use.

You can view the source code of the `Close All Orders.mq5` script in the `\MQL5\Scripts` folder.

Libraries

A *library* is an executable file that contains reusable functions for use by other programs. It is similar to an include file, but with several important differences. Unlike an include file, a library does not have classes or variables that can be used by other programs. You can define classes, structures, enumerations and the like in your library, but they will not be usable outside of the library.

You can use native Windows DLLs or other DLLs created in C++ in your MQL5 programs. The process of importing DLLs functions is similar to importing functions from an MQL5 library. Functions contained within libraries have limitations as to the types of parameters that can be passed to them. Pointers and objects that contain dynamic arrays cannot be passed to a library function. If you are importing functions from a DLL, you cannot pass string or dynamic arrays to those functions.

The advantage of a library is that you can distribute it without making the source code available. If you use a library in numerous expert advisors, you can make minor changes to the library without having to recompile every program that depends on it (as long as you don't change the function parameters, that is).

You can create a blank library file using the *MQL5 Wizard*. Libraries are saved in the `\MQL5\Libraries` folder. A library must have the `library` property directive at the top of the file. If it is not present, the file will not compile. Let's create a sample library with two exportable functions. The functions that we wish to export will have the `export` modifier after the function parameters:

```
#property library

#include <Mql5Book\Indicators.mqh>
CiRSI RSI;
```

```
bool BuySignal(string pSymbol, ENUM_TIMEFRAMES pTimeframe, int pPeriod,
    ENUM_APPLIED_PRICE pPrice) export
{
    RSI.Init(pSymbol,pTimeframe,pPeriod,pPrice);

    if(RSI.Main() < 30) return(true);
    else return(false);
}

bool SellSignal(string pSymbol, ENUM_TIMEFRAMES pTimeframe, int pPeriod,
    ENUM_APPLIED_PRICE pPrice) export
{
    RSI.Init(pSymbol,pTimeframe,pPeriod,pPrice);

    if(RSI.Main() > 70) return(true);
    else return(false);
}
```

This file is named SignalLibrary.mq5, and is located in the \MQL5\Libraries folder. The #property library directive indicates that this is a library file. This library contains two functions that will be used to return trade signals to the calling program. These functions use simple RSI overbought and oversold trade signals, but you could create a library with more elaborate trade signals that you can keep hidden from the expert advisors and programmers that use them.

We include the \MQL5\Include\Mql5Book\Indicators.mqh file and declare an object based on the CiRSI class. Note that this object is not visible outside of the library. The BuySignal() and SellSignal() functions take parameters that set the parameters for the RSI indicator. Note the export modifier after the closing parenthesis. Any function that will be imported into another program must have the export modifier!

This file will be compiled just like any other MQL5 program. To use our library functions in another program, we need to import them into that program. We do this using the #import directive. Here is how we would import these functions into an expert advisor program:

```
#import "SignalLibrary.ex5"
bool BuySignal(string pSymbol, ENUM_TIMEFRAMES pTimeframe, int pPeriod,
    ENUM_APPLIED_PRICE pPrice);
bool SellSignal(string pSymbol, ENUM_TIMEFRAMES pTimeframe, int pPeriod,
    ENUM_APPLIED_PRICE pPrice);
#import
```

The library name is contained in double quotes after the opening #import directive. Note the .ex5 in the library name indicating that this is a compiled executable file. You cannot import a source code file. All libraries must be located in the \MQL5\Libraries folder. Following the opening #import directive are the functions that we are importing from our library. A closing #import directive must be present after the last imported function.

Our imported functions are used just like any other functions. Here's an example of how we could use the BuySignal() function in an expert advisor:

```
if(PositionType(_Symbol) == WRONG_VALUE && BuySignal(_Symbol,_Period,14,PRICE_CLOSE))
{
    // Open buy position
}
```

The example above calls the BuySignal() function, and calculates the RSI value for a 14 period RSI using the close price for the current chart symbol and period. If the RSI is currently oversold, the function returns true.

If an imported function from a library has the same name as a function in your program or a predefined MQL5 function, the scope resolution operator (::) must be used to identify the correct function. For example, let's assume that our program already has a function named BuySignal(). If we import the BuySignal() function from our library file, we'll need to preface it with the library name when we call it:

```
SignalLibrary::BuySignal(_Symbol,_Period,10,PRICE_CLOSE)
```

Chapter 22 - Debugging and Testing

Every programmer makes mistakes, and almost every program contains errors. Whether they are compilation errors caused by mistyping a function, or an error in your program logic, you will need to learn how to test and debug your programs. This chapter will discuss errors and procedures for debugging and testing your programs. You'll also learn how to use the Strategy Tester to evaluate your program's performance.

Errors

There are three types of errors related to MQL5 programs. *Compilation errors* occur in MetaEditor when invalid source code is compiled. *Runtime errors* are logic or software errors that occur when a program is executed in MetaTrader. Trade server errors occur when a trade request is unsuccessful.

Compilation Errors

It is common to mistype a function call, omit a semicolon or closing bracket, or make a syntax error when coding. When you compile your program, a list of errors will appear in the *Errors* tab in MetaEditor. The first time this happens, it may appear daunting. But don't worry – we're going to address some of the most common syntax errors that occur.

The first thing to remember when confronted with a list of compilation errors is to always start with the first error in the list. More often than not, it is a single syntax error that results in a whole list of errors. Correct the first error, and the remaining errors will disappear.

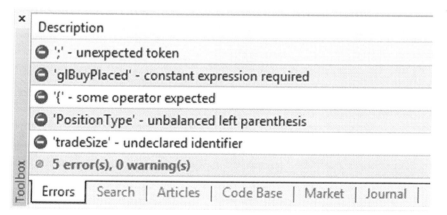

Fig. 22.1 – The *Errors* tab under the *Toolbox* window in MetaEditor. Note that all of these errors are due to a single missing right parenthesis.

Double-clicking the error in the *Errors* tab will take you to the spot in your program where the error was triggered. More than likely, the error will be right under your cursor, or on the previous line. A missing semicolon, parentheses or bracket may result in misleading compilation errors, so be sure to check the previous lines(s) for these when faced with an error on a line that otherwise looks correct.

Here's a list of the most common syntax errors in MetaEditor, and the most common reasons for these errors:

- **Semicolon expected** – A semicolon or left bracket is missing in the previous line.

- **Unexpected token** – A right parenthesis is missing in the previous line, or an extra left parenthesis is present in the current line.

- **Unbalanced right parenthesis** – An extra right parenthesis is present or a left parenthesis is missing in the current line.

- **Expressions are not allowed on a global scope** – A left bracket in a compound operator may be missing.

- **Some operator expected** – An operator is missing in the specified location.

- **Wrong parameters count** – Too many or not enough parameters in a function call.

- **Undeclared identifier** – A variable or object name is used without being declared first. Check the spelling and case of the variable name, and declare it if necessary.

- **Unexpected end of program** – A closing bracket is missing in your program. This is a tricky one, since the error refers to the end of the program. Examine the code that you edited recently and look for a missing closing bracket.

Runtime Errors

A runtime error is an error that occurs during the execution of a program. Runtime errors are logic errors – in other words, the program will compile, but is not operating as expected. An error message will print to the log when a runtime error occurs. The error message will indicate the cause of the error, as well as the line on which it occurred in your source code.

You can use the GetLastError() function to retrieve the error code of the last runtime error, in case you want to add error handling for runtime errors to your program. After accessing the last error code, use the ResetLastError() function to reset the error code to zero.

Programs will continue to run after a runtime error occurs, but there are a few critical errors that will end execution of a program immediately. A *divide by zero* error is where a division operation uses a divisor of zero. A *array out of range* error occurs when the program attempts to access an array element that doesn't exist. This usually occurs by trying to access an array element larger than the size of the array. Attempting to access an invalid pointer will also cause a critical error.

A complete list of runtime errors can be found in the *MQL5 Reference* under *Standard Constants... > Codes of Errors and Warnings > Runtime Errors*.

Trade Server Errors

Trade server errors are returned by the `ObjectSend()` function when attempting to perform a trade action. The `retcode` variable of a `MqlTradeResult` object passed to the `ObjectSend()` function contains the return code from the server. We've already discussed return codes on page 86, and our order placement and modification functions contain code to handle trade server errors. If you need to write a class or function that uses the `OrderSend()` function, be sure to add code that will handle trade server errors.

Debugging

New in MetaTrader 5 is a debugger that can be used to execute your programs interactively. By clicking the *Start debugging* button on the MetaEditor toolbar, your program will be opened on a chart in MetaTrader and tested in real time using live data. You can stop or pause the debugging process by clicking the *Stop* or *Pause* buttons:

Fig. 22.2 – Debugging buttons. From left to right are the *Start*, *Pause* and *Stop* debugging buttons.

The debugging process is entered when a breakpoint is reached. A *breakpoint* can be defined in MetaEditor by pressing the F9 key to toggle a breakpoint on the current line. You can also use the `DebugBreak()` function to define a breakpoint. When a breakpoint is reached during program execution, the program pauses and control is turned over to the programmer. Using the *Step Into*, *Step Over* and *Step Out* buttons on the toolbar, the programmer can observe the program execution line by line.

```
        // Open sell order
O       if(PositionType(_Symbol) == -1 && glSellPlaced == false
        {
            glSellPlaced = Trade.Sell(_Symbol,tradeSize);

            if(glSellPlaced == true && PositionVerify() == true)
            {
                double openPrice = PositionOpenPrice(_Symbol);
```

Fig. 22.3 – A breakpoint is set in MetaEditor on the current line.

The *Step Into* button moves execution to the next line of the program. *Step Over* will skip over any functions that are encountered during the execution, and *Step Out* exits the current function and returns control to the function that called it (or exits the current event).

Fig. 22.4 – Step buttons. From left to right are the *Step Into, Step Over* and *Step Out* buttons.

You can monitor the value of a variable during debugging by using the *Watch* window inside the *Debug* tab in the MetaEditor *Toolbox* window. The *Watch* window displays the current value of watched variables and expressions. To add a variable or expression to the watch window, place your mouse cursor over the variable name, or click-and-drag to select the expression you wish to add to the watch window. Right-click and select *Add Watch* from the popup menu, or press *Shift+F9* on your keyboard.

Expression	Value	Type
123 positionType	0	long
½ sar[1]	1.27947	double

Fig. 22.5 – The *Watch* window.

Debugging in MetaEditor is done in real time on live data, so you may need to modify your program to produce the result you are looking for immediately, especially if you are debugging a trading signal or trade operation. If you need to debug a program quickly, try logging and testing your program in the Strategy Tester.

Logging

Sometimes errors may occur during live or demo trading when a debugger is not available. Or you may need to test multiple trading scenarios at once in the Strategy Tester. You can use the `Print()` function to log information about your program's state to MetaTrader's log files. The `Alert()` function automatically prints the alert string to the log, so any alerts will be displayed in the log as well.

We have already added `Print()` functions throughout our trading classes and functions. These will print the results of trade operations to the log, as well as the values of relevant variables that are in use when an error condition occurs. This example is from the `CTrade::OpenPosition()` function in `Trade.mqh`:

```
Print("Open ",orderType," order #",result.deal,": ",result.retcode," - ",errDesc,", Volume:
",result.volume,", Price: ",result.price,", Bid: ",result.bid,", Ask: ",result.ask);
```

Here is the result as it appears in the strategy tester log:

```
Open Buy order #40: 10009 - Request is completed, Volume: 0.2, Price: 1.29693, Bid: 1.29678,
Ask: 1.29693
```

You should always build this kind of logging functionality into your programs, especially when performing trade operations or testing new code.

Debugging with `Print()` functions, while less interactive than using the debugger, allows the programmer to examine the output of many trades at once. You can view the Strategy Tester log under the *Journal* tab in the *Strategy Tester* window. Right-click in the *Journal* window and select *Open* from the popup menu to open the logs folder and view the files in a text editor. Or you can use the *Journal Viewer* (select *Viewer* from the right-click menu) to filter and view the logs by date.

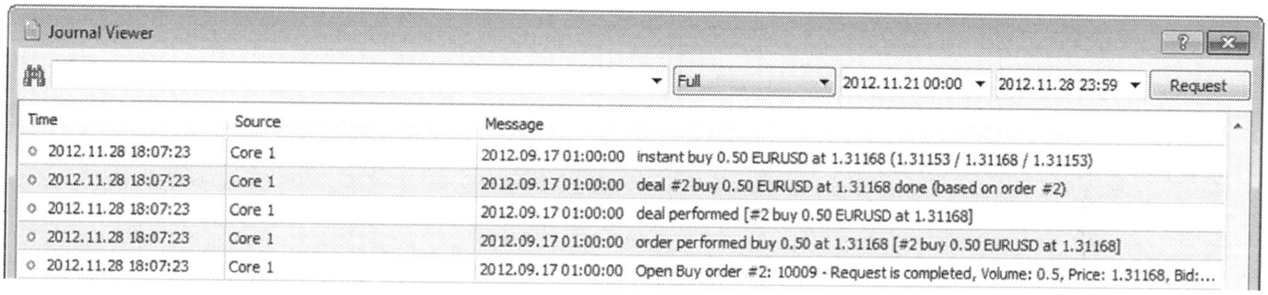

Fig. 22.6 – The *Journal Viewer* window.

When trading with an expert advisor on a live chart, MetaTrader uses two different log folders for output. The terminal logs, located in the \Logs folder, displays basic trade and terminal information. You can view this log under the *Journal* tab in the *Toolbox* window. The experts log, located in \Experts\Logs, contains the output of `Print()` and `Alert()` functions, as well as detailed trade information. You can view the experts log under the *Experts* tab in the *Toolbox* window. You can open the log folders by right-clicking inside the *Journal* or *Experts* tab and selecting *Open* from the popup menu, or view them in the Journal Viewer by selecting *Viewer* from the popup menu.

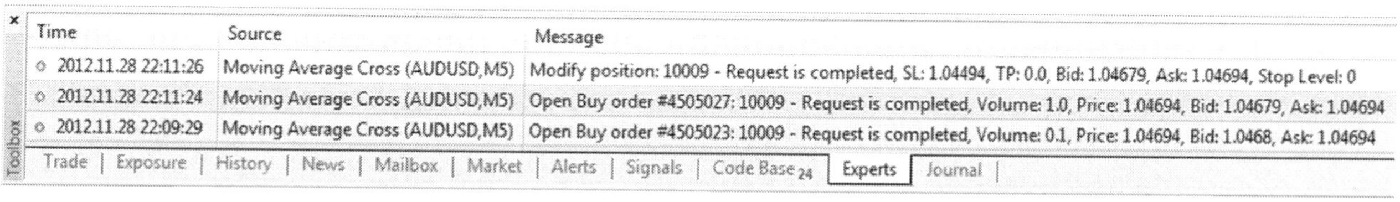

Fig. 22.7 – The *Experts* tab in the toolbox window. All `Print()` and `Alert()` output is viewable here.

Using the Strategy Tester

The Strategy Tester is the most important tool you have to test and evaluate your trading systems. MetaTrader 5 introduces new features to the strategy tester, including multi-currency testing, improved reports, and forward testing. To access the Strategy Tester, open the *Strategy Tester* window in MetaTrader from the *Standard* toolbar, or press *Ctrl+R* on your keyboard.

The *Settings* tab in the *Strategy Tester* window is where you'll enter the settings for testing. Most of the settings are self-explanatory, and should be familiar to you if you've used the MetaTrader 4 strategy tester. There are a few new settings worth mentioning. The *Execution* drop-down box allows you to incorporate a random delay when testing order operations, which mimic the natural delays in live trading.

Fig. 22.8 – The *Settings* tab of the Strategy Tester.

To the right of the *Execution* drop-down box is the tick generation mode. *Every tick* attempts to model every incoming tick from the server. It is the slowest mode, but the most accurate. *1 minute OHLC* uses the open, high low and close of each M1 bar in the testing period, providing a rough approximation of intrabar price changes. It is quicker than *Every tick*, but less accurate. *Open prices only* uses only the OHLC of each bar of the selected chart period. This is the quickest mode, but the least accurate. This is useful if you wish to quickly test an expert advisor that only opens orders at the open of a new bar.

If you check the *Visualization* checkbox, a separate visualization window will appear when you start the testing. The Visualization window shows the testing tick-by-tick. All indicators are drawn, and you can see orders opening and closing on the chart. Fig. 22.9 shows the Visualization window. The speed of the visualization is also adjustable.

The remaining settings in the *Settings* tab are for optimization. We'll discuss optimization shortly.

Fig. 22.9 – The Strategy Tester *Visualization* window.

The *Inputs* tab is used to adjust the input parameters of the expert advisor. The *Value* column is used to set the values for the current test. The *Start*, *Step* and *Stop* columns are for optimization, and will be addressed shortly. You can save the current settings to a file, load settings from a file, or set all parameters to their defaults using the right-click menu.

Variable	Value	Start	Step	Stop	Steps
☐ Fast MA					
☐ FastMAPeriod	10	10	10	50	
☐ FastMAMethod	Simple	Simple		Linear weighted	
☐ FastMAShift	0	0	1	10	
☐ FastMAPrice	Close price	Close price		Weighted price	

| Settings | Inputs | Results | Graph | Agents | Journal |

Fig 22.10 – The *Inputs* tab of the Strategy Tester.

Once your testing settings and input settings are configured, press the *Start* button in the *Settings* tab. After the testing has completed, a chart will open and the results will appear under the *Results* tab. The *Results* tab displays a testing report showing the profit, drawdown, profit factor and other statistical measures of performance. If you scroll down in the *Results* tab, there are additional trade statistics and graphs.

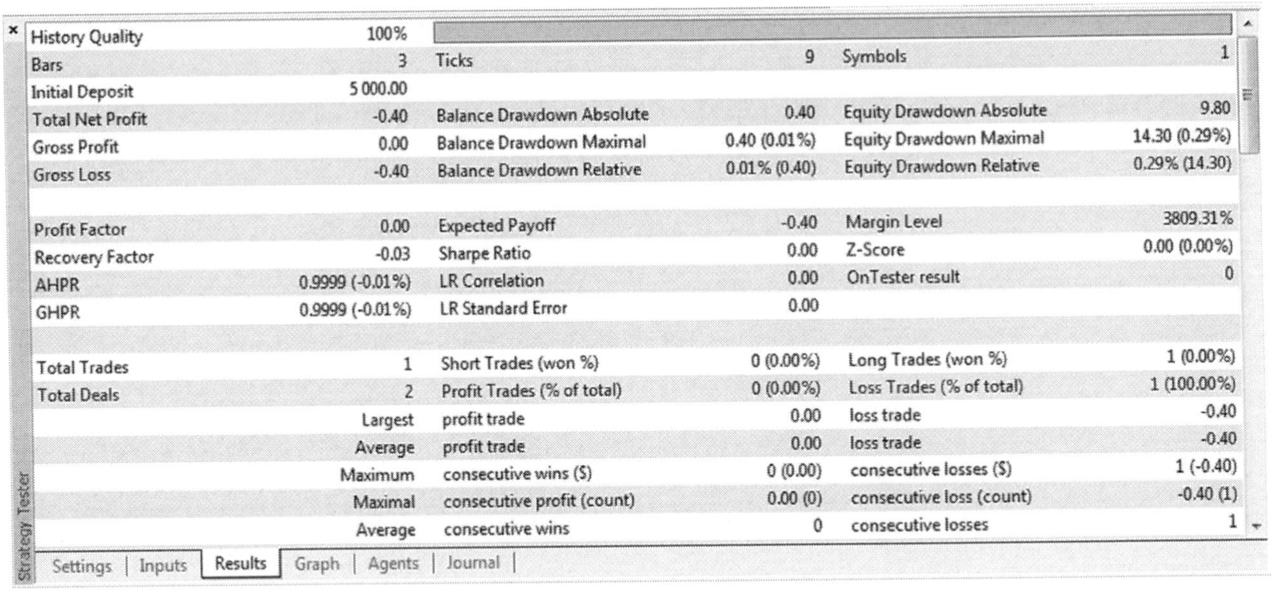

History Quality	100%				
Bars	3	Ticks	9	Symbols	1
Initial Deposit	5 000.00				
Total Net Profit	-0.40	Balance Drawdown Absolute	0.40	Equity Drawdown Absolute	9.80
Gross Profit	0.00	Balance Drawdown Maximal	0.40 (0.01%)	Equity Drawdown Maximal	14.30 (0.29%)
Gross Loss	-0.40	Balance Drawdown Relative	0.01% (0.40)	Equity Drawdown Relative	0.29% (14.30)
Profit Factor	0.00	Expected Payoff	-0.40	Margin Level	3809.31%
Recovery Factor	-0.03	Sharpe Ratio	0.00	Z-Score	0.00 (0.00%)
AHPR	0.9999 (-0.01%)	LR Correlation	0.00	OnTester result	0
GHPR	0.9999 (-0.01%)	LR Standard Error	0.00		
Total Trades	1	Short Trades (won %)	0 (0.00%)	Long Trades (won %)	1 (0.00%)
Total Deals	2	Profit Trades (% of total)	0 (0.00%)	Loss Trades (% of total)	1 (100.00%)
Largest		profit trade	0.00	loss trade	-0.40
Average		profit trade	0.00	loss trade	-0.40
Maximum		consecutive wins ($)	0 (0.00)	consecutive losses ($)	1 (-0.40)
Maximal		consecutive profit (count)	0.00 (0)	consecutive loss (count)	-0.40 (1)
Average		consecutive wins	0	consecutive losses	1

Settings | Inputs | **Results** | Graph | Agents | Journal

Fig 22.11 – The *Results* tab in the Strategy Tester.

To view the trade details, right-click in the *Results* tab. You can select *Deals*, *Orders* or *Orders &* Deals from the popup menu. The *Deals* report is the most useful, as these reflect the actual trade results. Note the *Direction* column in the *Deals* report. A direction of *in* means that a deal is adding to the current position. A direction of *out* means that the deal is closing out part or all of the position. An *in/out* direction refers to a reversal in position.

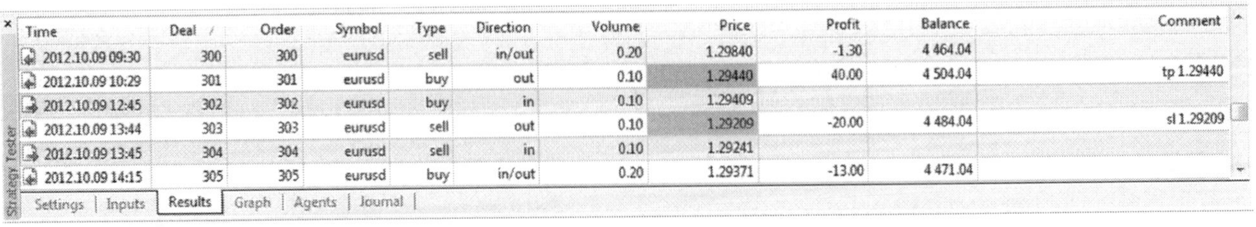

Time	Deal	Order	Symbol	Type	Direction	Volume	Price	Profit	Balance	Comment
2012.10.09 09:30	300	300	eurusd	sell	in/out	0.20	1.29840	-1.30	4 464.04	
2012.10.09 10:29	301	301	eurusd	buy	out	0.10	1.29440	40.00	4 504.04	tp 1.29440
2012.10.09 12:45	302	302	eurusd	buy	in	0.10	1.29409			
2012.10.09 13:44	303	303	eurusd	sell	out	0.10	1.29209	-20.00	4 484.04	sl 1.29209
2012.10.09 13:45	304	304	eurusd	sell	in	0.10	1.29241			
2012.10.09 14:15	305	305	eurusd	buy	in/out	0.20	1.29371	-13.00	4 471.04	

Settings | Inputs | **Results** | Graph | Agents | Journal

Fig 22.12 – The *Deals* report inside the *Results* tab of the Strategy Tester.

Note that the reports do not list the stop loss or take profit placed on a position! If you need this information, check the log under the *Journal* tab and search for the order/deal number. If a position closes out at a stop loss or take profit, that will be reflected in the *Deals* report with an entry in the *Comment* column, a red or green background in the *Price* column, and a *Direction* of *out*. Note that when a position is closed out, it is listed as a separate deal. You can save the contents of the *Results* tab to a report file by right-clicking inside the *Results* tab and selecting *Open XML* or *HTML* from the *Report* submenu.

The *Graph* tab shows a graph of profitability over time. The *Agents* tab allows you to manage multi-core processors for testing, as well as utilize remote computers and the MQL5 Cloud Network for running resource-intensive optimizations. Finally, the *Journal* tab shows the testing log, which is located in the \Tester\Logs folder. The results of your testing, including all log entries and errors, will appear in this log.

Optimization

Running an *optimization* on an expert advisor involves selecting the input parameters to optimize and testing every possible combination of parameter sets to determine which parameters are most profitable. This is usually followed by a *forward test* that tests the optimization results on out-of-sample data. Optimization and forward testing is the process by which you will evaluate the profitability of your expert advisors.

Let's start under the *Inputs* tab. The *Start*, *Step* and *Stop* columns are used to set the optimization parameters. To optimize a parameter, select the checkbox to the left of the parameter name in the *Variable* column. The *Start* value is the starting value for the parameter. The *Step* value increments the parameter by the specified amount, and the *Stop* value is the ending value for the parameter. For example, if we have a *Start* value of 10, a *Step* value of 5, and a *Stop* value of 50, then the parameter will be optimized starting at 10, 15, 20... all the way up to 50 for a total of 10 steps.

Select each parameter that you wish to optimize, and set the *Start*, *Step* and *Stop* values for each of them. You may want to limit the number of parameters to test, as well as the step value for each parameter. The more parameters/steps there are to test, the longer the optimization will take.

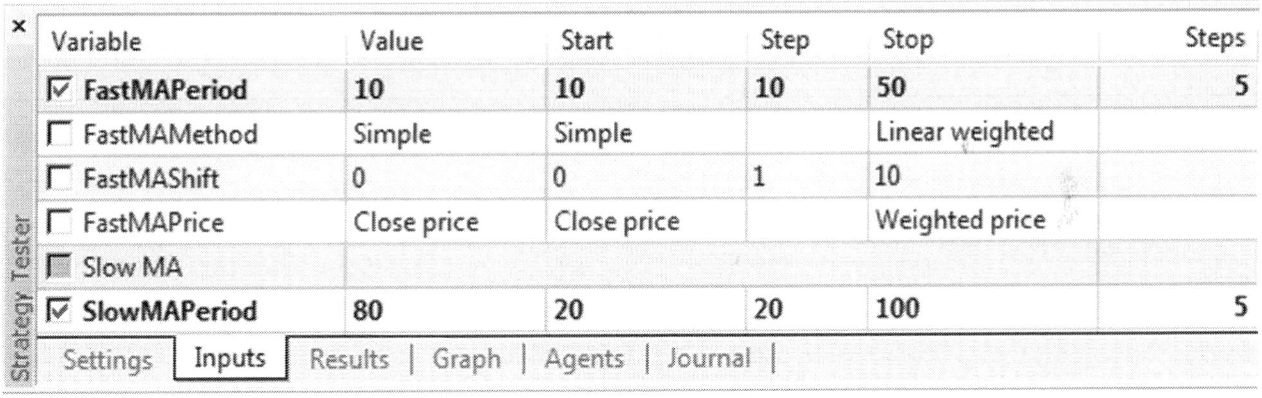

Variable	Value	Start	Step	Stop	Steps
☑ **FastMAPeriod**	10	10	10	50	5
☐ FastMAMethod	Simple	Simple		Linear weighted	
☐ FastMAShift	0	0	1	10	
☐ FastMAPrice	Close price	Close price		Weighted price	
☐ Slow MA					
☑ **SlowMAPeriod**	80	20	20	100	5

Settings | Inputs | Results | Graph | Agents | Journal |

Fig 22.13 – The *Inputs* tab in the Strategy Tester, using the *Start*, *Step* and *Stop* columns for optimization.

The optimization settings are at the bottom of the *Settings* tab. If an optimization is not being performed, the *Optimization* drop-down will be set to *Disabled*. If you wish to perform an optimization, select one of the other options. *Slow complete algorithm* tests every possible combination of parameters, and can take a very long time if there are a lot of parameters to optimize for. *Fast genetic based algorithm* uses a genetic algorithm to narrow down the range of parameters to test. The results are comparable to using the complete algorithm, and should be your default choice. *All symbols selected in MarketWatch* will test all symbols in the *Market*

Watch window. You can add and remove symbols from the market watch window using the right-click menu inside the *Market Watch* window.

Fig. 22.14 – The optimization settings in the *Settings* tab of the Strategy Tester.

The drop-down box to the left of *Optimization* is the optimization criteria for the genetic algorithm. The default is to sort by max balance, although you can sort by max balance combined with other criteria, such as profit factor, drawdown or expected payoff.

The *Forward* drop-down selects the forward testing period. If *Forward* is set to something other than *No*, then the selected fraction of the optimization period will be set aside for forward testing. You can select your own start date for the forward testing period by selecting *Custom* and then setting the start date in the date entry box to the right. If forward testing is enabled, then each of the optimization results will be tested individually in the forward testing period.

You can view the results of the optimization in the *Optimization Results* tab. Compare the optimization results to the forward testing results to see how well the optimization results hold up. If the forward testing results are comparable to the optimization results, then your system may perform well in trading. If the two sets of results are not comparable, then you may need to adjust your optimization parameters, your trading system or both.

Pass	Forward ▽	Backtest	Profit	Total trades	Profit factor	Expected pa...	Drawdown %	Recovery fa...	Sharpe ratio	FastMAPeriod	SlowMAPeriod
12	5534.55	3967.36	534.55	14	1.98	38.18	6.58	1.48	0.30	30	60
13	5342.55	4572.73	342.55	12	1.55	28.55	7.41	0.84	0.21	40	60
18	5160.90	4336.43	160.90	8	1.37	20.11	5.32	0.60	0.16	40	80
15	5081.73	4899.70	81.73	10	1.16	8.17	5.17	0.30	0.08	10	80
2	5065.50	4726.76	65.50	23	1.06	2.85	9.49	0.13	0.04	30	20

Settings | Inputs | Results | Graph | **Optimization Results** | Optimization Graph | Agents | Journal |

Fig. 22.15 – The *Optimization Results* tab in the Strategy Tester, showing both forward and back testing results.

Right-click in the *Optimization Results* tab to select between *Back Test Results* and *Forward Test Results* if applicable. You can also enable additional columns in the report such as the profit factor, drawdown, expected payoff and optimization parameters. The optimization results can be saved to an XML file that can be opened by any spreadsheet program by selecting *Export to XML* from the right-click menu. The *Optimization Graph* tab shows a scatterplot of optimization results. You can select a 2D or 3D graph from the right-click menu, and set the parameters to use for the X-axis and Y-axis.

Evaluating Testing Results

The *Results* and *Optimization Results* tabs present a variety of statistical measures to evaluate the profitability and stability of your trading system. MetaTrader 5 has added a lot of new statistics to the Strategy Trader report. In this section, we will examine the most important statistics that appear in the trading and optimization reports:

- **Net Profit** – The *net profit* is calculated as the gross profit minus the gross loss. This is probably the most important statistic, and should always be considered in relation to other statistics. Obviously, a higher net profit is better.

- **Drawdown** – The *drawdown* is the maximum peak to valley loss during the testing period. The absolute drawdown is the maximum drawdown of balance or equity below the original starting balance. The maximal and relative drawdown is the maximum drawdown of equity of balance from the maximum profit to the maximum loss. Relative drawdown is the most important value. Lower values are better.

- **Profit Factor** – The *profit factor* is a simple ratio of gross profit to gross loss. A system that makes zero profit has a profit factor of 1. If profit factor is less than 1, then the system has lost money. A higher profit factor is better.

- **Expected Payoff** – The *expected payoff* is the average/profit or loss of a single trade. Higher values are better.

- **Recovery Factor** – The *recovery factor* determines the risk of a trading strategy, and how well it recovers from a loss. It is a ratio of profit to maximal drawdown. Higher values are better.

- **Sharpe Ratio** – The *Sharpe ratio* also determines the risk and stability of a trading system. It uses a sophisticated algorithm to compare the returns of a system versus a risk-free method of return (such as a Treasury Bond). Higher values are better.

Index

11164240R00176

Printed in Great Britain
by Amazon.co.uk, Ltd.,
Marston Gate.